Machiavelli and the Problems of Military Force

Also available from Bloomsbury

A History and Philosophy of Expertise, Jamie Carlin Watson
Certainty in Action, Danièle Moyal-Sharrock
Early Analytic Philosophy and the German Philosophical Tradition,
Nikolay Milkov
Exploring the Philosophy of R. G. Collingwood, Peter Skagestad

Machiavelli and the Problems of Military Force

A War of One's Own

Sean Erwin

BLOOMSBURY ACADEMIC
LONDON · NEW YORK · OXFORD · NEW DELHI · SYDNEY

BLOOMSBURY ACADEMIC
Bloomsbury Publishing Plc
50 Bedford Square, London, WC1B 3DP, UK
1385 Broadway, New York, NY 10018, USA
29 Earlsfort Terrace, Dublin 2, Ireland

BLOOMSBURY, BLOOMSBURY ACADEMIC and the Diana logo are trademarks of Bloomsbury Publishing Plc

First published in Great Britain 2022
This paperback edition published 2023

Copyright © Sean Erwin, 2022

Sean Erwin has asserted his right under the Copyright, Designs and Patents Act, 1988, to be identified as Author of this work.

For legal purposes the Acknowledgements on p. vii constitute an extension of this copyright page.

Cover image: Vintage engraving of a Macedonian Phalanx. Duncan1890/Getty Images.

All rights reserved. No part of this publication may be reproduced or transmitted in any form or by any means, electronic or mechanical, including photocopying, recording, or any information storage or retrieval system, without prior permission in writing from the publishers.

Bloomsbury Publishing Plc does not have any control over, or responsibility for, any third-party websites referred to or in this book. All internet addresses given in this book were correct at the time of going to press. The author and publisher regret any inconvenience caused if addresses have changed or sites have ceased to exist, but can accept no responsibility for any such changes.

A catalogue record for this book is available from the British Library.

A catalog record for this book is available from the Library of Congress.

ISBN: HB: 978-1-3501-1571-2
PB: 978-1-3503-2381-0
ePDF: 978-1-3501-1572-9
eBook: 978-1-3501-1573-6

Typeset by RefineCatch Ltd, Bungay, Suffolk NR35 1EF, UK

To find out more about our authors and books, visit www.bloomsbury.com and sign up for our newsletters.

Contents

Acknowledgments — vii

Introduction: The Problem of Hiero II — 1

1 Atomic War: The Influence of Lucretius on Machiavelli's *Art of War* — 13

2 Practical Proportions: Aelianus Tacticus in Machiavelli's *Art of War* — 37

3 Industries of Failure? Mercenaries and the Arms of Others — 53

4 Instrumental and Aleatory Aspects of Auxiliary Force in Machiavelli — 73

5 Transforming Compounds: Machiavelli's Analyses of Mixed Force — 99

Conclusion: Captains of Critique — 121

Notes — 129
Bibliography — 185
Index — 193

Acknowledgments

I would like to thank Mario De Caro, Ioannis Evrigenis, Gabriele Pedullà, and Vickie Sullivan for their generosity, encouragement, and valuable insights into various stages of this manuscript. I am grateful also to scores of scholars at the annual meetings of the Renaissance Society of America and the American Philosophical Association for their feedback on earlier stages of this work.

Thanks too to Julie Regan, Celeste Landeros, Kellee Weinhold (and Elif, Elizabeth and Sarah) for their ongoing support of my writing process. Finally, this book could not have been written without the consistent support of Letizia Cutino and Tim O'Brien, to whom I owe much.

Introduction: The Problem of Hiero II

Hiero II[1] performs an ambiguous role in Machiavelli's works. The Syracusan king appears at key moments in both the *Prince* and the *Discourses* as an important example of a private individual who became prince, as Machiavelli explains, through possessing "arms of his own." In the *Prince*, Machiavelli cites the example of Hiero at the close of Chapter 6 as someone who even exhibited a certain proportionality with the likes of new princes like Moses, Cyrus, Romulus and Theseus, who acquired new principalities through their own arms and virtue when presented with the opportunity to do so.

Machiavelli cites the example of Hiero II again in Chapter 13 of the *Prince*, during the discussion of different qualities of armed force. Here he discusses why arms of one's own are always to be preferred over employing mercenary or auxiliary arms. Machiavelli invokes the example of Hiero during this discussion as someone who destroyed the mercenary arms he inherited when he became captain of Syracuse, "and then made war with his own arms and not with alien arms."

Machiavelli inserts the discussion of Hiero between discussions of Cesare Borgia and the Biblical David. The career of Hiero resembled that of Borgia, the illegitimate son of Pope Alexander VI, in that the careers of both leaders began with their using the arms of others. According to Machiavelli, when Borgia detected the risks that came with making war with the arms of others, he replaced them and made war with his own.

Machiavelli then examines the example of David, who abjured the use of Saul's armor and sword and went to meet Goliath with arms of his own. On Machiavelli's account, David's arms included his sling and his knife. Of course the story of the battle between David and Goliath from Samuel I makes no mention of David fighting with a knife. In fact, Samuel kills Goliath and then cuts off his head using the Philistine's own sword.

Machiavelli's error paraphrasing the well-known story of David asks the reader to take a closer look at these examples. David's own arms were not enough to defeat Goliath. David had to employ Goliath's own sword to defeat him. Machiavelli also silently glosses over the detail in his presentation of Cesare Borgia that at every major engagement throughout his career, Borgia employed in a significant way mercenary or auxiliary troops.[2] Finally, Machiavelli overlooks a key detail in Hiero's own career as narrated by Polybius. Hiero did contrive to rid himself of the Syracusan militia's veteran mercenaries by withdrawing his citizen infantry and cavalry during a battle with the Campanians. Left vulnerable, the seditious mercenaries were cut to pieces in the ensuing battle. Relieved of their burden, Hiero then hired *another mercenary army* to supplement the Syracusan citizen militia.[3]

The problem posed by Machiavelli's use of the example of Hiero is only exacerbated by turning to the *Discourses*. In the dedicatory letter, Machiavelli offers Hiero II as a positive example to Zanobi Buondelmonte and Cosimo Rucellai in terms that recall the *Prince,* Chapter 6: "Hiero lacked nothing to being prince other than the principality."[4] However, his subsequent references to him in the text are not as positive. Later he mentions Hiero II in connection with the career of his grandson, Hieronymus, whom Hiero carefully cultivated to be his successor. Hieronymus proved a spectacular failure and was assassinated shortly after acceding to the throne.

Machiavelli also lists Hiero II among those leaders who behaved as faithful allies to the Romans. He asked in return only that the Romans protect and defend his kingdom. In other words, apart from the dedicatory letter, the sole references to Hiero II in the *Discourses* feature him bungling his succession and basing his career and legacy as King of Syracuse on acting as a reliable Roman client state.[5]

Far from serving as an unproblematic case study for a potential prince pursuing arms of their own, Machiavelli's use of Hiero II as a model complicates what Machiavelli presents as a straightforward set of categories laying out the qualities of armed force. For Machiavelli, princes and republics can deploy four different types of force. They can go to war by hiring mercenaries or borrowing auxiliaries from another prince or republic. He calls the use of these two force qualities employing the *arms of others* (*arma alienis*). Princes and republics can also deploy forces that belong to them, and he terms the use of such forces deploying *one's own arms* (*arma propriis*). Finally they can also deploy troops that are mixtures of these three principal categories, which he terms the use of *mixed forces*. For instance, Polybius describes Hiero II employing a combination of Syracusan citizen and mercenary troops. According to Machiavelli's typology of forces, Hiero II then did not employ arms of his own but rather mixed forces compounded from mercenaries and his own militia. Though not ideal, mixed forces constitute an improvement over fielding unreliable mercenaries or auxiliaries alone. Still, by highlighting the case of Hiero II, Machiavelli problematizes the very distinction he makes between the *arms of others* and *arms of one's own* that the example of Hiero supposedly clarifies.

The importance of the topic is evident for reading texts like the *Prince* and the *Discourses*, both at least in part addressed to "potential princes." For the potential prince, the use of mercenary or auxiliary arms would seem a necessary and logical first stage in the process of crossing the threshold from being a potential prince to becoming something more. As if to underline the importance that mercenary arms can play in making a private individual into a new prince, the very first proper name introduced by Machiavelli in the first chapter of the *Prince* is the mercenary captain, Francesco Sforza—who transitioned from *condottiere* to Duke of Milan by plying his trade and whom Machiavelli cites as an example of a successful new prince.[6] Consider, too, that the only text published by Machiavelli during his lifetime, the *Art of War*, contains sustained discussions with Fabrizio Colonna, a mercenary captain but also the dialogue's acknowledged authority on military practice and theory. These considerations added to how Machiavelli forefronts the example of Hiero II as a prince worthy of imitation by potential princes reveal unanticipated complexity to the distinctions Machiavelli draws between what seem at first glance relatively straightforward force categories.

1. Machiavelli and the Military

Scholars have long acknowledged that Machiavelli treats politics as an analogue of war and that for him the spheres of the political and the military overlap. However, Machiavelli's discussions of the specifics of war—particular conflicts, troop compositions, logistics, etc.—as well as his critiques of different types of military force – mercenary, auxiliary, mixed forces, one's own – have not been the subject of sustained reflection. As Timothy Lukes argues, scholars are, "hesitant to embrace [Machiavelli's] unambiguous recommendation to privilege warfare, often avoiding it or offering a perfunctory explanatory paragraph." Lukes warns against attributing the importance Machiavelli accords military matters as excessive rhetorical emphasis, since it leads to treating Machiavelli's discussions of warfare as secondary to his decidedly more important political doctrines and theories.

Recently, however, scholars have begun re-evaluating the importance of Machiavelli's discussions of the military and military forces in his major works. Mikael Hörnquist, Yves Winter, Harvey Mansfield, Gabriele Pedullà, Timothy

Lukes, John McCormick, John Najemy, Robert Black, and others, have made the issue of the military, military force, and violence central themes of their investigations. Though their motivations for addressing these themes differ, most agree that Machiavelli's distinction between the spheres of the political and military needs to be re-conceived not as a hard distinction between exclusive institutions but as a porous and even fluid threshold between intrinsically compatible spheres of activity. As Yves Winter argues, "Machiavelli treats war as a profoundly political practice and the military as the site of potential political upheaval and popular revolt."[7] For Winter, Machiavelli's emphasis on military discipline is the key to the interpenetration of military and political spheres. The "disparate and heterogenous patchwork of practices, routines and disciplines"[8] that Machiavelli frames in texts like the *Art of War* is certainly a condition of the physical force the militia generates in the city's defense; but the continuous performance of the choreography of movements and displays of visual and aural signs that organize the militia's disciplinary regime proves a source of shared values that transcends the militia as an institution. Through performances of practices, military force and political power forge channels where features from one sphere shuttle into the other.

Felix Gilbert arrives at a similar conclusion when he assesses that the importance of the army to the life of the state implies for Machiavelli a process where other state institutions continue to change to augment the functioning of institutions devoted to the military.[9] Similarly, Harvey Mansfield notes that even in Machiavelli's texts like the *Art of War*—apparently committed to investigating the military as its sole object—political issues constantly arise even when they are only implied. Louis Althusser goes further when he affirms that Machiavelli's army is a popular army and the state apparatus *par excellence* whose constitution, formation, and employment must be considered before all else in terms of the political ("sous la rapport de la politique") and as a realization of politics in the part of the state which employs violence.[10]

Investigating the military's organization for its political features even means that decisions made concerning features of military policy, from its disciplinary regime, processes of recruitment, selection of equipment, exercises and tactics, possess implications for the military both as an organization of force relations and as a social unifier that transcends institutional limitations as a source of shared associations and values. For instance, concerning the function Machiavelli's military captain assumes when recruiting for the militia, Mansfield argues that Machiavelli "almost makes his captain into a Machiavellian prince." He emphasizes that Machiavelli's captains will need the authority of a prince if their selection of soldiers is to be effective given that the art of war is so intimately dependent on political authority.[11] John McCormick expresses a similar position when he states: "the logic motivating Machiavellian popular government, whether a democratic republic or governo largo, is fairly simple: arm the people militarily with weapons and collective discipline and politically with tribunes and assemblies."[12] Arming the people requires a prince achieve both these overlapping, institutional-shifting objectives.

However, analyzing Machiavelli's discussions of military force involves more than merely assessing the strengths and weaknesses of his definitions of different forms of military organization. It also calls for textual and historical interpretation of the events and characters that Machiavelli associates with the definitions he offers for different force categories. Machiavelli's account of military conflicts and military forces are marked by historical and textual inconsistencies. His accounts of the course of conflicts, the force compositions involved, and the behavior of leadership can differ greatly from descriptions of those same events in other sources. Further, Machiavelli's retelling of the same event in different locations within his own texts can also show variations. These differences have received little attention by commentators. Given that Machiavelli played an active role in many of the military conflicts he describes and/or had privileged access to actors who took active roles in these events, contextualizing his presentations of conflicts, battles, and the performances of different types of troops and military technologies is critical to clarifying the valuations he forms of different types of military forces and their effectiveness. This is especially important because Machiavelli often appears intentional in his communication of historical inaccuracies or his misapplications of his own force labels. Often Machiavelli's glaring errors, when examined more closely, telegraph important nuances to his understanding of force, the structure and mutability of military forces, and possible tactics for exploiting or accommodating their strengths and weaknesses.

A reason for the scarce attention of these inconsistencies has been the lack of importance accorded to Machiavelli's practical involvement in the creation of the new Florentine militia. Christopher Lynch importantly cautions against believing too seriously Machiavelli's self-deprecating claim in the preface to the *Art of War* that he lacked experience in war. In the process, Lynch emphasizes the centrality of Machiavelli's practical experience of war:

> Over the course of his fourteen-year tenure Machiavelli bore the longest sustained responsibility for military matters of any government official. He was

immersed in virtually all areas of military affairs; he personally observed and reported to his government on the size, composition, weaponry, morale, and logistical capabilities of the most effective militaries of his day; he created Florence's first native fighting force in over one hundred years, writing the law on its composition, handpicking its troops, and vetting its potential "captains" (as Machiavelli called military leaders); and he planned or observed significant sieges and skirmishes.[13]

Recently, scholars have made strong cases for reassessing Machiavelli's pronouncements on the conflicts and militaries of his time from the perspective of Machiavelli's diplomatic and political service.

For instance, Hörnquist, Najemy, and Black examine the relationship between Machiavelli's early writings, his period organizing and advocating for the Florentine militia, and how these experiences colored his reasoning on warfare in the *Art of War*. Mikael Hörnquist argues that Machiavelli's silence concerning the Roman army as the model for his militia must be heard as his nuanced approach to the political debates around the militia project.[14] John Najemy evaluates the significance of the appointment of Cesare Borgia's lieutenant, Don Michele, as captain of the new militia and assesses whether or not the intentions of Machiavelli and Soderini in creating the militia aimed at tyranny.[15] Najemy discusses the debates among the Florentine *ottimati* over the use of *sudditi* as militia recruits, but also how these debates often operated as a façade concealing the political objectives of these same *ottimati* and their desires for a change of regime.[16] On the other hand, Robert Black argues against Najemy, highlighting the controversy that ensued at the appointment of Don Michele as evidence that Machiavelli together with Francesco and Piero Soderini weighed the militia's potentials for political intervention.[17] Hörnquist, Najemy, and Black also highlight how the Florentine debate over restoring the militia in the early 1500s was shaped by the awareness of the city's leaders of the challenges involved in sustaining the city's continued dependence on stipendiaries to fight its wars.[18]

From another perspective, Jean-Louis Fournel's recent work shows the precision with which Machiavelli deploys the Latin and fifteenth-century Italian vocabulary describing armaments. Fournel explores how Machiavelli's employments of different terms for hand cannons (*scoppietti*) differed in nuanced ways depending on the context of his description and the audience intended.[19] Despite Machiavelli's criticism of armies relying on artillery, Fournel emphasizes the political implications raised by Book 3 of the *Art of War*, where Machiavelli includes 1,000 infantry as part of his legion of 6,000.[20] Machiavelli includes the hand cannons as a counter-measure to cavalry assaults, but arming his new recruits with this weapon has an additional consequence: "Including firearms in the infantry transforms in this way the *scoppietto*...into an arm of the poor and free people that fight the nobles on horseback."[21] Since training and equipping units of *scoppietti* took much less time and cost less than equipping units with crossbows, peasants armed with hand cannons possessed a weapon that could effectively shift the conflicts between the classes when ranged against horse-mounted troops generally formed of the urban elite.

Bernard Wicht argues along similar lines when he examines Machiavelli's use of the Swiss as a political and military model. Wicht contends that Machiavelli's deployment of the Swiss model allowed him to formulate a new concept of liberty: "The Florentine discovered that in matters concerning the militia, it is necessary to reason in terms of social energy ("en termes d''énergie sociale'"), or otherwise said, "of popular effervescence ("d'effervescence populaire"), and that these qualities are maximized under the form of the people in arms."[22] In a way that recalls Winter's analysis, Wicht links popular violence as a support of the state with his analyses of the discipline at the basis of the success of the Swiss pike squares on fifteenth- and sixteenth- century battlefields.

Gabriele Pedullà also locates in Machiavelli's interest in the Swiss pike squares clues to the political implications of Machiavelli's reasoning on warfare. As Pedullà points out, scholars as diverse as Chabod and Gramsci have read the *Art of War* and Machiavelli's discussions of the military only from the standpoint of his political writings, often dismissing the *Art of War* for its emphasis on the technical details of warfare. Pedullà recasts the technical character of the *Art of War* as one of the text's principal strengths and an outgrowth of Machiavelli's meaningful engagement with the second-century military treatise on Greek phalanx tactics—the *De instruendis aciebus* of Aelianus Tacticus. Pedullà argues for the complete interpenetration of the spheres of the military and political when he states: "The *Art of War* is a technical work because anyone who says that the main political problem is to be able to fight in the open field must discuss even the smallest details if he hopes to prove the effectiveness of his theory."[23] Pedullà holds that even though the *Art of War*'s fine-grained discussions of recruitment, logistics, and training undercut its availability to specialists and non-specialists alike, these same discussions when examined closely also display the disciplinary foundations through which the militia experience of soldiers transcends the institutional limits of the military.

The *Art of War* would appear to be the text where Machiavelli most concretely lays out what it means for a prince or republic to possess their own arms, and it can be read as an apolitical "how-to" guide to that goal. However, recent discussions of Machiavelli's selection of the mercenary captain Fabrizio Colonna as chief interlocutor of the dialogue, situate the *Art of War* as a text whose discussions of the military clearly telegraph the short- and long-term political implications linked to the institution.

For instance, Marcia Colish shows how Machiavelli's choice of Colonna as chief interlocutor for this apparently technical discussion of warfare communicates both Machiavelli's very political criticism of the papacy, on the one hand, and his criticism of Savonarola, on the other.[24] Winter teases out the political implications of even Fabrizio's name, connecting it to *fabbro*, "blacksmith." As Winter suggests, blacksmiths know how to induce a form within *materia*, and blacksmiths are one of the main categories of recruits proposed by Fabrizio.[25] Frédérique Verrier argues that the figure of Colonna undergoes a radical shift of dimension during the course of the dialogue from that of a competent condottiere to that of "a prince or a counselor of the king, whose horizon would not be war but peace and whose competence would not already be polemology but the political." Verrier argues that Machiavelli transforms "the historical Colonna into a fictional persona, the mercenary condottiere into a Machiavellian prince, the counter model into the model."[26]

Machiavelli and the Problems of Military Force follows in this recent trend toward scholarly reassessments of the importance of military force in Machiavelli's works. It reverses the traditional approach to Machiavelli's military thought that positions it as a supplement of his political doctrines by forefronting the militia's disciplinary regime for its capacity to generate values that exceed the military as an institution. By examining closely Machiavelli's definitions of force categories, it addresses directly the problem raised by Machiavelli's use of the figure of Hiero II in Chapter 6 of *The Prince* as a model for new princes. *How does a prince or a republic transition to employing arms of their own?* This book addresses this question and in the process offers a new approach to the theme of armed force in Machiavelli.

First, it argues that Machiavelli's discussions of the qualities of armed force—mercenary, auxiliary, mixed, one's own—are most accurately understood as a set of open-ended problems and not as a set of stable categorical determinations to be applied.

Second, it argues that Machiavelli's reasoning on the concrete tasks involved in raising and retaining a militia by a prince or republic are a response to the distinction he makes between the *arms of others* and *arms of one's own*. It is by drawing this distinction that Machiavelli generates the problem—the problem posed by different qualities of armed force and just how and when precisely a force qualifies as being of a certain kind and under what conditions it changes. Articulating and analyzing the circularity evident in Machiavelli's reasoning on this issue is the focus of this study. It contends that Machiavelli's discussions of the *arms of others* and *arms of one's own* are based on the Florentine's recognition of the fluid character of force which fluctuates according to internal and external variables, themselves in flux. Far from achieving independence of time and respect, armed force for Machiavelli arises as a set of only relatively fixed strata made stable for an indeterminate duration by the internal and external variables that generate, condition and support it. As such, Machiavelli's militia constitutes a differential of quantitative and qualitative force factors in flux because themselves in conflict.

This book argues that Machiavelli's presentations of mercenary, auxiliary, one's own, and mixed forces are not intended to function as stable or even scientific categories. Rather, Machiavelli's discussions of armed force are meant as a scaffolding for the investigation and evaluation of problems posed by analyzing the qualitative dimension of armed force.

In order to generate this scaffolding, Machiavelli breaks from the tradition of writings on war through the influence of two writers—the Roman poet, Lucretius, and the Greek mathematician, Aelianus Tacticus.

Machiavelli and Lucretius

This study argues that Machiavelli's logic of armed force cannot be properly understood without weighing the influence Lucretian natural dynamics exercised on him. It is generally accepted that Machiavelli began to transcribe his copy of Lucretius' *De rerum natura* sometime between 1497 and 1500.[27] While many scholars acknowledge that Lucretian influence can be detected in texts like the *Discourses*, the *Prince*, the *Florentine Histories*, and his long poem, *The Golden Ass*, few scholars have considered in depth possible Lucretian influence on the *Art of War*, which was composed during the same time period as these other texts. This study assumes that Lucretian natural dynamics influenced Machiavelli's reasoning on warfare in the *Art of War* as an investigation into the conditions necessary for generating a special kind of composite body—the militia.[28]

Machiavelli and Aelianus Tacticus

Machiavelli's *Art of War* styles its concerns for the minutiae of warfare after another military author available in the fifteenth and sixteenth centuries—the second-century Greek writer, Aelianus Tacticus, and his text on Macedonian phalanx tactics, *De instruendis aciebus*. Its influence on Machiavelli appears in numerous features shared by the two texts. For instance, both *The Art of War* and *De instruendis aciebus* are distinctive in that they include diagrams that detail the placement of individual soldiers to supplement descriptions of unit formations and movements. Both texts share the goal of communicating the knowledge of military tactics usually reserved for professionals with considerable field experience to readers without a practical experience of war. Investigating the overlapping intentions of these two authors, and the structural similarities of their texts, reveals that both considered the study of tactics to carry transformative implications for its reader, and, in the case of Machiavelli, offered the potential prince the opportunity to acquire the *scientia* of tactics.

2. The Outline of the Book

The book is divided into two sections. Chapters 1 and 2 anchor the distinction Machiavelli draws between *arms of one's own* and the *arms of others* in his discussion of military force in the early books of the *Art of War*. Chapter 1, "Atomic War: The Influence of Lucretius on Machiavelli's *Art of War*," examines Fabrizio Colonna's discussion of the differences between the phalanx form utilized by the Greeks and the manipular legion of the Romans in Books 2 and 3 of Machiavelli's *Art of War* from a Lucretian vantage point. In the *De rerum natura*, Lucretius describes the composition of the *animus* and *anima* in terms of the interactions of the smallest and most mobile elements. These elements then play a key role in the mechanics of sensation, the passions and in explaining how thought sets the human body in motion. In this chapter, the Lucretian mechanics of *animus* and *animo* act as a frame for examining the meanings of *anima* and *animo* in Machiavelli's *Art of War* and the disciplinary physics Machiavelli relies on to explain the factors that unify the militia as a composite body.

Chapter 2, "Practical Proportions: Aelianus Tacticus in Machiavelli's *Art of War*," examines the analyses conducted by the mercenary captain, Fabrizio da Colonna, in his discussions of small unit tactics and the role the intermediate officer structure plays in the project of generating *arms of one's own*. The chapter compares discussions of small unit formations in the *De instruendis aciebus* of Aelianus Tacticus to Colonna's discussions of the proper training of fresh rank-and-file recruits. I argue here that Machiavelli's critical reception of the second century Greek author on military tactics upends the relationship of officers like *conestabili* and *capitano* to foot soldiers and lower level officers from that of top down managers of force deployments to principal relays in a grammar of corporeal, visual and audible signs cued through bodies, flags, numbers, costumes, and music.

Chapter 3, "Industries of Failure? Mercenaries and the Arms of Others," shifts the direction of the inquiry with an analysis of Machiavelli's claims about the defects of mercenary forces. It argues that Machiavelli's arguments against relying on mercenaries serve both a practical function and as a platform for critiquing the theoretical commitments within whose horizon employment of mercenary force appears like good policy. The chapter examines in detail the examples Machiavelli furnishes of princes and republics employing mercenary forces in the *Prince* and the *Discourses* and shows that answering the question whether a prince or republic makes use of the arms of others or makes use of their own forces involves more than knowing whether the arms they employ are composed of contract forces or obedient subjects. As the cases of Hiero II and Francesco Sforza show, mercenary forces—for all their faults—can clearly prove effective transforming a potential prince into an established one.

Chapter 4, "Instrumental and Aleatory Aspects of Auxiliary Force in Machiavelli," examines the topic of auxiliary arms and argues that Machiavelli understands his militia project to possess both an instrumental and an easily overlooked aleatory aspect rooted in a Lucretian reading of the humoral conflict that Machiavelli identifies to be at work in all states. Close reading of the theme of auxiliaries presented in the *Prince*, Chapter 13, and the *Discourses* at 2.20 reveals that Machiavelli's analysis of auxiliary arms articulates the phenomenon from the standpoint of the prince where such forces serve as an instrument for the projection of power but also from the standpoint of the people. Further, Machiavelli's depiction of auxiliary force reveals the people to be an unpredictable factor that opens up political relations to a field of uncertainty. Acknowledging the aspectival function played by the definition of auxiliaries in Machiavelli's texts offers a new vantage point for re-reading Machiavelli on the nature of authority, power, and the humoral-driven conflicts of *popolo* and *grandi*.

Chapter 5, "Transforming Compounds: Machiavelli's Analyses of Mixed Force," returns to themes raised in the first two chapters and examines Machiavelli's discussions of the employment of mixed forces—forces comprised of mercenaries, auxiliaries and arms of one's own. Machiavelli's discussions of mixed forces show that he considers these forms of armed force important and valuable—much more so than either auxiliary or mercenary forces employed on their own. This chapter argues that the categorical limits Machiavelli draws between mercenary, auxiliary, and arms of one's own behave as porous thresholds between types of organization distinguished by their different qualities. Machiavelli uses the category of mixed forces to account for how bodies of military force experience changes due to both subjective and objective factors. His use of this category highlights how determining the quality of a force involves not only identifying the factors that unite it, whether economical in the case of mercenaries, authoritative in the case of auxiliaries, or disciplinary in the case of *arma propriis*. It is also a matter of accurately assessing whether the force being analyzed is in the process of strengthening or declining due to factors ranging from institutional and historical to material, technical and psychological.

1

Atomic War: The Influence of Lucretius on Machiavelli's *Art of War*

1. Introduction

Sergio Bertelli first wrote of the 1961 discovery in the Vatican Library of Machiavelli's hand transcription of *De rerum natura* (*Rossiana* 884),[1] which contained a copy of Lucretius' text bound with the *Eunech* of Terence.[2] Scholars accept that Machiavelli began transcribing his copy of Lucretius' *De rerum natura* around 1497.[3] Alison Brown, Paul Rahe, Robert Roecklein, Ada Palmer, and Vittorio Morfino, among others, have argued convincingly that the influence of Lucretius and Epicurean philosophy can be discerned in Machiavelli's texts like the *Discourses,* the *Prince,* the *Florentine Histories,* and his long poem, *The Golden Ass,* and that Machiavelli's notions of free will, religion, and natural philosophy exhibit Epicurean influence.

For instance, Brown argues that Lucretius' influence on Machiavelli spans his works and shows up especially in Machiavelli's reasoning on ethical themes.[4] Weighing the marginal notations Machiavelli made in the *De rerum natura,*[5] Brown establishes numerous parallels between the Roman poet and the Florentine, especially in their understandings of free will and the role they ascribe to religion as an instrument of politics. Brown's analyses detect Lucretian influence throughout Machiavelli's works, from texts like the *Discourses* to his plays, and she concludes that Lucretian Epicureanism forms the cornerstone of Machiavelli's philosophy.[6]

Paul Rahe also argues that Lucretius influenced Machiavelli and locates in the Roman poet the reason for Machiavelli's break from the Aristotelian political tradition. Rahe finds the clearest sign of Lucretian influence in Machiavelli's repudiation of religion and natural teleology.[7] In addition, he highlights passages where he sees Machiavelli to be critical of Lucretius and Epicureanism in general. For instance, Rahe hears irony behind Machiavelli's setting the *Art of War* in the sheltered gardens of the Oricellari family given the observations the *condottiere* captain, Fabrizio Colonna, makes in Book 1 about the softness of those accustomed to fight in the shade. Rahe assembles evidence that Machiavelli would not support the withdrawal from political life necessary to achieve Epicurean *ataraxía*—i.e., the pleasures taken in calmness of mind and freedom from the pains of emotional disturbance advocated by both Lucretius in the *De rerum natura* and Epicurus as transmitted through Diogenes Laertius.[8]

Rahe goes further and argues that Machiavelli's silence on the question of the famous Epicurean atomic swerve—the *clinamen*—should also be read as his rejection of this Epicurean position and his willingness to embrace natural determinism.[9] However, Rahe does not work with Machiavelli's transcription of the *De rerum natura* directly. Rahe's analysis does not acknowledge Machiavelli's marginal comments in Book 2 of *De rerum natura*, where Machiavelli clearly links the possibility of freedom of the will to Lucretius' description of the atomic swerve.

On the other hand, Ada Palmer analyzes the fifty-four manuscripts of the *De rerum natura* that remain from this period, including Machiavelli's manuscript. Her investigations show that Machiavelli is the only one of the Renaissance Lucretian annotators to include in his copy extensive marginal notes on the section of *De rerum natura* Book 2 that addresses the technical details of Epicurean atomistic physics, including the nature of the *primordia* and the discussion of the *clinamen*.[10] Palmer's study shows that Machiavelli was unusual among Renaissance transcribers of Lucretius in the attention he gave to passages in the *De rerum natura* that discuss atomistic natural principles like the *clinamen*.

Robert Roecklin would extend Palmer's line of reasoning even further.[11] Roecklin hears the reference to mixed bodies in these chapters as a challenge to approach Machiavelli's philosophy "from the vantage point of the theory of body that underlies his philosophy."[12] For Roecklin, Machiavelli's references to the physics of mixed bodies in these chapters are important because in them it is evident that Machiavelli relies upon Epicurean terminology.[13]

Vittorio Morfino argues that Machiavelli accepts the Epicurean physics of mixed bodies. Morfino contends that Lucretius and, following him, Machiavelli, adopt a notion of corporeality that subordinates considerations of a body's form to its susceptibility to mutate and change. On Morfino's reading of Lucretius, an individual body occurs as an event generated from the ongoing exchange of relations among the aggregated *primordia* that compose it and those in its environment that support it. Morfino argues that agency in a Lucretian context must be understood from this basic fact.[14] For Morfino, Machiavelli's narratives describe the actions of agents like Cesare Borgia from several different perspectives because multiple layers of different kinds of interacting bodies take part in the event. As with Roecklin, Morfino's readings of Machiavellian exemplars like Borgia would depend greatly on accepting the thesis that Machiavelli unconditionally adopts Lucretian atomism.[15]

A notable lacuna in these analyses concerns the *Art of War*, composed during the same time period as these other texts. The difficulty of establishing potential lines of influence between the *De rerum natura* and the *Art of War* is compounded due to the highly technical nature of the discussions on warfare that dominate the latter text. Scholars often neglect the *Art of War* on the basis of its focus on the minutiae of Renaissance military practice, which they judge a limitation of the text when measured against Machiavelli's more genuinely political works.

On the other hand, scholars like Gabriele Pedullà argue that the *Art of War* is critical to understanding Machiavelli's notion of the political, not despite, but *because of* these highly technical discussions; argues Pedullà: "To be a good political leader is not enough, because you have to become a military expert as well: this is Machiavelli's fundamental belief."[16] For Pedullà, Machiavelli's obsession with saddle construction, the angle of wagon wheels, and the proper width of roads and ditches in fortified towns and encampments shows his concern for the "microphysics of action" and how the concrete domains of practice and discipline serve as vectors for understanding his political thought.[17] Machiavelli's attention to the filigree of warfare signals his conviction that the spheres of practice and discipline forge chains of association that map onto subjectivity itself.[18] On this reading, military discipline acts as the foundation for the domain of subjectivity by generating, and then capturing, that domain.

Machiavelli's historical concerns with the atomistic physics and psychology spelled out in the *De rerum natura* offer a powerful vantage point through which to re-examine Machiavelli's treatment of the transformational power of military discipline as spelled out in the *Art of War*. This chapter and the next examine Fabrizio Colonna's discussion of the differences between the phalanx form utilized by the Greeks and the Swiss and the manipular legion of the Romans in Books 2 and 3 of the *Art of War* from a Lucretian framework. This chapter investigates two points of contact with Lucretius that emerge from the mercenary captain's analyses. First he favors his neo-Roman brigade over the Macedonian phalanx and Swiss pike squares on the basis of "its greater life," which it owes to materialist principles immanent to its organization. Second, the greater effectiveness of the brigade over the phalanx consists in its capacity for renewing itself, a theme that links Machiavelli's discussion of battalion organization to passages in the *Discourses* and the *Florentine Histories* where the Florentine's reasoning also exhibits a strong atomist influence.

As we will see, of all Machiavelli's texts, the *Art of War* most offers itself to being read as a project of Lucretian bioengineering.[19] As a dialogue between young Florentines and a mercenary captain, it begins by enumerating the ills following from the current state of military affairs on the Italian peninsula that stem from the reliance princes and republics have on professional mercenary and auxiliary troops, or what he discusses exhaustively in the *Prince* and the *Discourses* as the dangers of relying on *arma alienis*. It concludes by relying on both narrative and diagrammatic elements to generate a functional fighting force from ordinary citizens sourced from all parts of society who, at the end of the process, will be distinguished from mercenaries and auxiliaries by being highly disciplined, but *non-professional*, combatants.

2. Lucretius and the Bodies of War

Lucretius refers to martial bodies and martial actions frequently in the *De rerum natura* as examples,[20] so the Latin poet clearly does not consider these types of bodies as somehow outside the physical dynamics he applies to the basic building blocks of matter. Also recognizing the influence of Lucretian naturalism on Machiavelli's thought generates several consequences for reading Machiavelli on the theme of *arma alienis* and *arma propriis*.[21] Even considered superficially, military formations of whatever sort qualify as Lucretian composite bodies. A line of soldiers, a cavalry wing, or an army compounded of legions represent progressively more complicated mixed bodies in a way that parallels how fluids, organs, and tissues progressively combine to form the human body. For Lucretius, higher order composites piece together countless lower level composites which, themselves are textures of many different kinds of bodies linked with various kinds of bonds, differing widely in character but all originating ultimately with the *primordia*. For Lucretius, there are three principal features of atomic reality: the first is the simple fact of atomic motion. Atoms move and, when unobstructed, travel faster than thought. Second, atoms retain this fact of being in motion even when they are so tightly packed into formations they seem frozen in place. Third, no matter how trapped, atoms retain their potentiality for declining from their ultra-rapid, rectilinear, straight-line trajectories.

Three passages in Machiavelli's main works directly invoke the distinction between simple and mixed bodies and describe natural mechanics consistent with those articulated by Lucretius. These occur at *Discourses* 2.5 and 3.1 as well as the opening of Book 5 of the *Florentine Histories*. The Lucretian allusions in these passages make important references to themes also important to investigating possible Lucretian influence in the *Art of War*, so it makes sense to examine them first to show how Machiavelli adapts Lucretian principles in them to fit his purposes. For instance, Machiavelli reaches the conclusion at *Discourses* 2.5 that all mixed bodies necessarily undergo periodic purges, which result in the near total destruction of the human race and the partial or complete collapse of civilizations.[22] On the other hand, he reasons in the first chapter of the third book of the *Discourses* about the need for bodies like republics, kingdoms, and sects to undergo periodic renewals in order, presumably, to suspend the occurrence of these catastrophes.[23] When set side by side, the two passages present an argument for the importance of the return to beginnings for republics, kingdoms, sects, and institutions so that the experience of regular renewals strengthens them against those external and internal shocks that could trigger their ruin. Extending this reasoning to the *Art of War*, the complex militia Machiavelli constructs in that work would certainly qualify as one of these mixed bodies, confronted by the possibility of the shocks of battle prompting the need for ongoing renewals.

3. What Constitutes Primordia?

However, the fit between Machiavelli and Lucretius on the notion of mixed bodies is not a relationship of congruence. Notable in his reasoning in each of these three passages is that Machiavelli uses the Lucretian distinction between *composite* and *simple* bodies flexibly, as relative determinations whose specific meanings derive from the scope of the investigation. Machiavelli frequently takes the human body for his fixed *minima* and not the Lucretian atom. It remains to be seen whether his flexibility with atomist principles places him at odds with Lucretian naturalism.

For example, in Book 5 of the *Florentine Histories*, the Florentine exile Rinaldo degli Albizzi argues from the distinction between simple and mixed bodies when he begs the Duke of Milan to invade Florence. He initially contrasts the human body as a simple entity with cities as composite bodies. However, in the course of the passage, he also suggests that even cities could be considered a simple body when considered in certain contexts. On the basis of these passages, what counts as a *corpo semplice* for Machiavelli may depend on the order of aggregate being investigated. Thus, from the standpoint of a highly aggregated body like a city, the individual human body would serve as its functional minima, i.e., the *primordia*, of the inquiry. Palmer's analysis of Machiavelli's hand transcription of *De rerum natura* strengthens reading Machiavelli's *corpi misti* this way. Palmer highlights Machiavelli's marginal notation at *De rerum natura* Book 2, line 522 where he writes: "principia cuiuslibet formae esse infinita" (the fundamental elements are infinite whatever their forms). As she notes here:

> *cuiuslibet*, not present in the text, could simply be intended to say that each type of atom, whatever its shape, is in infinite supply, as the text states. But the powerful vagueness of Machiavelli's *cuiuslibet* suggests something broader, that this logical proof stands whether these *principia* are spheres or spiky rods, atoms or something else entirely. This is materialist logic applicable beyond atomism.[24]

Palmer interprets the passage to mean that Machiavelli is willing to posit the atom as a kind of logical exercise simply to arrive at a useful conclusion. As Palmer continues: "Machiavelli may have been an atomist, but he does not have to have been one for Lucretius to have been a key enabler of his revolutionary ethics."[25] Extending Palmer's reasoning further, Machiavelli does not have to have been an atomist for him to have based his theory of warfare in the *Art of War* on atomist logical principles and methods as tools for assessing the relative strengths and weaknesses of complex bodies like the battalions, brigades and armies he builds up on the basis of neo-Roman principles of combat.

If Palmer's thesis is correct, then Machiavelli's tendency to adapt atomist logic to complex bodies should be apparent elsewhere in his works.[26] Machiavelli's discussion of mixed bodies at *Discourses* 3.1 is important both for its conspicuous employment of atomistic language to describe the dynamics of mixed bodies and for its insistence on the importance of *renewal* for ensuring the greater life of a mixed body.[27] As the passage opens:

> It is a thing most true how all the things of the world have an end to their life (*il termine della loro vita*), but those go the entire course that is ordered for them by heaven that do not disorder their body but hold it in an ordered mode, or that do not alter, or, if they do alter, it is to their health and not to their harm. And because I speak of mixed bodies (*corpi misti*), as are republics and sects (*come sono le republiche e le sètte*), I say that those alterations are for their health that lead them back to their beginnings (*che le riducano inverso i principii loro*). And, further, those are better ordered and have a longer life that by means of their own orders are able to renew themselves often, or by some accident outside of the said order come to the said renewal (*rinnovazione*).

And it is a thing clearer than light that, not renewing themselves, these bodies do not endure.[28]

The opening of 3.1 expresses two themes compatible with Epicurean physics: 1) that mixed bodies exist with fixed durations; and 2) whether or not bodies reach the limit of the time fixed for them by heaven (*dal cielo*) depends on whether the body is renewed by being returned to its principles.[29]

The quotation from *Discourses* 3.1 suggests that Machiavelli has relativized the Lucretian hypothesis concerning what constitutes nature's fundamental building blocks and applies it as a convenient paradigm to explain the periodic returns to principles that institutions like republics, sects and kingdoms as well as cities and the human race undergo.[30] Sections like *Discourses* 3.1 offer strong support to Palmer's two-sided argument that Machiavelli is influenced by the concepts and methods of Lucretian physics, while his employment of these principles drifts from the strict axis of absolute *primordia* at the basis of aggregates Lucretius maintains throughout the *De rerum natura* to more like relative determinations of *minima* and *maxima* that are context dependent. This reading gives a substantial basis for analyzing the *Art of War* not only as having something to contribute to Machiavelli's notion of the political, but also as potentially acting as a Trojan horse by which Machiavelli introduces Lucretian methods for reasoning about complex bodies using a more flexible understanding of what constitutes a minimal building block.[31] After all the *Art of War* was published in Florence in 1521—four years after the *Concilium Florentinum* banned the teaching of Lucretius in schools.[32] The ban followed in the wake of the 1513 promulgation of Lateran V that made belief in the afterlife a requirement for all Christians. In this climate, a cautious author like Machiavelli might be inclined to conceal any links to the Roman poet in the only text he had published during his lifetime.

Acknowledging Machiavelli's tendency to adjust Lucretian dynamics is especially important to reading accurately the *Art of War*. If the *Art of War* demonstrates that Machiavelli incorporates the foundations of Lucretian natural principles and an anti-teleological physics then this text, too, reasons according to an atomist methodology starting from the human body as the *primordia*. The principles of unit formation the mercenary captain Fabrizio Colonna proposes to his interlocutors during the dialogue take on an importance that extends beyond historical questions on the extent of Machiavelli's involvement in the Florentine militia project. Reading Lucretian physics as background to the *Art of War* emphasizes the character of special composite bodies like military lines, battalions, brigades, and legions and the character of the bonds that hold them together to constitute an effective fighting group. Since these higher order bodies owe their characteristics to the qualities of the human bodies which, as building blocks, compose them, the disciplinary practices Colonna proposes as the core training for his recruits assume special importance. These practices target the formation of reflexive habits and associative thought chains on the basis of frequent repetition of colors, numbers, flags and sounds. The strength of these habits and associations form the basis of Machiavelli's claims of the superiority of his neo-Roman legion to the Greek phalanx and the Swiss pike squares, which will be investigated in more depth in Chapter 2.

4. Problems with Fifteenth-century Italian Warfare: *uno impeto* versus *rifarsi*

Fabrizio Colonna's discussion of the differences between the phalanx form utilized by the Greeks and the Swiss and the manipular legion of the Romans in Books 2 and 3 of the *Art of War* offers a promising starting point in determining any indebtedness Machiavelli might have had to Lucretian atomism in his theory of warfare. At least two points of contact with Lucretius emerge from the mercenary captain's analyses. First, he favors his neo-Roman brigade over the Macedonian phalanx and Swiss pike squares on the basis of "its greater life," a preference that stems from materialist principles immanent to its organization. Second, the greater effectiveness of the brigade over the phalanx consists in its capacity for renewing itself, a theme that links Machiavelli's discussions of tactics to *Discourses* 2.5 and 3.1, as well as the *Florentine Histories* at 5.1, where his discussions of the destruction and renewal of mixed bodies also exhibits a strong atomist influence.

In Books 2 and 3 of the dialogue, Colonna assesses the state of contemporary weapons, armor, and the forms of organization favored by Italian, French, and German armies. After highlighting their defects he then proposes a new form of organization that combines features of the Roman legion, the Greek phalanx, and Swiss pike squares. He equips his soldiers in swords and shields following the Romans, pikes following the Swiss, and adds a contingent of archers and arquebusiers to round out his brigade that numbers in total 3,000 swordsmen, 2,000 ordinary and extraordinary pikemen, and 1,000 ordinary and extraordinary velites. He reinforces the infantry with a contingent of 300 cavalry and a structure of 681 officers composed of decurions, centurions, constables, heads of velites, and a brigade captain along with sixteen squads of musicians and flags to accompany the senior officers.

Ten battalions of 600 soldiers form the building blocks of the brigade of 6,000. Colonna's argument begins by tackling the problem of how best to train, equip, and organize these battalions. He dismisses the contemporary mode of arranging soldiers that stretched them out in a single line because it gives the army one front and allows it only a single thrust and, therefore, one try at fortune ("*uno impeto e una fortuna*"). Contemporary armies fight this way only because the ancient Roman mode for receiving lines into one another has been lost.

However, he also rejects the other ancient form of organizing armies—the Macedonian phalanx. Colonna attributes its principal shortcoming to its inability to remake (*refarsi*) itself. This defect was due to the use of the Greek lance—the *sarissa*—whose extension was so long that the first three lines of the phalanx formed a threshold of engagement that could be maintained only as long as soldiers remained to step into the spaces vacated by the fallen. The phalanx form was definitely superior to the single-line formation. Colonna even allows that the Romans in their maniple formations experienced difficulty defeating King Perseus of Macedon due to the virtues of the Greek form[33] and that the Romans made use of the phalanx formation up to the second Samnite War.[34] Even the success the Swiss enjoyed in the fifteenth and sixteenth centuries with their pike squares was due to their study and imitation of the Macedonian phalanx.[35]

Colonna then explains that the Romans became dissatisfied with the order because of issues adapting it to uneven terrain, and so they broke their legions into multiple bodies having different functions, which could operate independently of one another. The Roman order of combat presented four waves. The first involved missile combat on the part of the velites. If this was successful—which happened rarely—the battle concluded, but when repulsed the velites would withdraw through empty spaces in the lines. He then continues:

> After their departure, the *hastati* came to hands with the enemy. If these were seen to be overcome, they withdrew little by little through the spaces in the orders between the *principes* and together with those they renewed the fight. If these too were forced back, they all withdrew into the spaces between the orders of the *triarii* and, having made one pile, they renewed the fight.[36]

He then contrasts the Roman mode with the Greek mode. The Greek phalanx was a body built up out of many smaller bodies each of which had its own nominal commander or "head." Despite all its subdivisions and large quantity of commanders, the phalanx made only "one body, or rather, one head,"[37] and so the Greek phalanx and the Swiss pike squares display the same defect because the different parts of the formation cannot receive the other.[38]

However, the Roman mode did not suffer this defect. Colonna ascribes this to the function played by the flag and *capidieci* for assuring that each soldier could instantly position themselves in their battalion; he states:

> Therefore, it is necessary that there are many bodies in an army, and that every body has its own flag and its own guide. Because having this, it must be that it also has many souls (*anime*), and as a consequence, many lives.[39]

Colonna's use of *anima*—or *soul*—in the passage is neither haphazard nor metaphorical but states an idea that will be echoed in Book 3.[40] The greater life of Fabrizio's formation is a function of the many bodies his brigade contains and how the responses of those bodies have been programmed. Colonna's recruits have been disciplined to orient themselves with respect to the *capidieci* and the positioning of their flag. In the logic of the passage, the so-called "souls" of the formation stem from the readiness of the soldiers to locate themselves in space relative to the formation's flag and sergeants. Colonna criticizes how flags are used in contemporary armies where they serve, "to make a beautiful show rather than for another military use."[41] The other way to employ flags is to follow the example of the ancients who used them,

> as a guide and to reorder themselves. For when the flag had stopped, each knew the place that he kept near his flag and always returned there. Each also knew that when it moved or stood still, they had to stop or to move.[42]

The flags for each battalion served as a marker both the soldiers and their commanders used to reorder themselves and to move or stop in their battalions as a single body, "judging their place at a glance" ("*giudicare a occhio il loro luogho*").[43]

But the flags were not the only ordering element. The soldiers retained their place in the order relative to the disposition of their battalion flags by constantly evaluating their position and actions according to the positions and actions of their guide (*guida*). The "guides" Colonna refers to here are the lowest-ranking officers, the *capidieci*, who rank below the centurions, the constables and the brigade captain—and who occupy the role of master sergeants in the battalion's officer structure. Colonna criticizes how these officers are used in contemporary armies where they are simply an infantry soldier paid more than the rest.[44] Colonna argues that in ancient armies, the *capidieci* guided their units of ten men by being constantly in contact and fighting, marching, and living with them. The *capidieci* were those soldiers who, "with his spirit (*animo*), with his words, and with his example keeps the others firm and disposed to fight."[45] Like the flags, each of the *capidieci* performed as a "line and a guide" (*rigo e temperamento*).[46] When the *capidieci* assumed their position in the line, their soldiers only became disordered with difficulty and, if they did become disordered, their habituated responses spontaneously prompted them to re-order themselves at once.

In these two passages, Colonna defines the *anime* of the formation as a function of the soldier's discipline, which is itself a function of the programmed responses the soldier's body assumes relative to the placement of the battalion flag and the *capidieci* of their line. However, as it turns out the *anime* of Colonna's legion also contain a final element that proves all-important. Due to the sixteen "music" (*suoni*) units that accompany the sixteen flags, and the fifteen constables and the brigade captain, Machiavelli's assembled brigade of 6,000 infantry hovers somewhere between symphony and cacophony. Colonna details the importance the *suoni* perform in the militia's disciplinary regime at the level of both battalion and brigade. The battalions can learn what it takes to maintain their lines, whether in motion and at rest. However, the *suoni* tell them how they must move their lines within the larger formations when assembled with the other parts of the battalion, the brigade, and the army as a whole. As he states:

> From the (*suono*) like a galley oarsman from the whistle, they learn to know how to recognize what they have to do, whether they have to stand firm, or go ahead, or turn back, or where to turn their arms and faces.[47]

The troops change behaviors on the basis of shifting sound cues. These sonic cues not only order their motions relative to their formation but also regulate the discrete parts of their bodies down to the position of arms and torso, feet, chest, and face. Through the *suoni*, "[the soldiers] understand well the commands of the head (*capo*) by means of the sound."[48] Included among the *capi* are not only the captain of the brigade but also the *conestabili* of each battalion, each of whom possess their own flag and sound corps. The upper level officers coordinate the centurions and *capidieci* by signaling them in sounds, and the lower officer grades act as an example and guide to the rest. As Colonna concludes: "For without this discipline, observed and practiced with utmost care and diligence, never was an army good."[49] What begins as a show of purely external factors—*capidieci, bandiere, suoni*—forms an economy of signs that maps onto the domain of subjectivity itself.[50]

A similar set of considerations accompanies the third and last occurrence of *anima* in the *Art of War*, which happens in Book 3 where Machiavelli contrasts the organization of the Macedonian phalanx with the structure of the Roman legion. He then explains,

> They [the Romans] divided the legions into more bodies; that is, into cohorts and maniples. For, as I have said a little while ago, they judged that that body had more life which had more souls (*anime*) and was composed of more parts, in such a way that each one regulated itself through itself ("*in modo che ciascheduna per sé stessa si regesse*").[51]

Machiavelli refers to the earlier occurrence of *anima* here and reaffirms that the greater life of the legion depends on it having "more souls." Machiavelli does not mention the ordering principles indicated in Book 2—the music, flag, and guide—but he does identify the condition of having multiple souls with the Roman legion whose discrete parts could operate independently in ways not possible for the Macedonian phalanx or for the other formation he frequently reasons about: the Swiss pike squares. The structure of the Roman legion owed its greater life to the greater independence of its maniples and cohorts, and this greater independence was due to how "each one regulated itself through itself." The capacity for self-regulation did not stop at the level of the formation, however, but extended down to each soldier on his own who was habituated to operate automatically within a network of signs generated from sounds, flags, and the physical position of low-ranking officers. This network of signs guided the aggregate with the immediacy of a "galley oarsman responding to a whistle."

Colonna then explains to Cosimo that when flags, low-ranking officers, and music function in their ancient mode of employment, it becomes possible to revive the Roman tactic of having lines receive one another and renew the fight during battle. This capacity of the brigade to renew itself does not derive from the top. It derives from principles immanent to the army at the level of the line and the individual soldier. As Colonna sums up the discussion at this point:

> For in the armies one observes two orders: one, what must be done by the men in each battalion; and the other, what the battalion must then do when it is with others in one army. And those men who know the first well observe the second easily; but without knowing the former, they can never attain the discipline of the second.[52]

The organization of Fabrizio's brigade is superior to that of the phalanx or pike square because it is a highly composite body whose minimal constituent —its *primordia*—are soldiers whose common discipline acts as the bonds organizing and uniting the battalion and the brigade together into a composite body. Colonna argues that his legionnaires possess skills lacking among Greek hoplites or Swiss pikes because they coordinate their places in a mobile and fluid space where their bodies have been conditioned to instantly self-regulate relative to their line guide, the position of the flag, and the sounds made by the music corps.

5. Lucretius and the Soul of War

But where does Lucretius lurk in the midst of Colonna's extended discussions of the proper angle of wagon wheels and the correct procedure for compressing a line of infantry? The immanence of the principles that organize Fabrizio's brigade, and his limited but suggestive use of the mechanics of the *anima* to describe martial composites, recall the distinction Lucretius makes between soul (*animus*) and body in the *De rerum natura*. Palmer shows how Machiavelli's copy of the *De rerum natura* stands out among the fifty-four still extant fifteenth-century manuscripts of the work due to the high density of marginal notations the Florentine makes in Book 2. This happens to be the book where Lucretius focuses most on laying out the mechanics of atomist physics, and no other copy of the *De rerum natura* from this period shows the same concentration of marginalia in this section of the text. When Lucretius discusses the human body, he concentrates on the microphysics of atomic interactions with priority given to how they produce sensation and motion.[53] For instance, in Book 3, after explaining how thought affects the body Lucretius adds:

> This same reason teaches that the nature of soul and also the spirit are bodily; for indeed it (*animus*) is seen to propel forward the limbs, snatch the body from sleep, change facial expression, and also to guide and steer the whole human being, of which we see none of this can come about without touch, nor can there be touching without body; must we not confess that the soul (*animus*) and spirit (*anima*) to consist in the nature of the body?[54]

If Colonna composes the *anima* of his battalion from circuits composed of *capidieci*, flags, sounds, and line soldiers programmed to respond to these cues, Lucretius defines the *animus* of the human body as a composite aggregate of "extremely round and extremely minute seeds,"[55] made of three named substances—breath (*vapor*), heat (*calor*), air (*aera*)—to which he adds a fourth, nameless, substance. As he describes their interactions:

> In fact, first this [the unnamed nature] is set in motion, being made of small shapes, then the heat and unseen power of wind receives the movement, then air; then all others are moved. The blood is agitated, then all the viscera begin to feel deeply, then last of all motion is given to bones and marrow . . .[56]

For Lucretius, as for Colonna, the soul is also a composite that serves as both a principle of sensation and of bodily movement. It accomplishes these things not by being a discrete separable substance capable of independent subsistence, but by being itself an aggregate whose components connect up with the other tissues, fluids, and structures of the body.

Examined through an atomist lens, these two spheres of concern—the Lucretian *animus* of the individual human body and the Machiavellian *anima* of a brigade—do not have to exclude one another. As both composite bodies, they form a natural continuum where Machiavelli's analysis of the bodies of war rests on and plays out the implications of Lucretian atomic principles as a *higher order aggregate*. The key to establishing a nexus point and plane of deep compatibility between Machiavelli and Lucretius depends on analyzing the relationship between Lucretius' usage of *animus* (soul) and *anima* (spirit) in the *De rerum natura* and Machiavelli's usage of *anima* and most especially the ubiquitous, *animo*, in *The Art of War*.

6. Lucretius and the *Anima—Maxima* of Motion

In the *De rerum natura*, Lucretius links *animus* to the powers of reflection, emotion, and sensation. On the other hand, he identifies the *anima* as the motive principle spread throughout the body, which sets its parts in motion. Lucretius presents both the soul and spirit as parts of the body, distinguished from other constituents by being the body's most rapidly moving elements.

Though Lucretius distinguishes between the *animus* and *anima*, he also identifies important points of continuity between them. For instance, he identifies *anima* as the principle of motion rooted in the body's heat and breath and, thus, in air as well. For Lucretius, *anima* is neither a harmony within the body or a substance separable from it. Like the *animus*, movement defines it. While the stomach serves as the seat for the *animus*, the *anima* spreads throughout the body.[57] The elements of the *anima* move the body by being in contact with its parts. Sufficiently strong motions of the *animus* may excite the *anima* as well or they may lack the strength to set its parts in motion. He also describes the two in terms of the *animus* commanding and the *anima* obeying.[58]

The bottom line is that, for Lucretius, the *animus* performs as an ultra-energetic particle field through which thinking and emotions arise, and the *anima* acts as the body's principle of motion, though both are aggregates composed of many of the same bodies.[59] The human body can be moved as a whole by these two because the *anima* is mixed throughout it and shares three of the four elements that compose the *animus* as well. These bodies are uniquely described by Lucretius in terms of their mobility and their capacity to transmit movement, as opposed to their solidity and their location in a place. Breath, heat, air, and the fourth (unnamed) nature share the character of being extremely rapid, extremely small, smooth in texture, and spherical in shape. The size, texture, and shape of these elements are attributes of their solidity that Lucretius takes pains to minimize. Instead, he emphasizes their extreme speed on the basis of their smallness, smoothness and sphericity. The attributes describing solidity give these substances the minimum corporeity necessary to be something that still can participate in networks of bodily motions, which they do through their most critical and defining feature—their swiftness.

The remaining element is the nameless fourth element.[60] Lucretius distinguishes this element from the other three by ascribing to it the three attributes ascribed to them but even more so, i.e., this element is even smoother, smaller, more spherical, and, therefore, yet faster. It is important to note here that by drawing the distinction between *animus* and *anima* this way, Lucretius consistently presents their difference as being one of degree, not kind. The fourth element is just that element of the *animus* which is the closest it gets to a minimum of extension and a maximum of mobility.

This is particularly important because Lucretius closely identifies the motion of this type of body with sensation itself. For Lucretius, motions of the fourth element do not produce sensations—sights, sounds, scents, and textures—as a separable effect. Rather, their motions *are* sensations. Motions of the soul's fourth element are compounded with the soul's other elements. When these interact, the soul undergoes sensations.[61] Further, motions of the *animus* broadcast toward the *anima* affecting it, and through it, other parts of the body. On the basis of the circuit of motions generated by the *animus* and *anima*, the body as a whole acts. Instead of serving as the *terminus* of perceptions, the fourth element acts as a site of re-distribution, broadcasting its motions back toward the body's other elements by being aggregated with the *anima*. As François Moreau describes this relationship, in Lucretius: "there is not here a theory of sensation. Rather, there is a theory of the unity of sensation and excitation."[62]

7. *Animo* and the Many Lives of Machiavelli's Legion

In the *Art of War*, Machiavelli constructs a legion–phalanx hybrid whose composition parallels enticingly the tri-partite structure of *animus, anima,* and grosser *corpi* whose exchange of movements Lucretius uses to explain features of the human body in the *De rerum natura*. At first glance, his militiamen appear to externalize performatively the functions Lucretius identifies to be at work in the human body itself. Where Lucretius concentrates on explaining the causes of the body's capacity for sensation and thought and the microphysics of excitation and movement through the interactions of the *animus* and *anima*, Machiavelli externalizes these relationships. He presents the militia as a compound of very different kinds of bodies united by a common set of bonds generated by the militia's disciplinary regime. Constant exercise in the practices that generate this common disciplinary framework prepares the human body to be integrated into progressively higher order aggregates like a brigade, battalion, or entire army.

Key to establishing greater depth to the relationship between the similar terms in the two authors is a closer examination of the use Machiavelli makes of the officer grades. Two important factors surface here. First, the low-ranking officers knit together the legion as a whole because they perform their role by occupying a place within each line. These officers are not simply paid more money. They distinguish themselves from the other soldiers by demonstrating more spirit ("*animo*"). The decurions (*capidieci*) anchor the lines and the centurions (*centurioni*) anchor the squares of the battalion.[63] They serve as anchors by being placed in physical contact with the other soldiers with whom they live. Only when these officers take their position do the rest discover their appropriate place on the field. Machiavelli describes the *capidieci* and *centurioni* as integrated into the military formation in a way that recalls how Lucretius describes the *animus* and *anima* in the structures of the human body. Again, these two groups of officers merit their rank not because they originate in a different economic class, have more honorable occupations, or have acquired seniority over the rest through sheer length of time in service. For Machiavelli, the lowest-ranking officers receive their positions because they possess "greater spirit"—the *animo* mentioned above—than the rank-and-file soldiers who emulate their lead.[64]

Machiavelli's use of the term *animo* here provides a potential clue to how Machiavelli's reasoning on the mechanics of the battalion lines up with Lucretius' reasoning on the mechanics of the aggregate soul. For these two discourses to align, the role of the *animo* in the *Art of War* would need to match with the part the Lucretian *anima* plays in the human body in the *De rerum natura*. For Lucretius, the *anima* acts as a threshold between the component of the soul defined most by mobility—i.e., the *animus*—and the body's grosser elements and compounds.

A survey of the occurrences of *animo* in the *Art of War* reveals a rich tapestry of meanings linked to Machiavelli's use of the term. First, he employs *animo* with much greater frequency than he does *anima*. Where *anima* only appears three times in the *Art of War*, *animo* and related terms like *animoso* appear thirty-five times.[65] Though they crop up in varied contexts, the occurrences of *animo* and its cognates roughly sort under five headings, but all refer to some type of motion whether of the feelings and passions, of a part of the body, or of the body (or a group of bodies) as a whole. These meanings of *animo* include (1) liveliness or energy level, (2) consciousness of pain or pleasure, (3) degree of certainty, (4) softness or firmness of intention (i.e., determination), and (5) character as source of intentions.

For instance, Machiavelli most frequently uses *animo* to designate degree of vigor and liveliness, which he does in twenty-two passages in the *Art of War*. For instance, *animo* occurs three times at 1.21 where Colonna stipulates that discerning the *animo* of potential recruits is a primary task of the militia's draft:

> Those who have given rules for war want men to be selected from the temperate countries, so that they have spirit and prudence (*animo e prudenza*). For a warm country generates prudent and not spirited (*animosi*) men, a cold one spirited (*animosi*) and not prudent ones.[66]

Or, again, he deploys it when discussing in Book 4 the effects a captain's speech can have on the behavior of the soldiers: "which not only did not disturb the army but grew its spirit (*animo*) so much that it remained victorious."[67] Or, again, in Book 2, Colonna employs *animo* to describe the effects that different sounds (*suoni*) can have on an army:

> ...they varied the sound (*suono*) according to how they wanted to vary the motion, and according to how they wanted to ignite or calm or firm up the spirits (*animi*) of the men.[68]

These passages reflect the dominant usage of *animo* when it has the meaning of energy level and liveliness. Certain emotions like fear and terror diminish or even force out the *animo*, rendering the person paralyzed, while certain sounds and rhetorically charged speeches by leaders energize and throw a person forward.

Linked to this usage, *animo* also denotes the experience of pleasure or pain. For instance, Colonna accepts the invitation to join the group for an afternoon of conversations in the Oricellari garden because, "it appeared to him an occasion to spend a day reasoning about those matters that satisfied his spirit (*animo*)."[69] This meaning of *animo* is often linked to occurrences of the term that convey a sense of certainty and uncertainty. Examples of this meaning occur in Book 1 when the narrator describes Colonna discovering some trees in the garden he doesn't recognize: "he was with his spirit (*animo*) in suspense."[70] It appears again when Cosimo Rucellai reacts to Colonna's assessment of the dangers of a class of leisured gentlemen with: "since this is almost the entire contrary to what I had thought of it until now, my spirit (*animo*) is still not purged of every doubt..."[71] Here the sense of motion ascribed to the *animo* shifts into a subjective index as deliberation between options or shifts among states of emotion.

As some of these examples imply, the first three meanings of *animo* often overlap. Sometimes the usage of *animo* in a particular passage implies at the same time an increase or decrease in energy level, the experience of pleasure and pain, and the state of certainty on the part of the agent(s). The interdependence of these first three meanings explains why *animo* frequently appears with the additional sense of "having an intention, being hardened of determination or firm of character." For instance, at the close of Book 4 the discussants address the means available to a leader to remove a "sinister opinion" ("*sinistra opinione*") that has infected the army. Colonna underlines the role a captain's address has on reducing the anxieties of the soldiers:

> For this speaking lessens fear, ignites spirits (*animi*), grows obstinacy, discovers deceptions, promises prizes, shows dangers and the way to flee them, reproves, entreats, threatens, fills with hope, praises, vituperates, and does all of those things by which the human passions are extinguished or ignited.[72]

In this passage, *animo* carries both emotional and volitional shades of meaning. This is not unusual since when *animo* possesses the sense of the volitional, Machiavelli often refers to emotional states to emphasize the described state. Thus, the first three effects of a captain's address of his or her troops in the above passage, i.e., that it "lessens fear, ignites spirits, grows obstinacy," often appear as different ways the captain's speech influences the listener's subjective dynamics.

For instance, at the end of Book 3, Colonna enumerates the drills soldiers practice to identify commands according to the sounds made by different musical instruments; he then adds:

Alexander the Great and the Romans used horns and trumpets, as they thought that by virtue of such instruments they were more able to ignite the spirits (*animi*) of the soldiers and make them fight more hardily (*gagliardamente*).[73]

The sense of *animo* in this passage is that of a determined mindset generated on the basis of emotion. Because their spirits were inflamed, the soldiers fought *gagliardamente*, i.e., hardily or lustily. Passages like the two above communicate the close connection Machiavelli forges between strength of emotion and steadiness of volition presenting them as two sides of the same vital energy.

On the other hand, the fourth and fifth categories demonstrate meanings of *animo* that exceed transitional emotional states. In these passages, *animo* carries the volitional overtones of determination, intention, and character. For instance, in Book 7 Colonna argues that when besieging a city, an attacker must either do so in a serious and determined manner or leave the city alone entirely. As he states: "For if the first attempt turns out in vain, the spirit of the besieged grows ("*cresce animo agli assediati*"), and then the enemy is forced to overcome those who are inside with virtue, and not with reputation."[74] The phrase "*animo cresce*" refers to the determination of the besieged city to resist the attackers, and it also acts as a warning to would-be besiegers not to engage in indecisive actions that could take away the fear the defenders already have of the aggressor on the basis of its reputation. The fear the besieged citizens have of the reputation of the attacking commander and troops can deliver the victory on its own. In this last passage, *animo* expresses an emotional state like steady confidence built up by prior conditioning. The attacking army's reputation instills fear and the confidence of the defenders decreases. Remedy this fear and that confidence increases. If those who attack a city make the mistake of removing the fear the defenders had of their reputation, the aggressors will discover that they have a real fight on their hands. In both cases, the practical measures that the besieged will take, whether to surrender or to resist, are entirely dependent on the relatively fixed condition of their *animo*, which now functions as a matrix for generating motion.

The final meaning of *animo* carries the sense of an "abiding disposition" or established "character." For instance, in Book 1 the narrator reflects on the loss of Cosimo Rucellai at such a young age: "...without having been able, in accord with his spirit (*animo*), to benefit anyone."[75] The narrator describes Rucellai's youthful character as altruistic in outlook, and this sense of *animo* appears again when Colonna a little later in the same book discusses the qualities that distinguish someone as a good potential soldier:

For no one believes that any virtue that is in any part praiseworthy can be discerned in a dishonest education (*educazione disonesta*) and base spirit (*animo brutto*).[76]

In both passages, *animo* carries the sense of an established way of being resulting from prior conditioning, which generates actions of a certain quality. Colonna even likens the *animo* to the body and its capacity to be shaped and disposed in a certain way by repeated actions when he states:

And they do not consider that those who anciently wanted to hold their states used to do and used to have done all those things that have been reasoned about by me, and that their study was done to prepare their bodies for hardships and the spirit (*lo animo*) not to fear dangers.[77]

Just as a body trained for hardship may suffer from illness and experience weakness while at the same time retaining its underlying dominant disposition to vigor so, too, the *animo* may waver from fear while still retaining its tendency to recover and reassert prevailing affects of confidence and certainty with respect to certain tasks and contexts.

Machiavelli's employment of the *animo* plays a key role in the mechanics of motion laid out in the *Art of War*, where it shares striking similarities to Lucretius' use of the *anima* in the *De rerum natura*. The *animo* functions in general to explain motion whether those motions occur in a subjective or an objective register. Further, he forefronts the *animo* as the explanatory principle for the quality of the performance of motion and situates both in a disciplinary subject generated and stabilized through repetitive performance. Finally, Machiavelli's explanations of the mechanics of *animo* situate it as a relay between individual and aggregate behaviors. Individual responses made routine through exercises prepare the individual to be compounded with other similarly disciplined individuals and to be taken up into increasingly complex structures like brigades, battalions, legions, or even cities.

8. Hints of Lucretius in the Swerve of the Horse

The level of generality implied with these meanings of *animo* has the added consequence of situating human beings on a continuum with the rest of the animal world, and this leads to the discovery of a final feature Machiavelli's disciplinary regime shares with Lucretian physics. For instance, Colonna identifies the defects of cavalry by pointing out that often a spirited (*animoso*) man will be paired with a vile horse or a vile man with a spirited horse.[78] He then concludes that "where this disparity of spirit (*animo*) occurs it makes for disorder."[79] In his reasoning on the limitations of cavalry here and elsewhere, Machiavelli argues that the difficulties introduced by cavalry occur in part due to a mismatch of spirits of the horse and rider. He argues the greater value of the infantry unit over cavalry is due to the greater reliability and flexibility of individual soldiers compared to the potential difficulties plaguing the horse and rider compound. Militiamen can be trained to respond with greater uniformity of *animo*, and this cannot be assured for equestrian units.

As compound bodies with disparate natures, cavalry units exhibit a *double animo* and, on Machiavelli's analysis, the conflict between the spirits of horse and rider can be so at odds that in some situations the compound proves both unreliable and a source of disorder. The absence of continuity of intention between a mismatched horse and rider is the apparent outcome of a difference between the two that is always there—the fact that horse and rider are *of two minds* about any action they undertake, even when they appear to act as one. Under some circumstances, the double *animo* of horse and rider will reveal itself as a spontaneous tendency to balk and swerve on the part of the horse if, for instance, steered toward a wall or a thicket of massed pikes. On the other hand, Machiavelli has Colonna imply that remedies can be found that will compel human infantry to run into—or at least *at*—a wall.

For Lucretius, the *clinamen* describes the unpredictable tendency of atoms to swerve spontaneously from their rectilinear paths.[80] Far from being a marginal element of atomic mechanics, both Epicurus and Lucretius postulate the atomic tendency to deviate ever so slightly from straight-line motions both as the ultimate cause for the origin of the worlds as well as providing the grounds for supposing the human will's freedom from pre-existing causal factors.[81] Machiavelli's critique of cavalry with its emphasis on the disjunct of spirit of horse and rider carries detectible echoes of the swerve as an atomic principle.[82] Lucretius even employs the example of the horse race during his explanation of the *clinamen* in *De rerum natura* Book 2. His example emphasizes the limitation of the action of the horse relative to the human mind's expectations of it when he describes the moment the gates snap open at a horse race:

> nevertheless the force of the horses cannot break forth instantly as the mind (*mens*) itself desires.[83]

These Lucretian echoes of the *clinamen* carry important consequences not only for Machiavelli's preference for infantry over cavalry but also for his evaluations of different types of warfare. In the *Art of* War, Machiavelli divides combat strategies into two major types—those developed for battles fought on land in tight, contained spaces as the Romans were used to do in Europe, and those developed to fight in wide spaces, as the Parthians fought.[84] Colonna admits that the Parthians engaged entirely on horseback and that their nomadic form of warfare was superior to that of the Romans for their kinds of terrain. But with more than a nod to Lucretius, Colonna then goes on to describe the Parthian mode of warfare as one entirely contrary to the Roman mode, based on horseback, which proceeded in a way that was "confused and broken" ("*confuse e rotti*); it was, "an unstable mode of fighting [that] was full of uncertainty."[85] On the other hand, the Romans fought in a mass as a tight-fitting solid, which was a style of combat suited excellently to tight spaces.

The very division Colonna draws between modes of warfare based on types of terrain depends on a set of considerations that teems with the Lucretian language of the *clinamen*. Certainty versus uncertainty, stability versus instability, dispersed (like a gas) versus a tight-packed solid, confused versus clear—these opposing categories present a basis for a critique of the Roman orders that Colonna proposes to the young assembled Florentines even as he works to persuade them to adopt an adaptation of the Roman orders.[86] Even when at the end of Book 5 he lays out the counter-measures Marc Antony devised to defend against the Parthians, he notes that Roman use of these measures did not enable Antony's troops to attack the Parthian horsemen successfully, much less defeat them.[87]

Machiavelli's critique of the equine swerve serves as a telegraphed but provisional exclusion of uncertainty, instability, and confusion from his account of the optimal orders for the militia even as he has Colonna acknowledge that forces organized around these values proved strikingly effective against the militia style he recommends.[88] Colonna's evaluation of the cavalry critiques these units on the basis of the operations of the *animo*. In the course of his critique, Colonna recalls the notion of the Lucretian *clinamen* as he establishes which values will serve as the basis for the style of militia organization he recommends to the young men in the cultivated, well-ordered confines of the Oricellari garden. As he does so, he reveals that where it concerns the subjective conditions necessary for generating motion, human beings and animals share much due to the mechanics of the *animo* which motivates them both. He also implies that the double *animo* of horse and rider introduces an irreducible limitation on the effectiveness of cavalry. But extending this logic one step further, Machiavelli's critique of the swerve that emerges from the mismatch in *animo* of horse and rider suggests another problem. Human beings themselves possess composite bodies whose elements may demonstrate both continuous and conflicting intentionalities. People can also be joined together to form lines, battalions, and brigades whose different parts may demonstrate areas of both continuity as well as discontinuity of execution. Differences like these are a source of disorder. Machiavelli's analysis of the problem of cavalry initiates an inquiry into a disciplinary regime's effectiveness in reducing, or at least channeling, the ineliminable fields of unpredictability that persistently appear when complex bodies engage in complicated interactions.

9. Conclusion

For Machiaveli, *animo* figures as a principle of movement whose quality, strength, and determination are affected by shifts of emotion and changing external conditions. Machiavelli's *animo* functions as a principle of movement much like the *anima* does for Lucretius. For both thinkers, these respective principles are responsible for inciting the motions in and of bodies.

Beyond the Epicurean allusions contained in Book 1, Machiavelli does not directly discuss Lucretius' account of atomic mechanics in the *Art of War*; this is not surprising given the text's practical objectives. The fact Machiavelli mentions "soul" (It., *anima*) only three times does not undermine the argument for an atomist influence operating in the text. In fact, it suggests the complexity of Machiavelli's engagement with atomism and that he may be involved in a critique of the very distinction Lucretius draws between *animus* and *anima*. Lucretius distinguishes the *animus* and *anima* on the basis of the mobility of the smallest and fastest bodies, a relative distinction which explains why Machiavelli does not refer much to the soul to explain practices, discipline, and behaviors in the *Art of War*. Not only would it unnecessarily complicate his exposition of his approach to warfare by entangling the discussion in philosophical and theological questions on the nature of the soul, it simply isn't necessary to explain the modes of training and the orders of warfare he advocates. For both Lucretius and Machiavelli, soul is a function of motion(s) and a consequence of the relationships of the very smallest bodies caught in the weave of the human body. This explains why *anima* in Machiavelli settles on an externally neutral meaning—*vita* or life. If there is *vita*, it is because the organizing motions of *animo* are detectible, as the continuing capacity of a composite being to mobilize effective responses to shifting external conditions.

However, my objective in this chapter has been only to establish the notion that the war-making bodies Machiavelli details in the *Art of War* exhibit the influence of the atomist physical mechanics Lucretius locates to be at work in the human body and mind in the *De rerum natura*. The next chapter expands this argument by reading the disciplinary regime outlined and implemented by Colonna as Machiavelli's re-reading of key authors in the theory of warfare through the lens of a materialist interpretative framework.

2

Practical Proportions: Aelianus Tacticus in Machiavelli's *Art of War*

1. Introduction

The analyses of Chapter 1 discussed the implications of Lucretian influence on Machiavelli on the subject of mixed bodies and the forces of nature. There I argued the compatibility of the Roman poet and the Florentine concerning their views on nature and linked these views to the arguments deployed by the *condottiere* captain, Fabrizio Colonna, to persuade his interlocutors that his soldiers *can* move as a unit despite the great diversity of bodies that compose the battalion, brigade and army. Rank-and-file militiamen, sergeants, and centurions *can* constitute a unified, fluid field of forces owing to the natural mechanics exhibited by all mixed bodies.

Machiavelli's orientation toward tactics emphasizes the foot soldier and lower level officers in a way that breaks with the military writers that preceded him, but what about the upper level officers that include the fifteen *conestabili* and the brigade's *capitano*?[1]

The present chapter argues that Machiavelli's critical reception of the second-century Greek author on military tactics, Aelianus Tacticus, and his text, *De instruendis aciebus*, redefines the relationship of *conestabili* and *capitano* to foot soldiers and lower level officers from that of top-down managers of force deployments to principal relays of a grammar of visual and audible signs cued through flags, numbers, costumes, and music.[2] In the *Art of War*, Machiavelli has Colonna outline the co-functioning of the militia's distinct strata where the performance of upper level officers both depends on and completes the circuit of martial practices internalized by line soldiers and lower level officers. The effectiveness of their co-functioning determines the militia's readiness to execute martial choreographies not only with the enemy on the field but with *any* potential enemy that may materialize within *any* site.

2. Aelianus Tacticus and *De instruendis aciebus*

Περί Στρατηγικῶν Τάξεων Ἑλληνικῶν (*On the Military Arrangements of the Greeks*), composed by the second-century AD Greek mathematician, Aelianus Tacticus, was translated into Latin by Byzantine immigrant Theodore Gaza and published in 1487 by Eucharius Silber in Rome under the title *De instruendis aciebus* in a small volume which included earlier military writers like Vegetius, Frontinus, Modestus, and Onasander. Why and, more importantly, *how* an obscure second-century Greek-Roman author could be important to Machiavelli is partly explained by a shift in the tactics and technology of war in the fifteenth and sixteenth centuries. Interest in Aelianus increased at this time due to the success of the Swiss pike square.[3]

Though Swiss pike squares possessed advantages over shallower medieval formations, their compact organization made them especially vulnerable to becoming disordered. Handguns were not as accurate as longbows or crossbows and took considerable time to reload.[4] Still, the poor accuracy of handguns little diminished their effectiveness when employed against a compact wall of soldiers only forty yards wide. Since the use of hand gunners could disorganize the ranks of pike squares, the Swiss complemented their infantry formations with units of arquebusiers. This tactic—along with developments in armor technology and the introduction of different kinds of firearms—caused the kinds of troops deployed on Renaissance battlefields to multiply. This led to an arms race fueled by infantry and cavalry specializing in different kinds of firearms.[5] The problem of small unit tactics grew increasingly prominent during the fifteenth and sixteenth centuries given the difficulty of coordinating effectively such a diverse array of forces.

Many of the techniques employed by the Swiss squares were modeled on the techniques employed by the ancient Macedonian phalanx. Both the square and the phalanx emphasized the discipline of infantry as critical to the survival of the formation during battle.[6] Under such conditions, classical military values like courage and valor were demoted given the importance of maintaining the cohesion of the square. As David Eltis makes clear, good order in such formations was not an ideal—"it was cruel necessity."[7]

The success of the Swiss and the need for soldiers with the skill set necessary to execute small unit actions with precision caused a revival of interest in the works of Aelianus. His thirty-page text stood out from the military literature of the time for two reasons: 1) it described phalanx strategy on the basis of the placement and movement of individual soldiers; 2) it used diagrams to illustrate those movements.[8]

In *De instruendis aciebus,* Aelianus attends carefully to the behavior of the individual soldier in small formations of ten to 200 men. For instance, in Chapter 19 he describes how to arrange the cavalry in the *rhomb* formation:

> The leader of the troop being placed at the head, the next succeeding horsemen, on either side of him, ought not to rank in a line with him, but to follow at due distance, so that the heads of their horses may reach to the shoulders of the horse on which the leader is mounted; [this is done] in order that the men may preserve due distance from each other, both those which are formed on the right and on the left, and likewise those posted in the rear; and [it is done] to prevent the disorder that might arise in case the horses should come in close contact.[9]

From here, Aelianus goes on to describe the number of men each line must contain in order to form the figure and maintain it while marching.

Machiavelli echoes Aelianus's focus on the details of the placement of individual soldiers when describing the placement of the infantry in numerous places in the *Art of War*. For instance, in Book 2 Machiavelli describes a simple maneuver to prepare a battalion to march:

> ...and wishing during the march to arrange them in the battalion so as to make a front [*testa*], you have to make it so that the first centurion stops with the first twenty files, and the second continues to march forward and turning to the right hand, goes along the flanks of the twenty stopped files, so that he comes beside [*si attesti con*] the other centurion, where he stops as well. The third centurion, turning also to his right hand, continues to march along the flanks of the stopped files, marches so that he comes abreast of the other two centurions.[10]

Machiavelli's narrative focuses on the actions of each centurion and the files that answer to him. The centurions, like the *capidieci* analyzed in Chapter 1, function as a *guide* through the placement of their bodies on the field. Machiavelli's focus on the movements of individual soldiers aims to lay out a precise pattern so that the brigade retains the integrity of its formations as it executes the maneuver.

Contrast these passages from Aelianus and Machiavelli with how the fourth-century Roman military authority—Publius Flavius Vegetius Renatus—describes a complex maneuver to counter the outflanking of the army's right wing in his *Epitoma rei militaris*:

> ...there is one remedy so that bend back and round off your wing and horn, so that your men, who have wheeled around, may defend the backs of their comrades. But in the angle at its very extremity gather there the most strong, because this is where the main impetus is usually made.[11]

Vegetius does not go into more detail about the specific movements the individual soldiers must perform to accomplish the complicated maneuver. Though often cited as a principal influence on Machiavelli's *Art of War*, throughout *De rei militaris* Vegetius is content to identify at most three parts in his army—*cornus dextrum, cornus sinistrum, media acies*. On only two occasions in the work does he mention the movement of individual lines.[12] On the other hand, Aelianus and Machiavelli focus their attention exclusively on the multiple layers of organization between the individual soldier and the battalion considered as a whole.[13]

Another feature the *Art of War* shares with *De instruendis aciebus* is the inclusion of diagrams to supplement narrative descriptions of unit formations and movements. In Renaissance military texts, illustrations of everything from field cannon to cavalry harnesses were not uncommon. For instance, the *condottiere* captain, Battista Della Valle, includes in his text *Vallo* (published in 1529) numerous illustrations depicting military implements ranging from field artillery to incendiary devices.[14]

On the other hand, *diagrams* showing formations that represented the placement of individual soldiers, whether by dots or Greek letters, were rare. So, for instance, Roberto Valturio's *De re militari* (1472)[15] and Egidio Colonna's poem, *De regimine principium* (1502)—two texts composed in the tradition of Vegetius—contain many illustrations but no diagrams. As Hale's research shows, no Roman military treatise was handed down to Renaissance theoreticians on war that gave visual clues to tactical formations.[16] On the other hand, the 1487 edition of *De instruendis aciebus* contained thirty-three diagrams. Each diagram depicts small units ranging from six to 200 men with most showing between thirty and fifty. The diagrams are closely interpolated with the text and each of the diagrams bears a title. The diagrams show how the individual soldiers should be arranged in the formation. However, they also explain to the soldiers how to *turn*, i.e., to advance, go back, or slide to the side.[17]

Machiavelli's project in the *Art of War* aims at the creation of a neo-Roman legion for the sixteenth century and not the resuscitation of the Greek phalanx. However, Machiavelli's use of diagrams in the *Art of War* goes beyond a simple adoption of a rarely employed textual device, and it is not the only place Machiavelli is in dialogue with the text of Aelianus. Aelianus directly incorporates diagrams into the narrative of his text. On the other hand, Machiavelli places his diagrams in an appendix to his. He explains there in an address to his readers:

I believe it to be necessary to wish that you readers can without difficulty understand the order of the battalions, the armies and the encampments according to how they are disposed in the narration [*secondo che nella narrazione si dispone*], to show you the figures of each of them [*mostrarvi le figure di qualunque di loro*].[18]

With that, he introduces the "signs or characters" ("*segni o caratteri*") of the different types of troops. He lays out two columns, one of Greek letters and one with a two- to three-word description of the kinds of troops to which the Greek letters correspond.[19]

Aelianus also explains why he included so many diagrams to illustrate his tactics. He ascribes his need for diagrams to the shortcomings of previous writers on war:

They have not addressed themselves to the uninstructed [*ignaros*], but to those skilled [*peritos*] in the art. It shall, therefore, be my study to remove out of the way of others, those difficulties which I myself encountered, when I first wished to know, and could neither find able teachers nor any treatise . . .[20]

Aelianus intends his work for the uninstructed, *ignaros*, i.e., those like himself who come to the study of tactics with no practical experience in war. As he adds, speaking of the diagrams for the first time:

As often as language shall fail me, I shall call in the assistance of figures [*figurarum*] to explain my meaning; so that a seen thing [*visum*] may be a help to the intellect [*ut ita visum intellectui adiutorem adhibeam*].[21]

On this point Machiavelli's *Art of War* converges with the treatise of Aelianus. Both Machiavelli and Gaza's translation of Aelianus use here the same word, "figures"—*figure* in Italian and *figurae* in the Latin—to translate the Greek term, σχῆμα.[22] Both authors intend the figures to remove difficulty and, in doing so, to aid the reader with no professional experience on the battlefield to grasp the subject matter.

Machiavelli's strategy behind the inclusion of diagrams is meant to overcome the same two obstacles Aelianus describes in his introduction: the diagrams allow him to instruct the uninstructed and to intervene on their behalf with a textual technique—the diagram—where they can grasp with the eye what otherwise could only be grasped through years of battlefield experience.[23] For the two authors, the diagram is not meant to act simply as a supplement to the narrative passages of the text.[24] Reading the diagrams and grasping them in the way the authors intend them is meant to be a kind of training.

But who are the uninstructed here? Are they the potentially semi-illiterate lowest officer grade—the *capidieci*—described first by Aelianus and later adopted by Machiavelli as a critical relay between commanding officer and individual soldier? Possibly. However, Aelianus goes further and explains why the science of tactics is so important that it requires the textual innovation involved in employing diagrams. He argues here that no science is more useful than tactics because of the importance it has for the survival of cities. He paraphrases as evidence for this claim a passage from the first book of Plato's *Laws*:

> ...but, by the deed, every polis is by nature always in an undeclared war with all (others). [τῷ δ'ἔργῳ πάσαις πρὸς πάσας τὰς πόλεις ἀεὶ πόλεμον ἀκήρυκτον κατὰ φύσιν εἶναι].[25]

In this passage from the *Laws*, Clinias the Cretan explains to the Athenian stranger the reason for certain Cretan citizen practices—like taking meals in common and engaging in specific gymnastic activities. For the Cretan, peace is merely a name [τοῦτ'εἶναι μόνον ὄνομα], since, by the deed [τῷ δ'ἔργῳ], all cities show themselves to be always at war. Aelianus paraphrases this passage from Plato to explain why he employs the innovation of diagrams in *De instruendis aciebus*.

Considering the implications of this passage reveals another reason for why Machiavelli would follow Aelianus here. These diagrams lay down a kind of grammar, vocabulary, and set of logical rules for the manipulation of signs. Both Aelianus and Machiavelli include diagrams as supplements for the limits narrative language encounters due to the detail rich and hyper-precise language needed to describe military choreographies in action. Further, both writers present their diagrams as supplements to aid the inexperienced reader. The diagrams are offered as a kind of textual technology. Through them, the non-professional can practice warfare even while their cities dream the illusion of peace. Whether engaging with this kind of textual technology constitutes a practice of war or an art of peace, or is even a kind of technique that somehow spans both, must yet be thought through.[26] The practice of war in peacetime may, in fact, appear as a kind of play.

And this is important because in Book 1 of the *Art of War*, Colonna argues that those who serve as his soldiers must practice another art in times of peace. This begins a series of observations that places the program outlined by Colonna at odds with, for instance, what Plato lays out in the *Republic* when he insists that his guardians will only take war for their art *and* that they will be financially supported by the other citizens, so that they won't have to practice the art of money-making as well.²⁷ Judged from a Platonic standpoint, Colonna's soldiers will be compelled to practice three arts: the art of war; their peacetime art; and the money-making art.

In setting up this problem, Colonna asks Cosimo to reflect on the *proportion* of those engaged in times of war compared to those engaged in times of peace and points out how the number of infantry employed to maintain the walls during times of peace is much less than the number needed during times of war.²⁸ In the *Art of War, proporzione* occurs only three times. This first appearance of it announces a problem—how does one maintain military readiness without professionalizing the military? During times of peace, there just does not exist a place for every trained soldier to practice their art. At the close of hostilities, those who make up the infantry must return to civilian pursuits. Colonna's reasoning here affirms that the type of militia he proposes is not, for instance, the type Plato proposes in the *Republic* when he asks Glaucon and Adeimantus to allow the guardians to devote themselves entirely to the art of war. Colonna argues that the most important provision is that the infantry not be allowed to engage in the art of war during times of peace.²⁹ If this is allowed, then those so practiced will take every opportunity they can to disturb the public peace to enrich themselves.³⁰ He concludes the discussion with a strong warning against the Platonic model: "because one does not find a more dangerous infantry than one composed of those who make war their art."³¹

3. Fabric versus graph: Machiavelli and Aelianus on Doubling by Rank and Doubling by File

Whatever the influence of Aelianus on Machiavelli, Machiavelli clearly does not simply follow in the steps of the Greek. Colonna does not propose the adoption of the phalanx formation or phalanx tactics for his army.³² He proposes a unit that combines the strengths and minimizes the weaknesses of both the Greek phalanx and the Roman legion. Further, the preferences Colonna silently expresses for putting his battalions in order reveal Machiavelli's critique of the tactics of Aelianus. This critique reveals as well the critical and redefined function played by the upper level officers in the formation and movement of the army.

His critique appears first when he considers how to transform his soldiers from marching order to a formation ready to give battle. When in marching order, soldiers are arranged in eighty files of five per file.³³ From this order,

Colonna explains that the battalion can be formed in two ways, either doubling by flank ("*raddopiargli per fianco*") or doubling by line ("*raddopiargli per retta linea*"). The first mode of combination—doubling by flank—conforms to the mode described by Aelianus in *De instruendis aciebus,* Chapter 28,[34] where he discusses doubling and halving the extension of the front to respond to issues of terrain and the enemy.[35] Machiavelli acknowledges doubling the flank as an acceptable way of forming up a battalion, but he also criticizes Aelianus on this point, remarking that doubling by flank forces one to obey the number ("*ubbidire al numero*").[36] Doubling by flank restricts the length of the line to only factors of two. The phalanx described by Aelianus is composed of men who are all armed in the same way with shield and sixteen-foot long *sarissa*. Aelianus places the velites and other lightly armed troops either behind the phalanx or on its flanks, but they do not occupy a place among the rank-and-file soldiers.[37] When all the soldiers are similarly armed, extending the formation by doubling the files occurs easily. However, Machiavelli silently overlooks the problem of equipment. He does not point out how in his battalion of 400, those armed with pikes compose the first five files and those armed with shield and sword the next fifteen.[38] When the arms are not of the same type, the tactic of doubling outlined by Aelianus for homogenously armed hoplites will not work.

Furthermore, the phalanx Aelianus describes is fundamentally committed to this arrangement since not only are the men all armed the same, but they are all distinguished in their placement by their *virtus*/ἀρετὴ.[39] For Aelianus, the Macedonian *decuria* who head each file of sixteen are not just veterans but also the most excellent of the soldiers. Counting off by twos, every second soldier is designated a "leader" by Aelianus and the other a "follower." This distinction is meant to describe the tested excellence of the soldiers in their relationships to one another. Aelianus constructs his phalanx by shaping from it a fabric of homogenous material woven according to a principle of sameness (of equipment) and a principle of difference (of *virtus*/ἀρετὴ). These two principles commit Aelianus to formations based on factors of two. Forming the phalanx as he does by doubling the flank does not disturb this underlying arrangement.

However, Machiavelli does not organize his battalion on the basis of either of these principles. He forms his battalion on the principle of heterogeneity of equipment (sword and shield versus pikes), which rests on a heterogeneity of combat techniques.[40]

However, more importantly, Machiavelli has Colonna argue that his formations are organized to value re-ordering over ordering and this occurs by instituting a system of signs to organize the battalion. Those signs include the prominent placement of the battalion's distinctive flag associated with its constable, the differently colored crests worn on the helmets of the constables and centurions, the numbers painted on the helmets of the *capidieci* and the numbers marking each soldier's rank and number in that rank. Machiavelli's objective is to organize his battalion so that it has the capacity to take and retake position and reform the square.

For this reason Machiavelli in Book 2 silently skips over the specifics of doubling by flank, since only doubling by line will preserve the diverse relationships and the system of signs that organizes his battalion square.[41] Every soldier who takes a position in the square is practiced in occupying that position on a coordinate field whose values are established in response to three factors: a) the disposition of the enemy; b) the disposition of the site; c) and the different armaments of the troops. In laying out his field of forces, Machiavelli implicitly argues that there are certain irreducible factors, or *atomic elements*, from which the theory of war must always take its bearings.[42] Machiavelli's ordering principles cannot be abstracted from their material conditions. For the mathematician, Aelianus, only one external factor could affect the numerical disposition of his phalanx—the nature of the levy.[43] Aelianus never mentions, for instance, the conditions of the terrain and how broken land like plowed fields or rocky land could decisively reduce the potency of his unit's organization. Entirely missing from Aelianus is Machiavelli's reliance on a system of signs to order his battalion.[44] When in Chapter 9 of *De instruendis aciebus* Aelianus describes the difference between the phalanx assuming open, close, and compact orders, he does so by simply specifying the different distances between files and the space occupied by each man.[45]

Machiavelli's formation does not depend on eyeballing distances or the physical principle of contiguity; nor does it depend on the commander modifying the distances between the soldiers in any way. Colonna leaves these kinds of adjustments and orientations to the lower level officers and, ultimately, to the soldiers themselves. Machiavelli replaces Aelianus's order formed from a fabric of homogenous forces with a coordinate system where each soldier occupies a determinate position on the field set up by a system of signs to which they have become practiced to respond.[46] Those soldiers who have internalized the significance of these signs can determine their position instantly like pinpointing a spot on a graph. A soldier's facility in determining their position when their signs are cued distinguishes the practiced "veteran" soldier from the new recruit, regardless of the number of campaigns they have experienced; as Colonna concludes:

Because the soldiers who know well how to do this are practiced soldiers, and even if they have never seen enemies, they can be called veteran [*vecchi*] soldiers.[47]

On the other hand those soldiers who lack the facility for determining their position when cued, even if they have been in a thousand battles, Colonna judges "new" soldiers. Machiavelli focuses on the inevitability of reordering the formation due to its encounter with the site, the enemy, and unforeseen circumstances during the battle. The discipline Colonna ascribes to his interlocutors in the *Art of War* stems entirely from recognizing the necessity of re-ordering. Interestingly, though he attributes the value he places on reordering to the ancient theorists on war, many of the recommendations he makes do not stem from the classical war theorists but rather supplement and correct what they failed to lay out.[48]

4. Roman Renewal Styles, by Grades of Experience and Styles of Formation

The issue of practice is central to the argument Colonna makes to his interlocutors in the Rucellai gardens. However, the discipline on which his militia is based depends intimately on consistent practice and exercise. The centrality of discipline sets up a conflict with one of the main themes of Book 1—the value Colonna places on the non-professional character of military practice. His soldiers would be more effective if they could be trained during both times of peace and war. However, as discussed above, Colonna also argues that such a solution is not advisable due to its cost and the effects a purely professional class of war-makers has on the society that supports it. Colonna then casually lets drop how the Romans managed to keep their legionnaires in the field for extended campaigns without experiencing adverse effects. They simply placed limits on the individual soldier's term of service. Soldiers served for only fifteen years, between the ages of eighteen and thirty-five.[49] Machiavelli implies that these term limits prevented the armies from gaining too much autonomy, since new men constantly circulated in, replacing the veterans.[50] Machiavelli's second use of the term, *proporzione*, occurs in this context where it connotes how a mixed body like a legion can remain the same by constantly infusing its parts with elements that are new and different.

On Colonna's argument, Rome's republican modes were preserved by the custom of regularly rotating in younger soldiers and retiring those older. This obligated Roman citizens to practice more than one art, since they would eventually be required to leave service. This was the case even during those stretches of Roman history when the plebs were enrolled in successive deployments due to Rome's wars of expansion. Even though the men were not the same, the legions remained in the same proportion of new recruit to experienced veterans because the new recruits were trained correctly and were guided by those who knew the ropes.[51] *Proporzione* here refers to the quantities the Romans monitored—term limits for the soldiers and a schedule of rotation that established temporal relationships between them.[52] This is seen most concretely in Colonna's endorsement of the Roman custom to divide the army into *principes, hastati,* and *triarii*.[53] The *principes* were the newest soldiers, the *hastati* those who had demonstrated their competency, while the *triarii* formed the seasoned veterans. The schedule of renewal concretely realized in rotation of service, during the period in Rome's history when it was consistently observed, helped to preserve Roman republican orders.[54]

The quantities of time described here are not arbitrary. They refer to dispositions the body passes through as it ages.[55] The proportions in the army are formed and preserved by observing these temporal markers. Further observing these markers preserves commensurable ratios between the bodies and lines that make up the formation—between bodies because all bodies between the ages of eighteen and thirty-five are postulated to exhibit coordination of "legs, hands, and eyes" and between lines because as practiced veteran is to trained recruit, so are the *triarii* to the *hastati* and the *hastati* to the *principes*. Renewal of the formation can happen on the basis of the proportions established by qualities of experience made commensurable due to shared discipline.

As the analysis above shows, Machiavelli organizes his militia squares based on time as a concrete quantity. However, proportionality operates along a temporal dimension as well as a spatial register. As noted above, Colonna's soldiers locate their place on the field according to the coordinates associated with that position. Machiavelli's diagrams map the potential location any soldier could occupy where the types of troop are all signified in a general way. For instance, swordsman are all equally represented by the Greek letter omicron. In the narrative, though, Colonna goes into further detail. Painted on the inside of each soldier's shield are two numbers: one corresponds to the file they occupy and the second identifies their position in that file. Not only are soldiers grouped into units according to equipment, but assigned to each soldier is a unique identifier that pinpoints their exact position. With the addition of these numbers, Machiavelli translates the field of deployment from a mass of soldiers loosely arranged into lines into a graph where each point in space comes assigned with its own coordinates.[56]

In a third passage in Book 2, Colonna combines these arrays of soldiers distributed according to time and space when the *condottiere* shows, starting from marching order, how a battalion can be arrayed in the square formation with its front formed on any side.[57] Colonna's description in the narrative is associated with diagram 2 in the appendix. The diagram shows eighty files of five soldiers per file arrayed in marching order as well as the 400-strong formed battalion square. The pike men make up the first five ranks of the left flank while the sword and shield compose the remaining fifteen. Machiavelli describes the figure in his introduction to the appendix with, "how a battalion is ordered that marches ahead and has to fight on its flank."[58]

Colonna considers this kind of arrangement the most effective of the three principal forms.[59] As he describes how to form a square with any side for front, the term *proporzione* reappears for the last time in the text. When Colonna describes this, he admits it is a more complicated maneuver than the first way of forming the square, where the pike men are already located at the front.[60] The second figure describes how to arrange the soldiers while on the march so that the front can be formed either on the sides or on the back of the figure. If the soldiers in Machiavelli's battalion were all equipped with the same weapons, this figure—and the maneuvers required to form it—would be unnecessary. However, Machiavelli's intent to combine both the advantages of phalanx and legion problematizes the placement of the 100 regular pike in the base square. The figure he constructs must be capable of transformations, and the rectangle of pikes within the square must appear on any side where the battle could be joined.

Machiavelli expresses the priority of the second figure over the first when he has Colonna state "it always happens" ["*Ma perché egli occurre sempre*"][61] that the front must be formed on a side other than the direction of travel. To respond to the unpredictability of marching through enemy territory, relationships of space and time must be mapped out in advance. For Colonna, the success of the maneuver depends on the elements of the battalion maintaining their correct *proporzione*. This can happen only by pre-placement of the pikes and the low-ranking officers among the four marching groupings. The pre-positioning of soldiers according to training and armaments in the order of march makes the figure maximally flexible for responding to the potentials for conflict in enemy territory. Pre-positioning and sequencing set the conditions for the troops to act on their well-engrained discipline while in hostile territory. The groups of pikes and shields are sequenced as they are in the line of march so that the square can perform a transformation of areas while maintaining constant internal relationships between differently equipped and trained troops, both conditions necessary for preserving the militia's disciplinary regime.⁶²

5. On the Importance of Observing Proportion

Machiavelli's emphasis on the importance of observing proportions spotlights two aspects of the discipline of the troops. The first emphasizes the soldiers' capacity for self-regulation.⁶³ Colonna expresses confidence that his soldiers will figure out for themselves how to make the necessary adjustments to maintain the proportions of the line.

The other way observance of proportion operates in the figure depends upon the officers. The soldiers find their places by orienting themselves in space according to the constable's flag and the plumes on the helmets of the centurions. Even the *capidieci* are identifiable to the rank-and-file soldiers by having their numbers painted on their helmets. The placement of the upper level officers lays out the dimensions of the field like axioms, postulates, and common notions orient a geometric inquiry.

Due to the unpredictability of the battlefield, Colonna expresses his preference for the second way of forming up the battalion over the first. Where an order like the phalanx championed by Aelianus is dependent on fixed horizontal and vertical sequences, Colonna's order depends on elements based on the individual soldier's relationship to a few, easily distinguishable rally points. Colonna's troops will be trained to situate themselves graphically, by spontaneously locating their place on a field given visual cues. An order based on this kind of discipline presents greater opportunities for regeneration despite becoming disordered.⁶⁴ In the logic organizing Machiavelli's formation, a large percentage of a unit could be destroyed and those who remain would still be able to discover their customary posts despite the vacant spaces around them. This can happen only because the soldiers have been trained to locate their position graphically, i.e., on the basis not of perception but through memory and imagination.⁶⁵

Where the order of Aelianus's hoplites hinges on their maintaining fixed horizontal and vertical sequences, Colonna's legionnaires form their square on the basis of visual and aural cues.⁶⁶ This has an important conclusion. The all-important discipline at the heart of Colonna's militia can effectively meet the enemy in real time in the ways he insists on only if it has already programmed how the soldiers will relate subjectively to space and time. This is why Colonna can conclude that the difference between the new recruit and the seasoned veteran does not depend on the number of their campaigns. For Colonna, a battalion, brigade, or army is an assemblage of heterogeneous forces that form a unified body due to the internalized conditioning of the atomic bodies—the individual soldiers—that compose it. The soldiers of his battalion compose a unified force due to their constant surveillance of the visual and audible signs that circulate the field. The very sign that their discipline has taken, so to speak, is that their time-sense and space-sense trigger them in predictable ways to respond to the changing conditions generated by complex bodies in conflict. Colonna's relentless prioritizing of troop conditioning acknowledges that the most important battle is the one for subjectivity itself.[67]

Chapter 1 argued that the Lucretian notion of mixed bodies plays an important role in Machiavelli's *Art of War*. Machiavelli's discussions of *anima* and *animo* consistently reflect the way Lucretius reasons about the *animus* and *anima* in *De rerum natura* and, though Machiavelli does not think of atoms as the ultimate building blocks of matter, he does reason about the human body as a *primordia* that anchors and orients the investigation of more complex composite bodies.[68] From the vantage point of Lucretian, mixed bodies discipline sets up the conditions where the pathways of the most minute seeds linked by the Roman poet to the experience of perception, memory, and thought are channeled according to increasingly internalized rhythms that grow more well worn the more they are performed. Machiavelli goes further than any other military theorist up to this point through his recognition that military exercises and practices are successful only when they imprint on the troops a shared subjective framework.[69] By conditioning them to respond to a grammar of signs, consciousness itself becomes one of the effects of military discipline.

For Colonna, the upper level officers perform a specific disciplinary role by populating the field of battle by flags, colorful crests, rhythms, and musical variations. The upper level officers function by generating a grammar of signs, both visual and audible, that both assembles the formation and saturates the field with constants that trigger specific movements. Machiavelli's higher level officers do not simply ply their troops with orders issued from above. They orchestrate their movements on the field by conducting them through fields of *segni*. Especially important for him is the music from the sound corps stationed with each of the upper level officers that functions to regulate the quality of those movements by igniting and calming the *animi* of the troops. As he has Colonna conclude later in *Art of* War, Book 2:

As one who dances proceeds with the time of the music and, going with it, does not err, thus also an army, obeying in how it moves to that sound, does not become disordered. And however they [the ancients] varied the sound, according to how they wanted to vary the motion and according to how they wanted to ignite or calm or arrest the spirits of the men.[70]

Colonna's martial discipline is successful when it conducts the soldiers through martial choreographies by enmeshing their subjective experience with the signs and cues that prompt and guide collective actions.[71] Disciplined soldiers are those that respond "at a glance" ("*a occhio*") and "like the oarsmen to the whistle" ("*come i galeotti dal fischio*"[72]) to the visual and audible markers that suffuse the battlefield. However, for Machiavelli, of the two kinds of signs, the musical cues with their cadences prove even more effective than the visual ones for coordinating and holding the troops as a unified body; disciplined troops are those that:

> Know well how to hold the file, so much so that neither rest nor motion disorders them and hearing well the commands of the head through the music, and through that knowing immediately how to return to their place, when brought together they can easily learn to do all that which their body must do together with the other battalions, to operate correctly as one army.[73]

Troops trained according to the exercises and modes of discipline outlined by Colonna will possess the capacity to renew their formations as a function of their having internalized the grammar generated from battlefield *segni*—*segni* which lead them by having become, in a Lucretian sense, part of the flow of their bodies.

Still, Colonna's soldiers do not come to him as a *tabula rasa* nor does he begin with a militia of ten-year-olds. If for Machiavelli to conquer objectively requires a commensurate taking hold of the subjective, what are the principal obstructions to ensuring the regularity and predictability of the kinds of martial notions Colonna proscribes?[74] What are the factors capable of disrupting his militia's all-important grammar of signs and disciplinary circuits his martial choreographies generate? At this point it is necessary to turn from Lucretius and Aelianus Tacticus and the roles they play in Machiavelli's project of "*arms of one's own*" and examine more deeply Machiavelli's analyses of those types of forces princes and republics should apparently avoid at all costs—mercenaries, auxiliaries, and mixed forces, i.e., the "*arms of others*."

3

Industries of Failure? Mercenaries and the Arms of Others[1]

1. Introduction

Treatments of the "arms of others" in Machiavelli typically concentrate on Machiavelli's discussions of mercenaries in the *Prince*. The discussions place special importance on the exaggerated disdain Machiavelli voices for mercenary arms,[2] sometimes passing over entirely the connected topics of auxiliaries and mixed forces,[3] and sometimes grouping these topics together with Machiavelli's treatment of mercenaries as constituting essentially the same issue.[4] Thus, a gap exists in the tradition of commentary on Machiavelli's works.[5] And yet, a deeper understanding of this topic is clearly important for texts like the *Prince* and the *Discourses*, addressed as they are to "potential princes."[6] Given the crucial role that gaining arms of one's own plays for Machiavelli in transforming the potential into an actual prince, the use of mercenary or auxiliary arms would seem to offer a pragmatic first step for many potential princes to take in that process.[7] Machiavelli emphasizes the role mercenary arms can play in making a private individual into a prince by making the mercenary captain, Francesco Sforza, both the first example he gives of the new prince and the first name cited in the first chapter of the *Prince*.[8] Thus, grappling with this theme, "*the arms of others*," can only enhance our understanding of Machiavelli's other texts where the theme, "*one's own arms*," and the whole process by which a new prince comes into her own figures so centrally.[9]

This analysis of force categories in Machiavelli opens with his treatment of mercenary arms and focuses on the *Prince* but drawing in relevant passages where the theme of mercenary arms appears in the *Discourses, The Art of War*, and the *Florentine Histories*. It begins with a sketch of the debate among Italian civic humanists around the status of mercenaries with whom Machiavelli's analyses are regularly included before turning to Machiavelli's explicit development of the theme in the *Prince*.

2. Citizen Militia or Band of Mercenaries?

Most commentators concentrate on Machiavelli's critique of mercenaries as a corrupting influence on civic virtue, seeing Machiavelli's thoughts on warfare as clearly a projection of a long and established tradition in Italian civic humanism. This tradition argued for the restoration and extension of the institutions of the citizen-militia and the encouragement of a renewed focus on martial discipline as a crucial part of the project for the revival and strengthening of republican institutions.[10] Among the early supporters of the project of a citizen militia was Leonardo Bruni.[11] Bruni clearly sees the use of foreign fighters and *condottieri* as the ultimate cause for the series of defeats suffered by the Florentine Republic in the early 1400s.[12] Bruni's funeral oration of 1428 for Nanni degli Strozzi, the Florentine commander and diplomat, relates the events leading to his death in an ambush with Milanese troops, and then states:

> now it quickly became clear how great the difference is between the sense of honor in a foreign soldier and a citizen. For the others, prizing nothing higher than their own salvation, gave way instantly; this man [Nanni degli Strozzi], however, holding the love up for his patria higher than his own salvation, threw himself into the fray immediately, attempted to block the way of the enemies, and, by inciting and admonishing his companions in resisting the enemy with his own body, checked for a while the general onslaught.[13]

Like many other writers both before and after him, Bruni saw the commutation of compulsory militia service in 1351 by the republic as a decisive mistake and the origin for the ongoing instability suffered by Florence in the century that followed. The direct consequence of this action was the disarming of the Florentine citizen who subsequently would have to look to others for defense.[14] For Bruni, republican liberty had no defense when citizens were barred from developing the competencies that came with intellectual mastery of and extensive experience in the art of war.[15]

In Bruni's eyes, evasion of militia service by the citizens was the prelude to military disasters and civic upheavals; it was also the prelude to a spirit of servitude that diffused itself throughout the political body. Thus, Bruni´s critique of the Florentine dependence on stipendiaries is done on psychological, social, and historical bases. Bruni linked the increased Florentine dependence on stipendiaries to a shift in the internal balance of power between the *populares* and the *optimates* in favor of the *optimates*.[16] The *optimates* enjoyed power over the military due to the size of their contributions to the public treasury.[17] The ongoing dependence of the republic on *condottieri* allowed the *optimates* to dominate the Florentine middle and lower classes whose direct participation in Florentine political life was effectively checked.[18] A host of writers like Matteo Palmieri, Stefano Porcari, Benedetto Accolti, Giovanni Villani, and Francesco Patrizi, followed Bruni and were, like him, deeply critical of the reliance and use of mercenary arms by the Florentines, in particular, and by Italian republics and principalities in general.[19] They understood themselves in their criticisms as clearly basing their observations on similar assessments of the ineffectiveness and dangers of the employment of mercenaries by Plato, Aristotle, Vegetius, Thomas Aquinas, Petrarch, and Boccaccio.[20] And yet, these humanist writers were compelled to acknowledge the need, in the light of the loss of a functional militia, for the ongoing employment of stipendiaries in the republic's defense.[21] As chancellor of the Florentine republic, Coluccio Salutati—like his disciple, Bruni, after him—voiced great concerns over the increasing reliance of the republic on stipendiary troops. However, Salutati fully acknowledged the difficulty of doing without mercenary troops entirely, especially in the light of the Ciompi rebellion of 1378 in Florence.[22] The issue was complicated further even among militia supporters when popular riots broke out again in 1382 and were followed over the next twenty years with numerous popular conspiracies.[23]

Given this military and political history, it is clear that Machiavelli's critique of the *condottieri*, far from being on the fringe of speculative trends on this topic,[24] was responding to a current of thought at the heart of the assessment of the proper conditions for civic life among Italian humanists in Florence and elsewhere. What remains to be seen is whether his critique of the *condottieri* is as patently negative as it appears on the surface, or whether Machiavelli does not greatly exaggerate the case against them.

3. One's Own Arms

Chapter 12 is the only one in the *Prince* where the term *mercenary* occurs in the title.[25] This chapter is set up by two earlier chapters—Chapters 6 and 7—in which Machiavelli introduces and develops the related theme of having "one's own arms" in his discussion of the new prince. In Chapter 6, the new prince is the kind of ruler who achieved his position not through hereditary succession, but from having once been a private individual before assuming the role of prince. In that chapter, Machiavelli cites both *virtù* and *fortuna* as causes for this change of status. Those princes having relied more on *virtù* and less on *fortuna* "have maintained themselves more" in the regimes whose rule they usurped or founded.[26] Machiavelli singles out the figures of Moses, Cyrus, Romulus, and Theseus as having been among the "most excellent" of new princes, having arrived at their position through their own virtue and not through reliance on fortune. After excusing himself from reasoning about Moses, "as he was a mere executor of things that had been ordered for him by God," Machiavelli goes on to reason about the others. He concludes that their virtue was so great that each one[27] needed only the "opportunity [to become prince], which gave them the matter allowing them to introduce any form they pleased." Moses needed to find the Hebrews enslaved in Egypt; Romulus needed to be abandoned at birth; Cyrus needed to find the Persians discontent with the Medes; Theseus needed only to find the Athenians dispersed. These new princes then acquired their regimes with difficulty but, because of their great *virtù*, they held them with ease.

Machiavelli also contrasts here the careers of Moses, Cyrus, Romulus, and Theseus as new princes who successfully introduced new "modes and orders" with that of Girolamo Savanarola who failed because he could not force men to obey him when they no longer believed he was divinely inspired. From this, Machiavelli concludes that armed prophets conquer and unarmed ones fail, a conclusion that contrasts the different outcomes experienced by Moses and Savanorola. The difference in the outcome of their ventures did not depend on some difference in the quality of their belief in God, but in how readily each one was able to use force to compel belief in their project from their followers in the absence of their enthusiasm for it.[28]

At the very end of Chapter 6 and, apparently, as almost an afterthought, Machiavelli includes the person of Hiero II (306–215 BC), who became king of Syracuse from having been a private individual in 270 BC. Machiavelli adds him here for consideration with the others because he holds a "certain proportion" ("*qualche proporzione*") with the rest. However it is only here, in the discussion of Hiero, that Machiavelli even refers to the phrase, *one's own arms*—the phrase that figured so prominently in the chapter title, "*De principatibus novis qui armis propriis et virtute acquiruntur.*"[29] Like the others to whom he is likened, Hiero, too, only received the "bare" opportunity to become a new prince from *fortuna*. His success in transitioning from a private individual to prince of Syracuse stemmed nearly entirely from his *virtù*. From being chosen captain of the Syracusan army, Hiero "proved worthy" to be made their prince. The phrase, "*having one's own arms*," then appears for the first time in Chapter 6 in connection with Machiavelli's conclusions about Hiero in the chapter's final line:

Hiero eliminated the old military and organized a new one; he left his old friendships and made new ones; and when he had friendships and soldiers that were his own, he could erect on such a foundation any building; so that he endured much fatigue acquiring, and little in maintaining.[30]

When Machiavelli again discusses the career of Hiero II in Chapter 13, his remarks there focus directly on the theme of mercenary arms. Hiero knew immediately upon becoming captain of the mostly mercenary Syracusan army that he would need to get rid of it because he could neither "keep them [the soldiers] nor let them go." He killed his former soldiers and replaced them with new ones with whom he was able to fight effectively, since they were "his arms" and not alien arms. Machiavelli emphasizes here that the mercenary soldiers Hiero possessed originally were not useful "because they were *condottieri* set up like our Italians." In Chapter 13, Machiavelli estimates that these mercenary soldiers would have made Hiero's transition from private individual to prince much more difficult if not impossible. Moreover, in neither passage does he specify in what specific and special sense we are meant to understand how Hiero's former mercenary arms were "not his own," nor in what specific sense his new soldiers were "his own." This is especially telling if we recall that Machiavelli, in recounting the story of Hiero, silently glosses over a key detail in Polybius' account of Hiero's ascendancy. Hiero certainly did have his former mercenaries cut to pieces by strategically retreating at a key point in a battle with the Campanians. However, having freed himself from his "old, unruly mercenaries," Hiero returned to Syracuse and subsequently secured his regime by hiring *new mercenaries* of his own.[31]

Machiavelli poses the theme of one's own arms and the arms of others more directly and more thematically in Chapter 7, which deals with the theme of principalities acquired through the arms and fortune of others. This chapter takes for its focus the career of Cesare Borgia. Machiavelli seems[32] to raise Cesare's career in central Italy as a pattern for imitation for anyone who receives a state from someone else. Such princes come to be:

> ...when a state is conceded to someone either for money or by the favor of whoever concedes it.[33]

Machiavelli explains this statement through the use of two examples: (1) Darius I; and (2) those Roman emperors who attained their empire by corrupting the soldiers. Machiavelli explains how Darius I (521–486 BC) gave cities to private individuals for the sake of maintaining his own security and glory; and through his action of "gifting" a city, he also made many new princes. These new princes owed their change in status and their continued "good fortune" directly to the *virtù* and *fortuna* of Darius. Even though Darius I is not cited again in the *Prince*, Machiavelli again refers to the Persian Empire in Chapter 4, when he describes the ease with which Alexander the Great held the Persian kingdom after overcoming a successor of the first Darius, Darius III. The Persian kingdom posed a peculiar set of difficulties for Alexander, and those difficulties had nothing to do with the brilliance of the Persian generals or the readiness of the Persian army. The Persian Empire, like the empire of the Ottoman Turks, both posed the same challenge—a prince who sought to acquire such a kingdom could not depend on the assistance of other princes within it. Unlike the kingdom of France, where each of the French barons within the kingdom enjoyed the allegiance and loyalty of his subjects, the Turkish and Persian "princes" were slaves of their sovereign.[34] In describing such new princes who held their position through the power of another, Machiavelli clearly describes their relationship in terms of dominance and obedience and, as he clarifies, such princes:

> rest simply on the will and fortune of whoever has given it [a state] to them, which are two most inconstant and unstable things...[35]

This kind of principality, gifted to a private person, has a clear-cut cost—it is held in service to that one or those from whom the gift originated. This state of affairs places this kind of new prince in a position of clear-cut dependency. Such new princes:

> Do not know how to hold and they cannot hold that rank: they do not know how, because if one is not a man of great ingenuity and virtue, it is not reasonable, that having always been in private fortune, he would know how to command (*sappia commandare*); they are not able [to hold the rank] because they do not have forces that can be friendly and faithful to them.[36]

This kind of new prince acts as an intermediary between the one who exercises and manages the actual conditions of power and those who are ruled. Their subjects accord allegiance to their principal ruler, whom they obey, and they feel no particular allegiance to their new "administrative" prince. The distinction between the princes who rule through their own *virtù* and *fortuna* and those who rule through the *virtù* and *fortuna* of another depends on whether those princes "would know how to command" (*sappia commandare*) and whether they have at their disposal friendly and faithful forces. Machiavelli expresses his high assessment for the art of war in Chapter 14, where he states:

And it is of such virtù that not only does it maintain those that are born princes, but many times it makes those of private fortuna rise up to that grade.[37]

For a prince "to be armed" is not determined simply by whether he has his own standing army, obedient subjects,[38] or is even a legitimate prince with official status. For a prince to be "armed" depends most immediately on whether he possesses the art of war.[39]

Understanding the importance of the art of command to the function of the new prince makes the apparent error Machiavelli commits in Chapter 7 much less surprising. The very next example Machiavelli cites in Chapter 7 is that of Francesco Sforza who, from private individual, acquired his state through his own *virtù*. This example raises difficulties here because, strictly speaking, Sforza's career and his rise took place independently of the virtue and fortune of others.[40] His example does not belong in this chapter, addressed as it is to a discussion of those who gained principalities through the arms and fortune of others. Sforza is noteworthy because "through proper means (*per li debiti mezzi*) and with a great virtue of his own, from private individual he became Duke of Milan." Having acquired Milan, he held it with little difficulty. In Chapter 14, Machiavelli tells us that Sforza's transition happened through his being armed ("*per essere armato*").[41] Earlier in the *Prince* Machiavelli tells us that Sforza's change of role with the Milanese resulted from his hire as a mercenary captain for that city.[42] For the same reason, Sforza's heirs lose Milan through not being armed.[43] Thus, using the examples furnished by Machiavelli as a guide here, whether a private individual transitions to the role of prince depends on whether that individual possesses the know-how of command and obedient forces. However, whether these obedient forces are an Ottoman army of converted slaves, a troop of Macedonian regulars, Swiss auxiliaries, or a sufficiently organized Northern Italian mercenary force stands in second place to the one factor predictive of whether the private individual becomes an independent new prince or a dependently slavish new prince: *the know-how of command*.[44] Even mercenary arms can function as "arms of one's own" if one happens to be Francesco Sforza.[45]

Chapter 7 then continues with a description of the career of Cesare Borgia, the career that Machiavelli appears to hold up as paradigmatic for new princes. However, exploring the relationship between Pope Alexander VI and his son Duke Valentino, i.e., Cesare Borgia, really serves to muddy the distinction drawn just now between independent and dependent new princes. Machiavelli tells the entire story of Alexander VI and Duke Valentino to show that the successes and ultimate failure of the younger Borgia were due not simply to *fortuna* but depended greatly on the relationship between the Duke and Alexander VI. Beginning with the very first statement describing Borgia's career, "Alexander VI, when he decided to make his son, the Duke, great, had very many difficulties, both present and future."[46] Machiavelli structures the entire story of Borgia's rise and fall to indicate how Alexander's powers of deception were so great that they lent his son the appearance of autonomy when, in fact, he was directly being employed in the systematic execution of his father's goals.[47] Later, in Chapter 11, during his discussion of ecclesiastical principalities, Machiavelli unambiguously states the relationship between father and son in his discussion of the temporal successes of the pontiffs:

> Then Alexander VI arose who, of all the pontiffs that have ever been, he showed how far a pope could prevail who had both money and forces. Using the instrument of Duke Valentino (*con lo instrumento del duco Valentino*) and the occasion of the invasion of the French, he did all the things discussed above in the actions of the duke.[48]

In Machiavelli's retelling of Borgia's career, Duke Valentino maintains the same relationship to Alexander VI that pertained between Duke Valentino and Remirro de Orco, a captain of Cesare's whom Cesare (or, indirectly, Alexander?) appointed to rule the Romagna after the events of Sinigaglia.[49] During his tenure, Remirro reduced the Romagna to peace, restored it to unity and earned a dubious reputation for himself in the process. Duke Valentino then convened a court whose aim was to convince the Romagnese that any cruelty committed in the province was the responsibility of de Orco rather than his. One morning, Remirro is found cut in half, left in the piazza, "with a piece of wood and a bloody knife beside him." The anonymous and ambiguous scapegoating of Remirro allows Valentino to exert the cruelty needed to bring this region to order and unity, himself evading a direct imputation for cruelty in the process. At the same time, Machiavelli in Chapter 17 ascribes the unity and orderliness of the Romagna to Borgia's *own* cruelty, and not to that of his appointee—Remirro, whose name does not even occur in the passage.[50] The principal actor in this drama that entirely escapes direct attribution for cruelty is, of course, Alexander VI and this despite the fact that in his telling of Cesare's story, up to the death of Alexander, Machiavelli consistently describes the advances and successes of Duke Valentino with either a direct or oblique reference to the interests and direction of Alexander VI.[51]

This dependency emerges even more fully with the reasons Machiavelli gives for Borgia's downfall. Machiavelli gives four reasons to explain why Borgia eventually lost everything acquired during the papal tenure of his father: 1) Borgia had not acquired enough empire to withstand attack; 2) the sudden death of Alexander; 3) the sickness that afflicted Borgia himself at the time of Alexander's death; 4) the danger that Alexander's replacement on the papal throne would prove an adversary to Borgia. In the concluding paragraph of Chapter 7, Machiavelli strikes out all but one of these causes. The remaining trigger for Borgia's downfall is the truly poor choice that Borgia made on his own when he allowed the election of Julius II as pontiff—a person whom Borgia had harmed in the past—and whom he allowed then to become his father's successor.[52] In Machiavelli's telling of the end of Cesare's political career,[53] the fact Borgia could have selected any successor to his father and yet made such a clearly bad choice critically exposes Borgia's direct dependence on Alexander for the successful decisions he made and successful strategies he employed throughout his career. Said another way: insofar as Machiavelli consistently reminds us of Alexander's presence in the career of Borgia; and insofar as the first decision Borgia had to make on his own brings about his complete downfall, Borgia's "dependence on the *fortuna* of others" needs to be read as his reliance on the acuity of Alexander VI for whatever success he did enjoy.[54]

Thus, Machiavelli's distinction between independently acting new prince and dependently slavish new prince itself depends on recognizing the institutional locations that anchor and manage the circuits of *effectual authority*[55] of the prince(s) in question. Ultimately, the meaningfulness of the very term, *principe*, in Machiavelli's usage clearly does not depend on someone holding a publicly visible, much less *legitimate*, office.[56] Thus, in the *Discourses*, Machiavelli discusses the dispute that arose in Syracuse upon the death of Hieronymous, successor of Hiero II. By doing so Machiavelli reminds his reader that the same Hiero who had exhibited a certain proportionality with the likes of those emblematically independent new princes—Moses, Theseus, Cyrus, and Romulus—was throughout his career one of Rome's most loyal *allies*, i.e., Hiero was a Roman pawn.[57] The message of Chapters 6 and 7 of the *Prince* is that those who rely on the arms of others become the instrument of those arms whose intentions they serve and accomplish. This instrumentality holds whether the relationship is a direct one, as it was with both Darius I and his provincial governors and the early Ottoman emperors with their *kul*; or is an indirect one, as it was with both the relationship between Duke Valentino and Alexander VI and Hiero II with the Roman Senate. The other message of Chapters 6 and 7, together with those passages in the *Prince* which refer to them, is that determining the quality of the autonomy of a prince's decisions and actions is not settled by simply answering the question whether the arms they employed were bought or were organized out of their own obedient subjects, i.e., whether these arms are slave or free. The crucial issue of the quality of a new prince's autonomy is *not* decided by whether the prince employs mercenary arms or obedient subjects; it is determined by who or what, in the final analysis, is in a broader sense the "author" of the intentions of those who have arms in hand.[58]

4. The Arms of Others

But if the factor determining princely autonomy and heteronomy is not simply reducible to whether a prince contracts for arms or employs obedient subjects then Machiavelli's whole discourse on mercenary arms in the *Prince* must have other functions in the text than what it appears to play at first glance. Machiavelli's critique of mercenary arms seems to operate as a warning to princes of what *not* to do, of how *not* to protect themselves and of how *not* to increase their states. Relying on mercenary arms seems to be *the* way to compromise princely autonomy. And yet, for Francesco Sforza, employment of mercenary arms was *the royal road* to achieving the duchy of Milan.[59] Thus, Machiavelli's critique of mercenary arms demands careful analysis to see in what ways this distinction, *the arms of others*, really does operate in his text. However, Chapter 12 does not begin with a discussion of the mercenary army: instead its opening passages discuss the relationship between good laws and armed force. These paragraphs finish with the famous formulation describing the relationship between the terms:

> The principal foundations that all states have, both new ones as well as old or mixed, are good laws and good arms: and because there cannot be good laws where there are not good arms, and where there are good arms it happens there are also good laws, I will leave to the side the reasoning about laws and will speak of arms.[60]

Following this introduction, his discussion of the category of mercenaries and the status of the *condottieri* in the passages that follow is the often-noted one that frames the question of arms in terms of the "ownership" of those arms. A prince either defends his state with his own arms or with mercenary or auxiliary arms. Unlike arms of one's own, mercenary forces and auxiliary forces threaten the security of the patron.[61] Thus, that prince is more secure the more he depends on his *own* armies. Yet by introducing this distinction between mercenaries and auxiliaries, Machiavelli re-orients the distinction between one's own arms and the arms of others according to a different trajectory that introduces a new criterion. We begin with the apparently straightforward criterion of whether the arms belong to the prince (or state) in question or somehow belong to some other(s). Then the critique of mercenary arms recenters the question around the *usefulness or uselessness* of the arms in question. This change is an important one since it introduces much greater flexibility into the discussion of having arms in general and employing the arms of others in particular. It is quite conceivable that even mercenary arms could be considered useful to someone, though perhaps not to the patron who employs them; or that they could even be employed usefully by a patron who was not naïve to the dangers of this kind of army; or that they could be usefully employed by some captain, like Hannibal,[62] who was able to rein in the bad qualities these arms exhibit through some feature of that captain's character.[63]

On the surface Machiavelli appears to criticize both kinds of army, mercenary and auxiliary, as useless and dangerous, but even these two kinds of contract army are not both dangerous or threatening to regimes in the same way. Silently bypassing the discussion of auxiliary arms,[64] Machiavelli enumerates the qualities of mercenaries:

> for they are disunited, ambitious, without discipline, unfaithful; bold among friends; among enemies, cowardly: they have no fear of God, no faith with other men; ruin is postponed only so long as the assault is postponed; and in peace you are despoiled by them; in war, by the enemy.[65]

These difficulties with mercenary armies stem from the fact that the small stipend received by them does not make them "want to give their lives" for their patron.[66] These men do, indeed, need a patron, since their livelihood and way of life depends on their continued employment which is only assured through the continuing threat of war.[67] Without at least the threat of war, there is no opportunity for the mercenary captain or soldier to market their labor.[68] On the other hand, actual war itself threatens their continued employment in a variety of ways, not the least of which is the possibility of personal death on the battlefield. Further, the logic of mercenary warfare implied that the decisive, i.e., *total*, loss of a battle could mean the loss of the employer's—their patron's—continued ability to keep forces in the field by depriving the patron of wealth, their state, or both. Even victory over the enemy endangers the next paycheck, since with the defeat of the opposing forces the patron has a valuable opportunity to stop the drain on their resources by canceling contracts or simply not fulfilling them.[69] However, even on Machiavelli's own estimation, the Italian mercenaries were indeed "successful" for a time:

> they once made some progress for some, and may have appeared bold among themselves; but when the foreigner (*il forestiero*) came, they showed that which they were.[70]

For a time, mercenary armies not only *seemed* to work but actually did work in Italy.[71] A logic[72] to mercenary warfare developed that made increasingly larger and more organized bands of *condottieri* useful to Italian princes and republics; this "logic" allowed them to maintain and even hope to extend their regimes through the use of this type of soldier.[73]

5. The *Condottieri*—Demonstrable Failures?

Machiavelli claims that his intention in the third paragraph of Chapter 12 is to "demonstrate more thoroughly why mercenary arms are unhappy (*infelicità*) failures." Examining the details of this "demonstration" reveals much about the status of Machiavelli's apparent indictment of the use of mercenaries. Paragraph 3 of Chapter 12 contains the statement of a general premise; the paragraphs that follow it elucidate particulars that support it before the argument's conclusion appears toward the end of the chapter. The general premise Machiavelli introduces is the following: *mercenary arms, whether excellent or not, always ruin their patron*. Machiavelli holds this general premise to be true for two very different reasons. First, if such arms are excellent and well-ordered they resist being controlled; they oppress their patron or the citizens themselves, at least when this is contrary to the patron's intention. Second, if the mercenary armies and captains are ineffective and incompetent they ruin their clients through both the cost of their employment and their failures in the field. Thus the complete *uselessness* of mercenary arms is of two types: 1) the *effective*; and 2) the *ineffective*. In both cases, such troops pose a danger to their patrons—they threaten the continued stability and even the form of the regime whether such arms prove successful or a failure. This would truly pose a problem if the *Prince* were a text addressed only to established princes, hereditary princes, or stable republics. However, the text addresses itself to the *new* prince in the *new* principality, for whom an exemplar is the mercenary captain Francesco Sforza. Given this focus, Machiavelli's distinction between effective and ineffective mercenary arms proves a useful distinction to make among such "useless" arms.[74]

Further, Machiavelli himself raises an objection to his own general premise when he states: "And if one responds that whoever has arms in hand would do this, mercenary or not..." He then addresses this anonymous objector by making another distinction, a distinction between kinds of patrons. The patrons of arms are either princes or republics. If they are princes, the ineffective prince has effectively replaced himself by allowing some other captain to lead his armies. Machiavelli is clear that a prince should always lead his own armies into battle.[75] In the case of the principality, the "performative" dimension of Machiavelli's point here hints strongly at the earlier point he made in Chapters 6 and 7 during the discussion of having one's own arms: those who have the know-how of command and obedient arms possess the foundation[76] necessary to make the transition from private individual to new prince. On the other hand, if the patron happens to be a republic the danger posed by the employment of mercenary arms is equally, if indirectly, clear. A republic should have good and well-observed laws to keep their citizens in bounds. Thus a republic with good laws never has to worry about any one citizen coming to dominate all the rest so long as its laws continue to be observed faithfully. If a citizen delegated to head a mercenary army should exhibit suspicious behavior, in a well-governed republic the citizen-captain would be promptly replaced. Yet, according to Machiavelli's general premise, a republic that employs mercenary arms in the first place would have neither good, or if good, then certainly not well-observed laws. Thus, effective mercenary arms present themselves as having clear utility for potential new, though perhaps illegitimate, princes whether they find themselves in a principality or a republic.[77] Mercenary arms are potentially useful in replacing ineffective princes and are potentially effective in transforming a republic into a principality. The transition in both cases would be contingent on money, opportunity and an ambitious captain.

6. Milan, Naples, Venice, and Florence—A Tale of Four Cities

The paragraphs that follow the general premise contain two occurrences of "*mercenario*." These paragraphs propose to continue the argument begun in paragraph 3 by introducing specific examples, ancient and modern, to elucidate the hypothesis that the failure of mercenary arms, and the tendency of such arms to end in disastrous failure for the patron, occurs no matter the actual capabilities of the mercenary forces in question. In execution, these statements accomplish two things: first, Machiavelli details the success of the Romans, the

Spartans, and the Swiss who were successful because they were armed republics. Then, he embarks on a list of modern Italian cities that all employed mercenary arms—Milan, Naples, Venice, and Florence. In describing the employment of mercenaries by two of these cities, Venice and Florence, Machiavelli refers to two cities that *successfully employed mercenary arms*. Even in the cases of Milan and Naples, whose employment of such arms ended in notable failures, the way Machiavelli relates their stories illustrates the fact that mercenary arms do tend to be useful *to someone*, if not to their employer. In fact, the example of Milan serves only to remind us again of the career of Francesco Sforza, who successfully exchanged his position as a condottieri for a dukedom. Further, the example of Naples describes how Queen Giovanna evaded the consequences of the success of Francesco's father, Muzio Attendolo Sforza—also a mercenary captain—only through marriage to the King of Aragon. Thus, the examples of Milan and Naples could be read as both a warning to cities and as subtle encouragement to aspiring new princes, since the use of the Sforza captains on both occasions brought about a change in regime.

However such a change did not occur for Florence and Venice. Machiavelli's analyses of these two examples then merits closer examination. The Florentine Republic is secured from the consequences of mercenary arms "by chance" (*"sono suti favoriti dalla sorte"*). Because of his failure in the field, mercenary captain, Giovanno Acuto, just happened *not* to win and, thus, the Florentines were spared (*"ma ognuno confesserà che, vincendo, stavano a Fiorentino a sua discrezione"*). Similarly Paolo Vitelli happened *not* to win at Pisa; should he have taken the city the Florentines would have been at his discretion.[78] However, in the midst of detailing the particulars of these two examples Machiavelli begins an apparent digression on another aspect of the use of mercenary forces—the known *intentions* of the mercenary commanders themselves. Because rival *condottieri* feared the consequences of the success of a particular commander on the dynamics of the market for force in Italy as a whole, mercenary commanders could be prevented from transitioning into the sovereignty of their patrons *by other mercenary captains*. Machiavelli in these paragraphs gives a genealogy of the rise of the *condottieri* and the Italian peninsula as a province whose market for force was managed by two students of Alberigo da Conio, the Sforza and the Braccio, who, according to Machiavelli "in their times were the arbiters of Italy."[79] Through the old school opposition of these rival clans, the gains of the Sforza were opposed by the Bracchesi, the successes of which were undermined by the Sforza.[80] Thus, the Florentines did not simply have *fortuna* to thank for their evading the consequences of their use of mercenary arms. The Florentines escaped the consequences of using mercenary arms by properly gauging, calculating, and playing on the ambitions—the signaled intentions—of their *condottieri*: Francesco Sforza ultimately desired Lombardy, not Tuscany; the Bracchio desired to possess the Romagna and the Kingdom of Naples, not Florence. Further, both of these captains needed continuous infusions of cash in order to keep their armies mobilized and their soldiers paid.[81] Thus mercenary captains were subject to easy manipulation by regionally prominent, mercantile powers that had the capital necessary to keep these captains in the field and engaged in campaigns whose success or failure very often did not threaten their own regimes.[82] At the same time, sponsoring such forces on their campaigns in other regions certainly could and did serve as disruptive objects of concern to their rivals in the Italian peninsula. Capital might be lost in the success or failure of a campaign, but capital could be replaced. The Venetians and the Florentines could both make use of these captains by making promises and tendering money to them in a way that ultimately benefited their own regional strategic interests.[83] Even though Machiavelli presents the Florentine and Venetian use of mercenaries as if it were a criticism of their having engaged such forces, attention to the *performance* of this criticism within Machiavelli's text suggests that Machiavelli greatly exaggerates the case against mercenaries here. The degree of his exaggeration intends to highlight the fact that the Florentines and Venetians both knew how to make use of mercenary forces such that their employment for a time proved useful and predictable to them.[84]

7. Fear of Success? Conspiracy and Patronage

Chapter 12 suggests that both republics and principalities are potentially made vulnerable through the use of mercenaries; it also suggests that there are indeed situations in which mercenary arms can be astutely employed. These cases would include: 1) if the mercenary captain isn't either decisively successful or entirely unsuccessful in their campaign, maintaining thereby the overall balance of power between their employer, themselves and the other powers in the region. 2) If one employs mercenary captains who, in their trade, are opposed by the ambitions of others plying the same profession, as the Sforza were opposed by the Bracchio. 3) If one knows that the ambitions of a mercenary captain ultimately lie elsewhere. This last (3) also suggests that mercenary captains, like the Bracchio and Sforza, may, indeed, have something like a "love" or at least a "cause" to keep them in the field beyond the stipend they receive. Machiavelli clearly attributes to *condottieri* like Sforza and Piccinino the aim of making the transition from being captains of Italian battlefields of questionable status to being legitimate princes in their own right. Their "desire for legitimacy" was thus a factor that rendered them useful and predictable to others.[85] Factoring in this "desire for legitimacy" was a clear strategy employed by the regimes of Italian republics and principalities, a strategy which, when utilized successfully, for a time made these mercenary "arms of others" their own.[86]

Further, if considered with care, the references made to the mercenary captain, Paolo Vitelli, in this chapter not only describe the risk the Florentines took in employing the *condottieri,* but also suggest—by *what is not said* about Vitelli's employment by the Florentines—another stratagem employers of mercenaries could employ against condottieri on those occasions when the decisive success of the captains in their engagements threatened the proportion of power between patron and *condottiere*.[87] Had Paolo Vitelli taken Pisa, in Machiavelli's estimation he would have ruined the Florentines. What Machiavelli does not mention here is that Vitelli was beheaded by the Florentines on October 1, 1499, for having been "overly cautious" in the midst of the siege of Pisa, revealing another stratagem, *betrayal* and *conspiracy,* that patrons of mercenaries employed against their captains.[88] Machiavelli describes both the Florentines and Venetians making use of the art of conspiracy as a way of securing themselves against the potentially negative consequences of their use of mercenary arms. Carmagnola, a mercenary captain, defeated the Milanese on behalf of the Venetians in 1432. The Venetians realized they could not, from that moment, win with him or dismiss him, so they tricked and killed him in a grand and thoroughly public manner.[89] In fact the betrayal of these captains is not, strictly speaking, even *betrayal* if by betrayal we intend to color these decisions and actions on the part of the regime as somehow immoral. For Machiavelli, the established legitimacy of the patron makes these betrayals a clear case of the patrons—the established republics and princes—conquering threats through the use of their established authority, i.e., of the use of fraud in warfare.[90] Effective mercenary captains thus also had to fear their own employers who could be clearly and reasonably threatened by the consequences following from a captain's overwhelming success.[91]

A final mention of mercenaries in Chapter 12 occurs at its close, when Machiavelli defines them as those who "were men without a state and who lived on industry" (*"feciono questo perché, sendo sanza stato e in su la industria. . ."*).[92] In these closing paragraphs, Machiavelli tells us here that in fifteenth- and sixteenth-century Italy war had become an "industry of mercenaries" because those who governed no longer had or practiced the art of war.[93] Machiavelli describes the process by which the Italian noble families were overthrown by their citizens with the support of the Church, and how, in other Italian cities, republics were overthrown when private citizens became princes. The story that Machiavelli tells here is interesting, both because it throws light on Machiavelli's understanding of the origins of this system,[94] and because it suggests limits to the security and success that possession of the art of war entails. As Machiavelli tells it here, the nobles, despite possessing the art of war, fail in their class struggle with the newly empowered mercantile class which, with the support of the Church, overcame their former rulers. Those who possess the art of war are overcome by those who do not: private citizens overcome their (presumably) *legitimate* rulers; citizens allied with the Church manage to overcome their nobility; the priests conquered the warriors. Through the support of the church—and the willingness to finance debt shown by the dominant mercantile families—an industry of conflict develops in the Italian peninsula, and this industry is of sufficient force to suppress the consequences simple possession of the art of war had previously entailed.

Chapter 14, the very chapter in which Machiavelli discusses the importance of the art of war, opens with yet another reference to the career of Francesco Sforza who, "through his being armed" (*"per essere armato"*), from a private individual became Duke of Milan; and his sons, by fleeing and shunning arms, from being Dukes "became private individuals." In this chapter, just the fact of the mercenary Sforza's being armed establishes a certain proportion between him and the esteemed figure of Philopoemon whom Machiavelli will praise in the following paragraph as someone who did nothing but think on the art of war.[95] With these varied statements Machiavelli signals both the importance of the art of war and suggests that this art, too, has its limits.[96] Generally speaking, the exaggerated character of Machiavelli's criticism of Italian mercenaries draws attention to the development of the reliance on mercenary forces by Italian princes and republics, and the history itself can be seen as a veiled response to an obvious question arising in the light of his overall criticism of mercenary forces: "why, if the Italian mercenaries are so awful and uncertain in the field would any prince or republic seriously depend on them?" The history Machiavelli tells of the genesis of the importance of the mercenary system describes its rise as a strategy to circumscribe the power of those who possessed the art of war. On his telling, the adoption, support and encouragement of mercenary forces was the expression of the *will-to-power*, so to speak, of a particular alliance of Italy's commercial, ecclesiastical and banking interests.[97]

Thus, Machiavelli's history of the use of mercenaries in the wars of the Italian peninsula is an interpretation of the multiple ways in which mercenaries were deployed to extend and routinize the arrangements of power requiring forces having the particular set of features mercenary arms exhibited. Employment of mercenary forces was not simply a bad decision on the part of republicans and princes who made their selection from among an array of choices available to them. The character of the arms are a function of the power(s) whose interests they were intended to secure. For fifteenth- and sixteenth-century Italian princes, contract forces were supported by state debt whose financing increasingly framed internal and external policy decisions.[98] Thus, Machiavelli's criticism of mercenary arms offers a critique of the decisions leading to the employment of such arms as well as a critique of the criteria and the conditions that prompted the employers, *themselves*, to choose such arms as an extension of their particular brand of state. Such a critique invites inquiry into the force of these values, which were such that they prevented serious practical development of more fruitful alternatives as, for, instance, the development of a citizen militia enabling a prince or republic to field at least mixed troops, if not an army of their own.

But if this assessment of Machiavelli's approach is correct, then this means that Machiavelli not only had worked out his idea of a citizen militia as a practical alternative to dependence on mercenary and auxiliary arms but had also fleshed out the conceptual framework and theoretical axiomatics that would encourage policymaking in the direction of this better option. What is the conceptual universe underpinning the practical possibility of one's own arms? This is the deeper question raised by Machiavelli's critique of mercenary force.

8. Conclusion

It is clear that Machiavelli's critique of the *condottieri* in the *Prince* is deliberately exaggerated by him and has not been perceived by commentators in a sufficiently nuanced way. The particularly exaggerated rhetoric Machiavelli employs in the critique of such arms compels his reader to attend to the conditions pressuring the policy-making processes that could have led anyone to employ mercenary forces in the first place. Thus, his critique of this sort of arms is at the same time a critique of those institutional arrangements and policy trends on the basis of which such arms possessed a consistent utility value.[99] The fact that Machiavelli dwells on how *condottieri* were not useful for repelling the French and Spanish armies from their incursions into the Italian peninsula after 1494 should not be read as a simple dismissal of them. In different passages throughout his works, Machiavelli points out limitations and defects possessed by the French, Spanish, and even Swiss arms. Each of these differently organized and equipped armies proved useful and effective in certain contexts while in other cases they proved easily overwhelmed and defeated.[100]

Thus, in Machiavelli, there are clearly certain contexts in which the use of the *condottieri* by acquisitive princes rendered their employment predictable, even effective, and their negatives manageable. As in the case of Francesco Sforza, mercenary forces could perform a key function in the transformation of a potential prince into an established prince. Further, *condottieri* could perform a key function for those wishing to transform a republic into a principality. Mercenaries were very useful for destabilizing a province, when a foreign prince or republic wished to disrupt or preserve the proportion of regional forces without directly engaging forces of their own. Mercenary soldiers were a way for those actually versed in the *know-how of command* to take away the regimes of others not so similarly versed. In his conflicting critique of the employment of such forces, Machiavelli at the same time illuminates the genuine, if limited, potential mercenary forces did possess for certain actors under certain circumstances. In fixing their limitations and the specific contexts where these forces exhibited effectiveness, Machiavelli's critique then subsequently foregrounds the ideological commitments that compelled continued reliance on such forces even in circumstances that clearly exceeded them.

4

Instrumental and Aleatory Aspects of Auxiliary Force in Machiavelli[1]

1. Introduction

For Machiavelli, mercenaries—for all their weaknesses—are not the form of the "arms of others" most dangerous to a prince or a republic who employs them. Auxiliary forces pose a much greater danger than mercenaries.[2] Contrasting the dangers of mercenary to auxiliary arms in Chapter 13 of the *Prince*, Machiavelli states:

> Auxiliary arms, which are the other useless arms, are when one calls a power that with its own arms comes to defend you…These arms can be good and useful in themselves, but they are, for those who call them, almost always damaging. Because losing, you are undone and, winning, you are their prisoner.[3]

For Machiavelli, auxiliary arms pose a specific type of problem. Auxiliary arms differ from mercenary arms in being more effective in combat. Their advantage here stems from their unity and their obedience to another. However, Machiavelli's description of auxiliaries includes another feature that he specifically excludes from the characteristics he ascribes to mercenary arms. As he states:

> Therefore he who wants to not be able to win, makes use of these arms, because they are much more dangerous than mercenaries. Because in these is conspiracy done, they are all united, at all times obedient to another.[4]

Though both types of arms pose a threat, auxiliary arms carry the added danger that they are subject to the intent of the prince or republic that loans them. The assistance they provide serves the interests of the loaning prince or republic, which might very well include designs on the party receiving the assistance. Given the uncertainties employment of auxiliaries poses, those who receive their aid have no easy way to counter their threat unless, of course, they possess arms of their own in sufficient strength and quantity to diminish the likelihood that betrayal would lead to disaster.[5]

Despite the many references to armies and kinds of soldiers in the *Prince* and the *Discourses*, only one chapter in each book refers directly to the theme of auxiliary arms. This happens in the *Prince* in Chapter 13, "Of Auxiliary, Mixed and One's Own Soldiers,"[6] and in the *Discourses* at 2.20 titled, "What Danger that Prince or Republic Runs that Avails Itself of Auxiliary or Mercenary Military."[7] Machiavelli links the two chapters at the beginning of *Discourses* 2.20 when he states, "If I had not dealt at length in my other work with how useless mercenary and auxiliary military are, and how useful is one's own, I would stretch myself in this discourse more than I will do."[8] In this way he signals the importance of reading together these two accounts of auxiliary force, examining them for their points of convergence and divergence.

Doing so uncovers that Machiavelli's analysis of auxiliary arms articulates the phenomenon from the standpoint of the prince (as is to be expected), where such forces serve as an instrument for the projection of power, but also, surprisingly, from the standpoint of the people. Further, Machiavelli's presentation of auxiliary force reveals the people to be an unpredictable factor that opens up political relations to a field of uncertainty. Acknowledging the aspectival function played by the definition of auxiliaries in Machiavelli's texts offers a new vantage point for re-reading Machiavelli on the nature of authority, power and the humoral-driven conflicts of *popolo* and *grandi*.

2. Auxiliaries in the *Prince*

In the *Prince*,[9] Machiavelli treats the categories of mercenary and auxiliary arms separately.[10] Chapter 12 discusses mercenary arms and Chapter 13 examines auxiliaries.[11] Over the course of the two chapters, Machiavelli describes mercenaries as arms that belong to anyone who can hire them. On the other hand, auxiliaries are arms whose obedience belongs solely with the prince or princes[12] to whom they are loyal.[13]

Both types of force are useless but in two different ways. Mercenary arms are useless owing to their unfaithfulness to the prince or republic that contracts with them, since money is not enough to make them want to die for the cause.[14] Auxiliary arms are useless because the authority their prince has over them makes them dangerous to those to whom they are loaned.[15] Thus, the core issue of auxiliary arms is the quality of their obedience to the prince or republic that is loaning them. As examined in Chapter 4, Machiavelli's analysis of mercenary armies provokes an investigation of the causes that would motivate princes and republics to make use of such apparently pointless arms. Similarly, his analysis of auxiliary arms requires an examination of the particular quality of obedience exhibited by auxiliary troops in order to explain the behavior of arms that are not so much useless (or at least not in the way mercenary arms are) as they are *dangerous* to whomever calls for and relies on their aid.[16] On the surface, Machiavelli's analysis of auxiliary arms appears to be a practical assessment of a category of military force that identifies the consequences that typically follow from their employment. Examined at greater depth, his analysis of this type of force reveals limits to the instrumental deployment of arms of one's own.

Machiavelli analyzes three examples of the employment of auxiliary force in Chapter 13 of the *Prince*. These examples concern Pope Julius II and the Spanish, the Florentines, and the French, as well as the Emperor of Constantinople and the Turks. In the cases of auxiliary force cited in the *Prince*, it did *not* always happen that negative consequences followed from the use of such troops for those who employed them. This ambiguity suggests that Machiavelli is signaling to his audience that his discussion of the theme of auxiliary force deserves more careful treatment than it may first seem to warrant. Recalling Machiavelli's description of this force category: "These arms can be useful and good for themselves, but they are, for those who call them, almost always harmful; because if they lose, you remain defeated; if they should win, you remain their prisoner."[17] It remains to be seen whether Machiavelli's description of this category of armed force yields unexpected interpretations in his texts.

For instance, in the discussion of Pope Julius II, it is telling that Machiavelli's presentation of the story is actually inconclusive concerning the consequences following from the use of auxiliary arms. As Machiavelli correctly notes in his retelling of this story, Julius II did *not* find himself the prisoner of his Spanish auxiliaries. On Machiavelli's account, because the Spanish troops supporting Julius were defeated and the Swiss mercenaries unexpectedly supported his cause, Julius II was spared the consequences of his bad decision to accept auxiliaries. This unanticipated consequence, "beyond every expectation both of his own and others" ("*fuora di ogni opinione e sua e d'altri*"),[18] prevented Julius II from being made a prisoner of his poor decision.[19] Thus, it was apparently nothing other than chance or *fortuna* that precluded the negative consequences of Julius II's use of auxiliary troops in his campaign. Although Machiavelli's re-telling of the battle of Ravenna may be at odds with a closer inspection of the events,[20] it is clear that the nature of the troops governed by the

Spanish on behalf of Pope Julius II did indeed satisfy the definition Machiavelli gives of auxiliary troops both here (in the *Prince*) and, again, at 2.20 of the *Discourses*.

Likewise, the negative consequences of employing auxiliaries did not follow the Florentine's use of French auxiliary troops in the siege of Pisa in 1500. On Guicciardini's account of this episode, the enterprise failed but the fault did not lie with the French troops. The failure occurred due to the soldiers' disorderliness and disobedience precipitated by the Florentine failure to send adequate ammunition and provisions.[21] Guicciardini clearly ascribes the failure of the expedition to the French captain's incapacity to "command the respect and obedience due him," and his failure to take the necessary steps to stop the disobedience of his soldiers. Had the enterprise succeeded, the Florentines may have had to face victorious French troops suddenly unwilling to relinquish the city. Still, in Machiavelli's second example as well, the specific danger he attributes to employing auxiliaries did not materialize.

The third example that Machiavelli considers is the reliance of the Byzantine emperor, John VI Cantacuzene (1292–1383), on the Turkish Osmanlis soldiers supplied by his son-in-law, Orhan. Orhan's own son, Suleiman, loaned Turkish support at various times to the different players in the factious politics of the Byzantine emperors. The auxiliary aid often took the form of assistance to both the Cantacuzene and Palailogos factions. The emperor's reliance on these troops eventually led to the Turkish occupation of a number of locations in the Thracian Chersonnese.[22] Thus it would seem that in this last example, Machiavelli describes circumstances where the use of an auxiliary army resulted in the negative consequences he predicts for a prince employing auxiliary force.

In the cases of auxiliary force taken up by Machiavelli in the *Prince*, it did *not* always happen that negative consequences followed from the use of such troops for those who employed them. This suggests that it may in fact even be possible to manage the dangers of auxiliary forces or make use of them instrumentally for the attainment of limited objectives.[23] Nevertheless, in each of these examples from Chapter 13, Machiavelli actually describes cases where auxiliary troops, as he defines this category of armed force, were used.

3. Auxiliaries in the *Discourses*

Although the title of *Discourses* 2.20 indicates it is devoted to an analysis of both auxiliary *and* mercenary arms, Machiavelli ignores the theme of mercenary arms[24] in this chapter and instead focuses on a discussion of auxiliaries.[25] Machiavelli defines auxiliaries here as, "those whom a prince or a republic sends captained and already paid for, for your aid,"[26] which parallels discussion of these forces in the *Prince*. However, he then interrupts the parallel by claiming to treat this subject once again in the *Discourses* only because Livy uses such an extensive example of it. He goes on to outline an episode from Livy's Book 7, Chapters 38–42, which lays out the story of the Roman legions during the period of the occupation of Capua following the first war between Rome and the Samnites.[27]

As Machiavelli retells Livy's account, after Roman legions defeated the Samnite armies, two of the legions were left behind as a garrison to protect the Capuans from future incursions by the Samnites. Because of their idleness and the richness of the land, the legions subsequently "forgot their Fatherland" and their reverence for the Senate.[28] They made plans to seize Capua and its inhabitants and to set themselves up as lords of the region. However, their schemes failed because, as Machiavelli states: "Which thing [the schemes] having presented itself, the Romans oppressed and corrected it."[29] Machiavelli then refers the reader to Discourses 3.6 for a discussion of how the soldiers' conspiracy was handled, and he concludes his discussion of this example from Livy with a restatement of the warning to princes and republics about accepting auxiliary forces along with the reminder that being in the position of loaning such arms is an opportunity for seizing the city or province that calls them in.

This story, as Machiavelli retells it, raises questions for at least two reasons. First, in Machiavelli's account it is not at all clear that the auxiliaries were indeed dangerous to the Capuans, the persons they were sent to protect. Yet the principal contention of Machiavelli's analysis of this type of army in the *Prince* is that such troops pose the highest of risks for the princes and republics that employ them.[30] The Roman auxiliaries posed a danger, which would have been realized if their plans had not been discovered, but even on Machiavelli's gloss these troops posed only a *potential* threat to the Capuans that, in the end, went unrealized. This is a strange example for Machiavelli to cite as a definitive illustration of the dangers inherent in the use of auxiliary arms.

Second, Machiavelli's retelling of the story suggests that the auxiliary soldiers were as much a potential danger to their *own* leaders—the Romans back home— as they were to the Capuans. The soldiers "thought to take up arms and to make themselves lords of the country," so that on Machiavelli's telling, the mutiny of the soldiers was a clear revolt against Roman authority as much as it was a potential disaster for the Capuans.

Thus—*even as Machiavelli tells this story*—it is unclear for whom the actions of the legionnaires posed the greater danger[31] and yet Machiavelli ends with a nearly identical restatement of the definition of auxiliary arms that introduced the story at the beginning of the chapter, as if this example is enough to confirm his argument.[32] However, given the particulars of the story, the Capuan episode seems to pose a clear instance where lending arms to others proved as dangerous to the very prince (the Roman Senate) that loaned the auxiliaries as it was to those whom they were intended to protect. Even on Machiavelli's telling, the episode appears to be an occasion that put Roman military authority to the test. During their sojourn in Capua, the Roman legionnaires became prepared to invest themselves as lords of the Campanians. Further, they conceived this temptation spontaneously, and they did so without having any clear leaders, captains, or heads of note named as instigators of the revolt.[33]

4. Livy: Rome's Capuan Adventure

Machiavelli directs the reader to consult Livy's account of the episode but doing so only multiplies the difficulties. Livy's version[34] unfolds a far different story than the one that Machiavelli's analysis in the *Discourses* would lead readers to expect. Even a cursory reading of Livy shows that this example, far from demonstrating the danger auxiliary arms pose for those who employ them, suggests an "unanticipated" danger of loaning auxiliaries—an implicit danger that exists for the prince or republic *who does the loaning*.

Again, the Livian story relates a conflict between the Romans and the Samnites.[35] The episode begins when the Samnites attack the Sidicini, the Sidicini seek the Campanians as allies, and the Campanians become involved in the conflict. Given the opportunity to wage war against the wealthier Campanians, the Samnium armies bypass the Sidicini and swiftly besiege the Campanians, confining them within the walls of Capua. The Campanians quickly recognize that they cannot handle this siege on their own.[36]

The Campanians send a delegation from Capua to Rome. During the course of two receptions, the members of the Campanian delegation first offer themselves to the Romans as allies[37] and then, when this is refused, they offer themselves as Rome's subjects. The Romans accept the second offer and immediately acknowledge this change of status, which figures directly in the reasons they give for offering assistance to the Campanians.[38] As the Campanians have become their subjects and Campania their property, the Roman Senate states their expectation that the Samnites should now be willing to relinquish their claims on Campania.[39] The Samnites do not comply. Thus, the Roman decision to accept the Campanian capitulation leads directly to war with the Samnites, which results in a victory for Rome and the Roman occupation of Campania.

This example from Livy describes forces that clearly fall outside Machiavelli's definition of auxiliaries. The cases of auxiliaries cited in the *Prince* presented a situation in which a prince or republic requested the armies of another prince or republic for assistance in a conflict. Thus, for example, Pope Julius II requested the assistance of Spanish armies. These armies were indeed provided by the Spanish king, Ferdinand I, and his captain, Ramón de Cardona, led them into the failed engagement against the French under Gaston de Foix.[40] Thus, despite the questions raised by his retelling of this episode, Machiavelli presents here a clear example of troops being furnished by one prince, Ferdinand I, for use by another, Julius II.[41]

In contrast, Livy indicates that with the Roman rejection of the Campanian offer of alliance, the Campanians were now considered "the property of Rome." Machiavelli compels the reader to consider the significance the Campanian capitulation has for the subject of auxiliary arms in the *Discourses* in two ways: 1) as Machiavelli paraphrases this episode from Livy in the *Discourses*, he refers to his discussion of auxiliaries in the *Prince*, contrasting the two treatments of auxiliaries; and 2) at *Discourses* 2.9, Machiavelli refers to the conflict between the Romans and the Samnites as a conflict that occurred because the Campanians had delivered themselves to the Romans. The conflict between the Romans and the Samnites would have been avoided, at least for a time, had the Campanians not freely surrendered themselves.[42] At the close of 2.9,[43] Machiavelli stipulates the Campanian surrender to the Romans as a tactic a prince or republic can use to defend itself from an oppressor if it is willing to employ any means to that end. Through this observation about the "defense" employed by the Campanians against the Samnites, Machiavelli signals to the reader that he is entirely aware of the Livian context in which the secession of the Roman garrison at Campania took place.

5. The People as *Auxilium*

The difficulty of categorizing these legions as auxiliary forces only increases with further consideration of Livy's version of these events. Two features of Livy's story deserve special attention. First, Machiavelli attributes to Livy the view that the proximate cause for the soldiers' defection was due to the pleasures of Capua. Livy, on the other hand, repeatedly links the general cause for the motivation of the soldiers to secede to their indebtedness and the burden incurred by the interest rates Rome charged them.[44] Insofar as the episode operates as an example in Machiavelli's text, this feature of Livy's story is important because it explains why the soldiers were so ready to "forget their fatherland" while in Campania.[45] It also indicates how economic issues can play a crucial part not only in understanding mercenary arms—where this is expected—but also in understanding the character of auxiliary arms and, therefore, "the arms of others" as a category of armed force. A key part of Machiavelli's definition of auxiliary arms is that these are arms *bought and paid for by another prince*. Escaping creditors was a key reason why plebeian Romans served successive deployments in the legions. Thus, the consequences of economic indebtedness temporararily suspended through military service was a way in which the continuing services of the legionnaires were secured. Economic indebtedness served to reinforce the Senate's authority with them, an authority that clearly had limits. Livy's story revolves around the relationship of the indebted plebeian soldiers to the senators, whom they viewed as oppressors, and their sudden shift to resisting that authority.[46] Using the theme of auxiliary arms to retell this story, Machiavelli intimates here that the very conditions through which state power is augmented and expanded rest on another power: that of the support of the Roman plebeians or, more generally, *the concurrence of the people*. He further intimates that Rome's patricians developed a broad set of strategies for securing that support.

However, the new and distinct orientation the account of auxiliaries presents in the *Discourses* compared to the *Prince* appears most clearly in the second narrative sequence from the Campanian adventure as Livy tells it. The soldiers' conspiracy ignites into outright conflict when it is uncovered by the new consul[47] who initiates a series of measures against the soldiers to defuse the conspiracy before it can do any harm. However, the soldiers come to suspect that they have been discovered and that discovery transforms them into open insurrectionists. Having formed into an army of their own, the troops march on Rome and would have attacked the city itself had they not been met by the second consul,[48] who opposed them with another Roman army. At this point, the conspiracy of the Roman legions is no longer a matter of concern for the Campanians only. Rather than referring us to an example of the employment of auxiliary troops, Machiavelli's use of this story refers to the conditions that set the stage for a possible civil war among the Romans.[49] On Livy's telling, neither of the two armies actually desired to fight and the conflict was resolved peacefully. Still, Livy shows through the conclusion of his story the seriousness of the threat posed by the insurrection, since the Senate acquiesces to nearly all of the soldiers' demands, including those Livy describes as unreasonable and unjust.[50]

In citing this example from Livy, Machiavelli has gone out of his way to provide us with an example in which auxiliary troops, as he defines them in the *Prince, did not play a part*. As Livy tells this story, the conspiracy of the legions[51] proves to be a conspiracy against Rome itself.[52] The discussion of auxiliary troops in *Discourses* 2.20, far from extending the discussion of the dangers of a prince employing them, raises decisive questions about the relationship between economy and authority, since the defining characteristic of auxiliary arms—the very thing that makes them "dangerous"—is that they are troops paid for, organized by, and obedient to the authority of some other.

But this episode reveals that a key ingredient of authority here is not simply the top down relation of command and obedience. In the *Art of War*, the disciplinary regime at the root of the effectiveness of the Roman legions did not derive its power from the upper level officer structure alone. The militia functions well when its practices are rooted in a shared subjective framework produced by a common discipline that includes the rank-and-file soldiers, lower and intermediate officers, and the commanding officers alike. A principal role of the captain and the other upper level officers is to remove obstacles that could impede the semi-autonomous functioning of the troops as when Machiavelli counsels potential captains on the importance of removing "*una sinistre opinione*" from a multitude.[53]

This episode in Livy[54] is so notable because it hinges on how the plebeian soldiers of the defecting legions are entirely responsible for bringing events to this point. On Livy's telling, the soldiers conceive the intention to wage war on Rome, organize themselves, and then march on the city *on their own* with only a figurehead for a leader. Far from being a case where soldiers of one state were loaned to aid another, Machiavelli refers here to a set of events where troops rebel against their leadership, going so far as to kidnap a general, instructing *him* how to lead them against their *patria*. They do this with the aim of negating oppressive economic conditions linked by Livy to the system of usury and of preventing the Senate from executing harsh penalties for their rebellion.[55]

6. Instrumentality—Captured by Debt

Read this way, Machiavelli reminds his reader to consider an armed people not simply as a fixed asset in the state's projection of power but as *a variable* in the relationship of forces constituting the state. As such, the phenomenon of auxiliary arms reveals another layer of significance. In the *Prince*, it is clear that auxiliary troops are analyzed in terms of the efficacy arms of this type have for the prince, or princes, involved in their use or their loaning—i.e., they are assessed for their *instrumentality*. As such, auxiliary arms resemble other forms of power like money, *condottieri*, cannon, and fortresses that Machiavelli critiques at great length in both the *Prince* and the *Discourses*. These instruments of war allow princes and republics to present the appearance of power in a way that increasingly detaches the projects of the *nobili* from the support of the people. Basing defense on money, cannon, fortresses, and bought or loaned forces can sustain the appearance of power. However, it can also suppress the contribution the people could make as active, armed participants to the state's capacity to generate[56] organized force. Reliance on instrumentalized forces may succeed in suppressing the political community's conflict of *nobili* and *popolo*, but this strategy unfolds as a kind of cultivated myopism around the external limit that accompanies all states no matter their size or degree of power. As Machiavelli states at *Discourses* 2.5, the flood—whether of waters or peoples—constantly threatens the existence of the state as an ever-present external limit. As Lefort phrases this: "A people can absorb or subjugate or exterminate other peoples: it does not cease abutting its outer limit: the latter is indifferent to the degree of power."[57]

For Jérémie Barthas, Machiavelli's critique of the arms of others is not only based on the dangers posed by a noble class that has ceased to weigh realistically the potentials that the "threat of the flood" poses to states no matter their size and strength; it is also a critique of the objectives of the ruling class itself whose employment of the arms of others signals a shift to instrumentalization of conflict as an ongoing mode for the accumulation of profits. For Barthas:

> While denying that money is the sinew ["nerf"] of war, Machiavelli engages in a critique of 'the rich,' of those who possess money and of the instutions by which the governing class consolidates its domination while maintaining the people disarmed in order to more easily dominate and loot them.[58]

Following the logic of Barthas, a state's dependence on the arms of others signals a generalized strategy on the part of the governing class to insulate its projects from the influence the people could have on them. And, analogous to the employment of mercenaries, employment of auxiliaries as a generalized policy presents a tactic that aims, not at the defense of the state from the external threats that menace it, but as, in the formula of Barthas, "an instrument for the accumulation of capital."[59]

Interestingly, Machiavelli's analysis of economies of force shows surprising parallels with the function of debt presented in Livy's story of the Capuan legions. Both Barthas and Marvin Becker locate Machiavelli's critique of a defense policy based on state indebtedness in the relationship Florentine military commitments had to a blossoming public debt in the historical situation of Florence itself during the fifteenth and sixteenth centuries. Becker describes how, in the case of Florence, the public debt—named the *Monte*—and the management thereof gradually became the largest factor determining Florence's public policy. Becker shows how the public debt grew as a function of Florence's military obligations incurred through its system of alliances and the need to bear the costs of mercenaries; he then adds:

> Public life began to center itself on the funded communal debt until the officials of the *Monte* came to be numbered among the most important of the republic's elected officers. The state had become a giant corporation in which the citizenry had invested a very substantial part of its patrimony. Anything that adversely affected the welfare of the republic would also deal a cruel blow to the fortunes of the citizenry, for, in fact, the two were now inseparable.[60]

Barthas agrees with Becker here and argues that Machiavelli's discussions of "*danari*" in the title of *Discourses* 2.10 must be heard with the history of the inception and rapid growth of the Florentine *Monte* in the background. For Barthas in the *Discourses*, "money is a metonym for the *Monte*, for the system of finances reposing on a principle of indebtedness of the political body."[61] When in *Discourses* 2.10 Machiavelli denies that money is the sinew of war, he is denying that the dependence of the Florentines on their system of public credit is either necessary or an absolute and indispensable condition of their capacity to make war. He is also arguing against the organization of political institutions and policies with the goal of maintaining interest payments on the public debt.

Viewed from the standpoint of Machiavelli's critique of *arma alienis*, the *Art of War* is where Machiavelli developed the argument most concretely that the citizen militia offered an institutional alternative to dependence on the arms of others as a means for the accumulation of capital. The disciplinary regime of the citizen militia generates a war-making body from a set of subjective conditions established on the basis of the discipline the rank-and-file foot soldier shared with lower and upper level officer ranks. The battalion and brigade as a whole are united by their responsiveness to circuits of audible and visual signs and cues. The readiness and the quality of the militia depends on the subjective force of these associations. From selection and drilling of recruits to training and promotion of officers, the *condottiere* captain Fabrizio di Colonna affords no prominent role to public, debt-driven funding in raising and maintaining his militia.[62] In this way, Machiavelli's *Art of War* poses a tacit critique and alternative to the circuit of reasoning that only money, cannon, fortresses, and the military expertise of *condottieri* figure as signs of power and sureties of exchange in an economy of force relations that both attempts to police—i.e., to suppress and bypass—the state's internal divisions and acts as a buttress intended to regularize demonstrations of force between states.

An instrumentalized approach to war-making increasingly detaches the imperatives posed by the necessities of armed conflict from their anchors in recruitment, practice, and discipline of one's own forces. It generates alongside these imperatives a new circuit of increasingly concurrent necessities, principally the creation of new markets and channels of predictable and rapid access to them. Anthony Molho's analysis of Florentine banking innovations in the late fifteenth and early sixteenth centuries offers an example of one such concurrent necessity. Officials responsible for administering the *Monte* curated the expectations of the citizens to whom the state was most indebted by establishing a pattern of irregularities in loan repayment schedules, frequently re-negotiating the terms on loans that were on the point of maturing. These patterns coalesced into a series of tactics for managing the internal financial conflict of wealthy families whose prize was often the most favorable terms in the rollover of loans.[63] This internal conflict ran alongside the external conflicts waged by the state, since, again, the major driver for Florentine indebtedness in the fourteenth and fifteenth centuries was the cost of military expenditures.[64] Employment of auxiliary forces figure here as both a cause for the increase in public debt and as a way to sustain its costs. Where mercenary forces are mainly an expenditure, the services of auxiliary forces can be bought and sold as a way to increase state revenues where they perform as a commodity in the market of force traded like arms among states.[65] At the very least, placing auxiliary arms at the service of a client state shifts the cost of maintaining those units to the receiving state, either in whole or in part.

However, as a commodity, auxiliary forces can also serve to open new markets and guarantee access to them, since they remain instrumentally tethered to the prince or republic who loans them out. Paolo Malanima describes the circle based on war as a mode of capital accumulation and public indebtedness in these terms:

> Military expenses augment and impose the expansion of finance. In its turn, these [expenses] cannot increase infinitely by intensifying internal pressure; so it proves necessary to extend the financial basis by enlarging the tributary territories. Territorial expansion requires new [military] expenses which it is only possible to make with new revenues and, therefore, by an even greater expansionist effort.[66]

Auxiliaries function as a tactic of substitution that, like cannon, fortresses and money, attempts to bypass the role the people *could* play in the support of the state. The employment of instrumental forces is a way of removing and then policing the substitution of the people, exchanging the material force they could channel toward organizing the power of the state and replacing them with signs of power like money, fortresses, cannon and professional expertise.

On the other hand, auxiliary forces are also a tactic for managing the threat that an armed and organized people pose to the princes and republics which train and organize them by inscribing these forces in the circle of expansion where they figure as a commodity in the intra-state market for force alongside other technologies of conflict. Loaning of forces to foreign princes and republics that call for aid both presents an opportunity for territorial expansion and conquest as well as an attempt to politically neutralize an already armed people. In the opening of the *Art of War*, Machiavelli details the dangers professional soldiers pose to their home territory.[67] Later, he discusses the term limits Romans placed on military service and shows how the dangers of professionalization can be neutralized by contriving that citizens serve during a window of quasi-professionalization. By limiting a citizen's availability for service to between the ages of eighteen and thirty-five and by maintaining rolling enrollment renewals, Roman republican troops could attain professional effectiveness without the guarantees that an entirely professional class of soldiers could negotiate for itself, since soldiers rotated out of the militia into civilian life once they ceased to qualify for service.[68] This strategy of quasi-professionalization displaces the political uncertainties posed by an armed and organized people's legion by projecting the potential conflict between the classes externally as incessant incitement toward military campaigns of conquest, which the people are incentivized—both positively and negatively—to support.

Machiavelli frames the discussion of auxiliaries in the *Prince* in a way that leaves no doubt that princes and republics profit from possessing their own arms. However, the *Discourses*, with its more extensive treatment of the possibilities of collective action on the part of the people, unveils an entirely "other" standpoint for articulating the phenomenon of auxiliaries. In Livy's story, this other standpoint is that of the plebeian legionnaire who finds himself involved in furthering political projects at great danger to himself in exchange for questionable, deferred, or ultimately no benefits. Machiavelli's reference to Livy's story here describes the phenomenon of auxiliary troops not from the standpoint of the nobility (as is done in the *Prince*), but *from the standpoint of the plebeians as an armed and ordered people*. As such, they have the ability to resist the state's projects and to compel redetermination of its modes and orders. Simply by being armed, organized, and very numerous, they form a basis for confronting the oppressive demands of the *grandi* and resisting the means-end, proprietary frameworks of instrumentalized warfare in which they are captured. Their collective discipline and organized force can alter the flows of power in the state just by their resistance and sustained refusal to cooperate.

7. Umori

Machiavelli's treatment of auxiliary arms in the *Prince* and the *Discourses* appears to support opposing interpretations of the same political phenomena. However, in signaling this aspectival approach to this force category, Machiavelli goes a step further. By retelling this story as he does, Machiavelli forces into relief the opposition he argues elsewhere generates the character of all states—the conflict between the humors of the *nobili* and *ignobili*. For Machiavelli, every polity is composed of at least two humors–one motivated to dominate and command and one motivated to resist and avoid being dominated. As he states:

> Because in every city one discovers these two humours: and it springs from this, that the people [*popolo*] desire not to be commanded nor oppressed by the great [*grandi*] and the great desire to command and to oppress the people; and from these two diverse appetites are born one of these three effects: either principality or liberty or license.[69]

While the *grandi* are defined by their desire for rule, the people are defined by Machiavelli, both in the *Prince*, the *Discourses,* and the *Florentine Histories*, through their *desire not to be dominated*.[70] As he continues:

> If one considers the end of the nobles (*nobili*) and the not-nobles (*ignobili*), one will see in the former a great desire to dominate and in the latter only the desire not to be dominated (*solo desiderio di non essere dominate*), and thus a greater will to live freely (*maggiore volontà di vivere liberi*).[71]

Machiavelli often presents the opposition between the great and the people without complicating it with further gradations. For instance, at *Discourses* 1.4 he states the opposition using language very similar to that of *Prince* 9: "in each republic exist two distinct humours, that of the people and that of the great." As Jean-Claude Zancarini emphasizes, Machiavelli keeps this distinction simple whether it occurs in the form it does in these passages or in slightly varied terms using the synonyms he employs to describe the humors:

> Insofar as this thesis is expressed in these terms, no conceptual difference exists between "people" and "pleb," which are defined in opposition with the other humour of the city, the "great" or the "nobles" or the "Senate." The word, "pleb" in this context, possesses its Latin sense and is not distinguished from "people."[72]

However, Machiavelli elsewhere complicates the account of the humors. First, both humors seek to be satisfied, but they also can shift register. As Anthony Parel notes:

> On closer examination it appears that the oppressed of today always turn out to be the oppressors of tomorrow. It is only the factual inability of the oppressed to usurp power that keeps them from becoming actual oppressors. Had they the opportunity, they would certainly seek to dominate.[73]

When Parel analyzes Machiavelli's description of the tumults of Florence in the *Florentine Histories*, he shows how the conflicts between the *nobili* and the *popolo* up to the establishment of the *Ordinamenti della iustizia* of 1293 not only failed to reconcile the humors but also effectively de-classed the nobility. The immediate result of the people's destruction of the nobility was its own division into two warring humors—the *popolo* and the *plebe*. This division in the fifteenth century is important, since it factored as a main reason for the subsequent dependence of Florence on mercenaries and auxiliaries for the city's defense.[74]

Though Machiavelli draws a sharp distinction between the humors, elsewhere he suggests a shared ground to their drives—the passion for acquisition, broadly understood, which manifests differently because the conditions that satisfy the drive to acquire differ among people.[75] According to Vickie Sullivan, "some desire to command; as commanders, their power to acquire material goods may increase, but there are other rewards to be attained from their positions of authority such as honor and glory (D 2.2)." Both Sullivan and Markus Fischer contend that relatively few human beings desire honor and glory. However, the desire for property cuts across class lines. In short, most nobles want what the people want. As Sullivan shows, under the Gracchi's campaign to enforce the Agrarian Laws, the people began to desire and value what the nobles had valued all along—the "unseen goods" offered by those Roman acquisitions located geographically far from the city. As she adds: "because the Gracchi taught the people to covet unseen earthly goods that existed far from their homes, their efforts helped to make possible Christianity's triumphant reception in Rome."[76] Sullivan draws a straight line from the people's newly kindled desire for unseen goods as setting the stage for the ascendancy of Caesar and the end of the Roman republic. Where the Capuan legions were taken in by the very present delights of Capua and persuaded by them to forget their Fatherland, the plebs, infected by the spell of the Gracchi, began to consider even the impossible good something they could make their own.[77] In either case, Sullivan's point is that the humors motivating plebs and nobles alike aimed at possession of the same concrete, this-worldly goods.

For Machiavelli, the relationships between the state's humors are subject to shifts. Not only do the players change but so, too, does the economic-historic conjuncture which assembles them. At issue for Machiavelli is whether *and how* one group or the other succeeds in becoming dominant. Key to the shift to dominance for a group is the continuing experience of the functional oppression of an other collectivity, which has re-organized to resist it.[78] Whether or not a state aims to attain the common good does not determine its goodness or badness, but whether it satisfies or fails to satisfy the humors that constitute it.[79] The modes of oppression employed or the nature of the groups that constitute the humors can vary widely. Since the condition for being "noble" here is constitutionally defined as an *appetite* to rule, command, and dominate, those collectively motivated by the desire aim not simply to maintain a status or a rank but to inaugurate new projects, expanding their "domain," however this is defined.[80]

On the other hand, the *ignobili* constitute an "other" to those projects[81] that can figure either as a crucial element in furthering and realizing them or as a field from which resistance coalesces.[82] This aspectual character of the people— as both a means to profit and as a persistent threat of check—figures more prominently when the people are disciplined and organized as well.[83] As John

McCormick points out, in Livy the Roman plebs don't attack the great when oppressed by them despite being armed and ordered. They simply leave the city for one of the hills around Rome or refuse to enlist in military service. When oppressed, the people, though organized into legions, are rarely bellicose or even aggressive. Resistant, yes, but rather than *doing* anything they *refrain* from acting. As McCormick argues:

> the military ordering of plebeian life instills the kind of discipline that enabled the people to withdraw from the city without engaging in egregious looting or excessive violence. A citizen army, even one instutituted under a monarchy, inculcates in soldiers a disposition akin to that which Aristotle identified as characteristic of democratic citizenship: the disposition to rule and be ruled in turn. The alternation between command and submission among soldiers of all ranks and from both classes that operates within a popular army translates readily into a civic life characterized by discipline and reciprocity.[84]

McCormick's observation here that "the alternation between command and submission among soldiers of all ranks," recalls the continuity of leadership set down in Colonna's militia in the *Art of War*. There Machiavelli lays out two vectors of leadership: 1) the coordination between lower, middle and upper level officers forms a chain of command by meshing with the rank-and-file soldiers; 2) the popular army allows for alternating command because the militia's officer structure is permeable. Starting with the lowest rank—the *capidieci*—the brigade's promotion structure defines a clear path for the new recruit to transition from rank-and-file infantry to brigade captain. Even the professionalization problem is addressed through the militia's organization where the three battle groupings of *principes, hastati,* and *triarii* serve both as a basis for the veterans to hand down their experience to the new recruits and a way to reflect differences of skill. Reciprocity in command structure is rooted in the shared discipline that generates in the militia a shared subjective framework that integrates its distinct and very different parts.[85]

McCormick further argues that this condition of reciprocity would hold of a citizen army even if instituted under a monarchy. Evidence for this claim appears early in the first book of the *Art of War,* when Machiavelli has Colonna anchor the order of Rome's social classes in how Rome's kings organized its militia:

> If you read about the orders that those first kinds made in Rome—and chiefly Servius Tullius – you will find that the order of the classes is nothing other than an order [*ordinanza*] to be able to put together at once an army for the defense of that city.[86]

Whether McCormick's observation holds true may depend on whether the monarch serves, or at least has served in, the role of brigade captain or army general, but this proviso would apply as well in the case of republican citizen commanders. Otherwise a troubling and potentially consequential gap would open up between military and political leadership.[87]

Still, the ameliorating effects of alternating leadership point to another, deeper, issue that challenges the organizational structure of the militia. This more fundamental question concerns the relationship between the militia's disciplinary regime and the fundamental strata Machiavelli identifies at the basis of all political communities—humoral conflict.

8. Lucretian *Umori*

When Machiavelli describes at *Discourses* 1.4 and 1.5 the appetite of the *grandi* as a great desire to bend others to their will, he does not intend this as a moral condemnation but as the description of a natural fact.[88] But it is worth examining more deeply Machiavelli's humoral theory and its relationship to his militia's disciplinary regime. On Machiavelli's reading, humors must find outlets and they are as kinetically active as Lucretian *primordia*. The militia, as an institution, directly addresses the political problem of granting the humors sites of discharge by allowing both humors their expression through features of its organization. For Lucretius, human and animal *ethoi* both express a surplus of the micro-bodies like heat (*calor* or *vapor*), wind (*ventus*), air (*aer*), and the unnamed element (*nominis expers*) whose proportion in the soul and interaction determine the range of characters there are.[89] As a mixed body, the human body performs character as a spectrum of types. Similarly, as itself a mixed body, the popular militia also functions as a humoral engine. Just like the human body's components, the militia's basic elements differ as completely from one another in terms of functions and capabilities as pikemen differ from swordsmen and cavalry soldiers from arquebusiers. Even the officer structure displays vast functional differentiation, with certain officers like the *capidieci* and *centurioni* occupying a place within the unit they lead. Where these lower and intermediate officers relay signals to the rest through the position of their bodies, the constables and captain lead by generating signs through the positioning of their flags and, most especially, through the audible cues delivered by their sound corps.

Generally scholars locate the roots of Machiavelli's doctrine of the humors in the Galenic tradition where personal temperaments and disturbances in the body are traced to the four humors—blood, black and yellow bile, phlegm. However, Tutrone, Pigeaud, Grimal, and Moreau suggest an alternative to the Galenic tradition for Machiavelli's humoral physiology—the Lucretian account of the humors at *De rerum natura* Book 3, 2.262–332. These scholars have no difficulty reading the Lucretian account of the humors in a way that is consistent with Machiavelli's account by showing how the opposition of Galenic and Lucretian traditions on certain issues is a false opposition. For Tutrone, Pigeaud, and Grimal a clear line of connection can be drawn between the natural dynamics of Lucretian *primordia* and the ceaselessly kinetic character of the humors whose tendencies are notably un-Hippocratic and non-Galenic. For instance, where the Hippocratic/Galenic tradition in humoral medicine establishes the condition of health in the balance of the body's humors, Machiavelli's usage of them to describe the dynamics of the state focuses on their restlessness, their drive toward excess, and their ceaseless, dis-equilibrating conflict.[90] Moreau argues it is a mistake to describe the relationship of the four Lucretian micro-bodies that compose the soul as in any way balanced by nature or even tending toward balance. They function as factors of increasing mobility. In discussing the part the *nominis expers* plays with the other three elements in the Lucretian physiology of sensation, Moreau explains:

> What is the reason behind its being impossible to name? And what in this element makes sensation possible if its sole force is an extreme aptitude for movement? We may now suspect the answer: sensation is precisely only movement. The secret [of the unnamed element] is therefore not a mystery, and it is logical that it has its source in an element of pure mobility. If one does not say anything other of it, the reason is not because it is unknowable—but that there is nothing other to say of it because it is nothing other than [mobility].[91]

The compatibility of the Machiavellian and Lucretian account of the humors is reinforced by Machiavelli's tendency to situate the basic building block of his elements at a level greater than that of either Lucretius's seeds or Epicurus' atoms, i.e. the level of the individual body. From a Lucretian perspective, Machiavelli's account of the humors as building blocks of the state offers a short-hand way to speak of a mixed body after it has become sufficiently complex to begin consistently demonstrating politically significant features. Approaching Machiavelli's account of the humors for its potential Lucretian influence also suggests it is possible to think these two most obvious humors—the *popolo* and *nobili*—as both autonomous and potentially separable, their relationship running the gamut from toxically parasitic to flourishing symbiosis. In its character as resistant, the popular *humor* differs from that of the noble by the apparent finitude of its aims, which play out in part according to a dramatics of reactivity—desiring *not* to be commanded or oppressed. The *popolo* demonstrate their desires through performances of resistance and rebellion.[92] The popular humor and noble humor present those desires in theatrically distinct ways even if, as commentators like Sullivan argue, both humors for the most part desire the same things.

Unlike the Galenic approach to humoral physiology, for Lucretius the humors are not discussed as physiologically distinguishable much less subject to recalibration by re-balancing their oppositions. The mélange of Lucretian *primordia* generate the different humors along a spectrum of variations. This range is so extensive and gradated that Lucretius freely admits enough names do not exist to name all the *ethoi*.[93] Only reason (*ratio*) possesses the power to adjust the *ethoi* of human beings and minimize their influence on life and action.[94]

For Machiavelli, the militia's disciplinary regime performs the role of adjustment for its members that *ratio* performs for Lucretius within the individual human being. Its practices generate shared circuits of associations that compatibilize the individuals it organizes. This open-ended process of compatibilization proves important, because in its absence humorally driven conflicts flare. These fragment not only the body of the militia itself but also the *animi* of the individuals that form it.

9. A City of Flows

Nobili and *ignobili* seem at first glance to designate two distinct humors, each on its own possessing a consistent unity of character. Several passages in Machiavelli's works support the distinction he draws between the *nobili*, as those that seek to dominate and command, and the *ignobili*, those that resist being dominated. But the terms Machiavelli employs here to describe the humors can seem suspiciously broad. A glance at the *Florentine Histories* shows how Machiavelli invests this two-fold conflict with more nuance than he does in either *The Discourses* or *The Prince*.[95] For instance, the description of the fall of the Duke of Athens in Book 2 of the *Histories* sees the emergence of a politically significant actor from within the *popolo* when Machiavelli sheds light on the political importance of the discontent of the Florentine plebs. In the events leading up to and following the downfall of the duke, it became necessary to take into account the discontent of the Florentine plebs for the first time. In Book 2, Chapter 34 of the *Florentine*

Histories, Machiavelli names three groups—*mediocri cittadini, grandi,* and *plebe*—and their very different responses to the executions of Giovanni de' Medici, Naddo Rucellai, and Guglielmo Altoviti by the duke who does so to, "increase thankfulness in the plebs" (*"accrescersi grazia nella plebe"*).[96] Machiavelli several times in Book 2 refers to the *plebe* as a third persuasion whose activity both brings the duke to power and contributes to his downfall. Two chapters later, Machiavelli again describes three groups—*grandi, popolani,* and the *artefici*—whose discontent with the duke provokes them to conspire against him, which they do as three separate groups: "and in the three parts of the three sorts of citizens three conspiracies were made" (*e in tre parti di tre sorte di cittadini tre congiure si fecions*).[97] Further on, the years-long struggle between the *grandi* and the *popolo* concludes with the victory of the people and the functional de-classing of the *nobili*.[98] Machiavelli then names three distinct popular groups that emerge from within the victorious humor—the *grandi, mediocri cittadini,* and the *plebe*. Then, again, when the government is reorganized after the defeat of the great families, Machiavelli identifies three sorts of *popolo* who occupy places within the new government, namely, the "*potente, mediocre e basso*."

It is clear from these examples that Machiavelli's political humors allow for much more gradation and variation than is often acknowledged, a feature it shares with Lucretian humorology. Zancarini highlights how Machiavelli often unfolds the notion of the popular humor by substantively distinguishing between *plebe* and *popolo*. At *Prince* Chapter 10, he discusses how the Swiss withstand a siege by, "*pascere la plebe a quelli che vivono dalle braccia*." Similarly, he notes in his report on Swiss and German cities—*Le Rapporto delle cose della Magna*—that the goodness of the order of the Swiss cities derives in part from how they remain ready to withstand a siege by maintaining a standing supply of the materials that *la plebe*—whom he again describes as those who live *dalla braccia*—need to remain active in their trades for a year.[99] In the *Discursus florentinarum rerum,* Machiavelli argues that those wishing to order a republic must lead three diverse qualities of human beings, "that are in all the cities, i.e., the first, the middle and the last" (*che sono in tutte le città, cioè primi, mezzani, e ultimi*).[100]

But these gradations are not limited to the popular humor. Recalling here Sullivan's analysis of the noble humor, Machiavelli lays the groundwork for distinguishing within the *grandi* between those nobles who, like the people, want to dominate in order to extend their material possessions and those who want to command to acquire honor and glory. From this survey, it is clear that

Machiavelli's two-fold humoral physiology that opposes *nobili* and *ignobili* shows itself to be more complicated than it appears at first glance, a complexity that makes it consonant with the physics of Lucretian ethics. Machiavelli's humoral state is composed of some flows that are apparent and obvious and others whose presence may in fact be virtualized by the force of others. The *stato* may actually be nothing more than a mixed body of temporarily confluent humoral flows whose internal articulations are vulnerable to shifts, cancellations, and redetermination by external mixed bodies whose encounters can both support the state but can also check and menace its durability. A humor may retain the same name through time or from one place to another, but its consistency, and therefore its meaning, does *not* remain the same.

10. Back to Capua

In Livy, the conflict between the Senate and the plebs in the Capuan episode illustrates the mechanics of humoral conflict from two perspectives—that of the *ignobili* and the *nobili*. Livy's story shifts between the viewpoints of Roman plebs and senators framed by the orders and institutions of the military, the *unfavorable* distribution of land between aristocrats and plebeians,[101] and the increasingly burdensome economic debt that motivates the soldiers to defect. The dynamics shift as the soldiers resist, first as conspirators against Roman authority before transitioning to open insurrectionists. Machiavelli's aspectival approach to auxiliary forces overlaps with his notion of the *plebe* as a *humor*. As such, they are defined in the drama as a critical determining element within the Republic whose regime they can reinforce, shift, and annul. They can shift its mode of functioning intentionally and overtly with deliberately planned out, conspiratorial forethought or by being reactively triggered through fear or outrage to withdraw.

This range of potential responses of an armed *popolo* explains Machiavelli's amphibolous usage of the term *auxilium* to describe this type of force. The people figure in the Capuan episode as indeed an *auxiliary* of the state as Machiavelli defines them in the *Prince*, where they appear as a commodity subject to the market for force. Armed and organized, the legions take possession of Capua, which they defend easily from the Samnite threat. This part of the drama fits neatly with Machiavelli's definition of auxiliaries as a force that comes with substantial risks to those who receive the loan. To recall his opening description in *Prince* 13: "Auxiliary arms ... are *those of a power that is called to come with its arms to help and defend you.*"

But Machiavelli has the definition operate in two registers. In Livy's story, the factor that allows the Romans both to come to the assistance of the Capuans and securely "take possession of them"—the fact that the Roman plebs are armed and ordered—is precisely that factor which allows the plebs to withdraw their support and detach themselves from the designs that Rome's ruling class had on the neighboring republics of the peninsula. The very fact that the Romans were able to garrison their troops in Capua and leave their legions there could happen only because the Roman plebs had been armed and, as such, were made powerful.[102] Here freedom and force appear in their immanence.[103] The unpredictability of the legions rests on the force they represent because they are united through discipline and a commonly experienced fear of punishment. The force they represent confronts both military and civil authorities with an unforeseen set of complications made significant by the level of the soldiers' discontent. Like any other auxiliary force, they are indeed obedient "to some other," but during the course of the story their obedience shifts from their command structure. They act autonomously, even kidnapping a retired general to act as their figurehead as they march on Rome itself. The force of their shared discipline generates their autonomy and sustains their successful opposition to the authority of the Senate and the consuls.

In Livy's story, Machiavelli's account of the dangers of auxiliary troops certainly shows them to be a tool of conquest and, thus, dangerous to recipient princes and peoples who gamble when making use of Rome's power for their own ends. But because auxiliaries are armed and organized, they can also "forget their Fatherland" and defy the state. They can incite a metabolic movement in the state that compels institutional and policy shifts and whose drives, just like a Lucretian humor, will flourish until (or unless) successfully checked.[104] On Machiavelli's telling, even if the Roman legionnaires were the *auxilium* of the projects of the Roman Senate, the Capuan secession presented a window when the terms of that assistance were cancelled and then renegotiated.[105]

Conclusion

At *Discourses* 2.20, Machiavelli introduces Livy's story of two Roman legions who conspired to take Capua for themselves as a clear-cut example of the dangers involved in the use of auxiliary troops. However, even a cursory examination of Livy's story reveals the misapplication of the category of auxiliary arms to it. By telling the story in the way he does, Machiavelli articulates to readers of the

Discourses that an armed and organized people presents opportunities that princes and republics can capitalize on, but it also generates a field of uncertainty to which a prince or republic is constantly exposed. Contrasting Machiavelli's account of auxiliary force in the *Prince* and the *Discourses* shows how the *concurrence of the people* both anchors state institutions and exposes the state to the possibility of radical (and often unforeseeable) shocks and redeterminations.[106] Machiavelli's category of auxiliary force operates amphibolously; it manifests both instrumental *and* aleatory aspects.[107] In the case of the Capuan episode, it does so at the same time with respect to the same units of force—the same two legions. Reading for these different deployments of the category reveals that Machiavelli's project of assembling "arms of one's own"—the project of forming a popular army—not only furnishes princes and republican captains a tool of defense and conquest (both direct and indirect) but does so by establishing the people as a potentially resistant, armed multitude, united by disciplinary rhythms and suffused with martial orders.

Further, Machiavelli's aspectival approach to the category of auxiliary force— as both instrument of conquest and unpredictable factor of state support—also carries implications for Machiavelli's account of the *umori*. His discussions of the diverse aspects of auxiliary force overlap meaningfully with his account of the *humors* as drivers of political conflict. Resisting the traditional Galenic interpretation and hearing Machiavelli's account of the conflict between the *nobili* and *ignobili* from a Lucretian standpoint reveals the potential complexity of Machiavelli's humoral theory. For Lucretius, the humors figure as flows, i.e., degrees of mobility programmed for absolute discharge unless checked through conjunction and composed of parts by no means possessed of homogeneous drives. In mixed bodies, internal shifts and the presence (or removal) of external checks fracture states of equilibrium, allowing virtualized currents to emerge and shift toward dominance.

But a final issue emerges from sustained examination of the distinction Machiavelli draws between *arms of one's own* and *the arms of others*, the popular militia, on the one side, and the employment of foreign troops—whether mercenaries or auxiliaries or both—on the other. Machiavelli repeatedly cites the great danger of the arms of others. Such troops generate a field of uncertainty due to their potentials for forming sites of resistance, defection, and insurrection. Machiavelli frequently ascribes the cause behind this field of uncertainty to their capacity to act as sites of conspiracy. Recalling Machiavelli's reason for the danger involved employing auxiliaries quoted at the start of this chapter: "Because in these is *conspiracy* done, they are all united, at all times obedient to another." Machiavelli reinforces this connection both in the definition of auxiliaries cited in the *Prince* as well as at *Discourses* 3.6, where he again relates the story of the Roman legions in Capua among the exemplary conspiracies he analyzes there. Just how, then, is conspiracy related to the distinction between *one's own arms* and *the arms of others* such that it can transform troops that satisfy all the external qualifications of *being arms of one's own* into the condition of *being the arms of others* and back? This issue will be taken up after examining Machiavelli's final category of military force—that of mixed forces.

5

Transforming Compounds: Machiavelli's Analyses of Mixed Force

1. Mixtures in Machiavelli and Lucretius

Machiavelli identifies a fourth and final category of armed force: mixed forces. His discussions of them make it clear that he considers mixed forces important and valuable—much more so than either auxiliary or mercenary forces alone. However, the category of mixed force lacks the definition or stability of these other force categories. Some of the examples he describes as involving mixed forces emphasize the plasticity of force and its unstable character. For instance, in the *Prince* Machiavelli shows how Louis XI changed the ordinances on the infantry laid down by his father, Charles VII, and with that change created mixed forces out of *"arms of his own"* by making French men at arms dependent on Swiss mercenaries. In the case of the French, the application of the category of mixed forces signaled their decline. On the other hand, in both the *Prince* and the *Discourses* Machiavelli identifies Hannibal as a superlative captain due to his success at uniting "infinite generations of men" effectively enough to vie with Rome's republican armies for control of the Italian peninsula.[1] Here, Hannibal made mercenary arms function beyond their usual category limitations. The category of mixed forces admits the factor of change into Machiavelli's analyses of military force. His use of this category highlights how determining the quality of a force involves not only identifying the factors that unite it, whether economical in the case of mercenaries, authoritative in the case of auxiliaries, or disciplinary in the case of *arma propriis*. It is also a matter of accurately assessing whether the force being analyzed is in the process of strengthening or declining due to factors ranging from institutional and historical to material, technical and psychological.

Further, Machiavelli's reasoning on the character of mixed force exhibits several points of overlap with the problem of the identity of mixed bodies in

Lucretius. For Lucretius, networks of assemblages of intra-dependent, differently mobile mixed bodies constitute the soul and body. Human beings exist as mixed bodies whose composite nature occurs within an interval established by two extremes, the first set by the minute, wildly fast seeds of the *animus* and the *anima* and the other by the slower moving composites of the body's organs, tissues, and fluids. The individual human body exists *as* the integrated conjunction of these extremes and as composite assemblages of them. Captured and integrated, the Lucretian *animus* and *anima* still dominate these other substances through their extreme mobility, which allows them to affect the body's slower, thicker structures. For Lucretius, all of the behaviors exhibited by the human body from locomotion to thought depend on the effects of these networked flows.

With this reality in the background, Lucretius locates the individual identity of a mixed body like the human body in the continuity of its memories. Analyzing the causes behind the persistence of the fear of death, Lucretius establishes that an individual retains his or her identity as long as their memories retain their established associations. At *De rerum natura,* 3.843–61, he makes the continuity of memory the center point of his argument against any possible sense of an afterlife. After discarding the superstition-heavy notions of other worlds of eternal punishments or pleasures he moves on to attack an atomist-friendly notion of another life —the repeated Individual. He concedes that it is entirely conceivable, even probable, that the restlessly infinite re-combinations of matter at some future point would re-create the assemblage of atomic flows which constitute me as an individual. Still even should the assemblages constituting this "repeated me" recur, they will still be an entirely different person. As he states:

> For if time (*aetas*) collected back our matter
> after our destruction and brought it back and repeated it
> so that it is as it is now
> and also again the light of life were given to us,
> nevertheless nothing whatsoever would belong to us
> even should this have been done,
> when once broken was our memory (*repetentia*) of ourselves.[2]

For Lucretius, the extinction of an individual at their death is complete. Even in the great likelihood that matter's innumerable motions will trigger the re-emergence of a specific human body, the individual's experience of their repeated life would happen as if for the first time. Key to this argument is Lucretius' notion of identity, which depends on the individual's experience of their memories as continuous. The death of the body snaps the individual's experience of this continuity. In the event of the body's repetition due to matter's innumerable motions, life, memory, and identity would happen to that other "me" as if it were happening to someone else because *it would, in fact, be* happening to someone else. For Lucretius, identity depends on the continuity of our experiences. Interrupt that continuity and a new individual emerges.

Lucretius employs these notions of memory and identity linked to specific realities of the composite individual and argues that death, just like the world prior to our birth, can be nothing to us, since our identity stems from the experience of our memories as continuous. Certainly, people claim to fear death, but what they really fear is suffering in general and/or a diminished life.

Lucretius enlists the atomic mechanics of identity as a strategy within an overall palliative for both the detection and the treatment of the fear of death.[3] As Moreau outlines Lucretius' approach here:

> The first knot of this chain of identity, which serves as the bait for all reasoning, is the individual's insistence on fearing death, even when the theoretical arguments have convinced him [not to fear it]. There is therefore at basis a persistent illusion anchored in his very structure, the illusion of continuity to which Lucretius opposes the science of *limit*.[4]

Those who dread the hardships of death—from being consumed by wild animals to being stretched uncomfortably on cold slabs of stone—betray a mistake in their reasoning. To emphasize this, Lucretius poses a thought experiment at *De rerum natura* Book 3, 879–92, when he asks the reader to imagine someone pining beside their own corpse for the discomforts and lost pleasures their lifeless body experiences. He points out that to do this requires the griever to imbue their corpse with just enough vitality so that their dead body experiences sensations after death, i.e., that their dead body did not actually die with death. The fear of what happens to the body following death drives them to postulate this impossibility; it also: 1) betrays their failure to apply rigorously the conclusions of atomic reasoning to the body and extend them to the experience of memory and identity as features of body; and 2) it highlights the importance Lucretius attributes to the continuity of memory whose fragility is such that not only can it be ruptured by the death of the body but also by events like serious illness and powerful physical or emotional traumas. To echo Moreau here, the continuity of identity is an illusion.

Still, the precise focus of the Lucretian arguments in these passages is not to remove the fear of death in general but to confront that specific individual who has received the Epicurean arguments about the annihilation of the soul with the body's death and *who yet* persists in illusions like that of imagining their doubled self, experiencing the suffering of their corpse. Lucretius locates the root cause for this persistent, intractable fear of death in the nature of desire. The illusion arises because those who fear death fail to grasp the limits that nature places on the enjoyment of pleasures. This failure not only has implications for the persistence of the fear of death but also proves the cause behind human dissatisfaction with present circumstances. At *De rerum natura* Book 3, 931–78, Lucretius personifies Nature upbraiding an old person, fearful at death's approach. Her argument concentrates on their failure to recognize the limits placed on the duration and scope of pleasures available to human beings. Their failure to grasp those limits translates into the lack of contentment they experience with pleasures in general. Nature argues that to extend their lifespans will not bring them satisfaction, even if they should never die:

> Because you always long after what you lack,
> And scorn the present (*praesentia*)
> Imperfect life has slipped by, unappreciated
> And unexpected death stands by your head[5]

Lucretius then adds:

> For the old always gives way, thrust out by the new,
> and one thing must be made fresh from others,
> yet none whatsoever is lost to the abyss of black Tartarus.
> Matter is needed so that ensuing generations flourish.
> However, all things which follow your life will also finish,
> and no less than you who fell before them,
> so also they will fall.
> Thus one thing from another never ceases to rise,
> and none own life free and clear, but all as renters.[6]

From these observations, Lucretius concludes that future time should appear to us as inconsequential from the perspective of experience and suffering as those events that occurred before our births, which also were affectively nothing to us.[7]

2. Machiavelli on Desire, Judgment, and the Body in Flux

In both the *Discourses* and the *Prince* Machiavelli employs arguments structured similarly to those of Lucretius in the *De rerum natura* to emphasize the changeableness of identity as a function of the changing body. For instance, Book 2 of the *Discourses* opens with an extended discussion of the variability of judgment due to the changeableness of desires rooted in the decline of the body. Machiavelli's discussion of the theme is rich with Lucretian echoes. He first argues that people are often mistaken when they praise ancient times and blame the present. They make errors about which of the two—the present or the past—are worthy of praise since "human things being always in motion, either they ascend or descend."[8] He considers whether the root cause for the error lies in the proximity of the ills of the present and the tendency of writers who obey "the fortune of the victors." However, as the argument progresses Machiavelli locates another cause for error—the effects of aging on memory and desire. He argues that people cannot evaluate accurately the relative merits of their present circumstances and the conditions of their youth because judgments shift as appetites change with age. So, the source of the old person's judgment that presents ways of doing things now as inferior to how things were done in their youth reflects how their desires have changed, not objective reality. Things appear differently to them because, as they age, "they lack forces and grow in judgment and prudence."[9] As he states:

> But those things varying while the times do not vary, they cannot appear to men the same who have other appetites, other delights, other considerations in old age than in youth.[10]

Desires and pleasures change with the changes of the aging body, and these changes cause people to make errors when they assess the relative virtues of the present and the past. Machiavelli's emphasis here is on the changeableness of the body and how the deliberative evaluations people form reflect the changes the body undergoes. Machiavelli then concludes this line of reasoning in a way that further echoes Lucretius on desire:

> Beyond this, human appetites are insatiable. Receiving from nature the ability and will to desire everything, and from fortune the ability to obtain few of them, there results discontent in human minds and an annoyance with the things they possess. This makes them blame the present times, praise the past, and desire future things, even if to do this they are not moved by any reasonable cause.[11]

Here Machiavelli's thoughts on desire echo those of Lucretius in Book 3 of the *De rerum natura*. Human discontent with what they possess so infects their judgments that their assessments of the positive and negative features of present and past times are not reliable.

The message of these passages from *Discourses* Book 2 is that human judgment, desires, and the changes of the body are not exempt from the aging body's declining forces. The young judge things differently than the old because they possess greater force. As the body's capacity to generate force declines so, too, does the character of the evaluations the aging person makes. At this point the author even shifts into the first person and encourages the reader to apply his reasoning on the relationship between the body, desire, and judgment to his own praise of the modes of ancient Rome and his blame of present ways of doing things. At first Machiavelli seems to exempt his own evaluations from the vicissitudes of the aging body when he claims that the source of the certainty of his esteem for ancient practices depends not on his own subjective evaluation but on the fact that the difference between ancient virtue and present vice are "clearer than the sun" and so manifest "that everyone sees it." However, Machiavelli then transitions to *Discourses* 2.1 and opens the chapter by first citing the argument of a "very grave writer"—Plutarch—who does not share the consensus opinion of ancient Roman virtue just endorsed by Machiavelli. He paraphrases Plutarch's opinion that the Romans acquired their empire through fortune rather than their virtue. He then cites the testimony of Livy who also "seems to come close to this opinion." By quickly shifting from the hyperbole of his first person praise of the Romans to forwarding the contrary opinions of ancients—Plutarch and Livy—concerning the virtues of ancient Rome, Machiavelli makes suspect his own praise for ancient modes over modern ones. This frees the reader to assess the author's evaluations of the present and past according to the just-described mechanics of desire, judgment, and the body in flux.

3. Mixed Forces and Lucretian Echoes in the *Prince*

In the *Prince*, the first echo of Lucretian reasoning occurs during Machiavelli's discussion of mixed principalities in Chapter 3. Here Machiavelli attributes the difficulties involved with holding a mixed principality to the mechanics of desire, force, and judgment in ways that recall the Lucretian logic of identity, desires, and memory at the start of *Discourses* 2. The chapter begins by distinguishing between two different kinds of new principality—one to which the prince is altogether new and one formed when an invader adds a new state to their current one. In the second kind of state, even an established prince is considered *new* to the state they have captured. The resulting composite Machiavelli terms *mixed*:

> it is not altogether new but like an added member (*membro*) (so that taken all together one can call it almost mixed (*misto*))[12]

The ease with which the prince adds the new territory is due to the dissatisfaction people naturally have for the status quo. Their unhappiness with the present regime sets up favorable conditions for an invading prince to acquire the state because the people hope for something better from the invader. However, even when the invader successfully captures the state, the resulting composite remains unstable. Machiavelli links the instability of the captured state to the desires of men in a way that echoes both *Discourses* 2 and Lucretius' reasoning on the instability of identity at *De rerum natura* 3:

> Men willingly change lords believing that they will do better, and this belief makes them take up arms against that one about whom they have deceived themselves because they then see by experience that they have got worse.[13]

The people's belief that the new prince will bring better conditions motivates them to depose their current prince and support the invader. However, when they discover the new prince will not satisfy their desires as they would like they revert to dissatisfaction with the new regime and again figure as a potential site of resistance to it. The changeableness of human desire is at the basis for the instability in the new mixed body. A mixed principality describes a political situation still in transition whose outcome remains uncertain, since it is unclear whether the invader will manage to make the state his or her own or whether it will revert back to the former leader or to some other powerful interloper who takes advantage of the uncertain circumstances. Machiavelli links the uncertainties presented by the mixed state to the restlessness of human desires, the dissatisfaction of the citizens at their present circumstances, and their readiness to change what they have for the promise they locate in the new.

Machiavelli then cements his point by taking the case of Louis XII and his 1499 invasion of Italy as the paradigm of this type of new prince. On Machiavelli's telling, Louis easily acquired a new state—Milan—from its established prince—Ludovico Sforza—due to the people's desire for something better. He then lost it again when the people's disappointment at the change opened the door for Sforza to return to power.[14] The difficulties he encountered were due to a series of errors Machiavelli claims Louis committed during his campaigns. For instance, Louis did not support (and even harmed) the lesser states in Lombardy, strengthened already powerful players like the Venetians and the pope, and invited a very powerful foreigner—the Spanish—into Italy to assist in the campaign against Naples. He also failed to establish colonies in the lands he took or to go there in person to live. Machiavelli contrasts the errors of Louis with the practices of the republican Romans whose successes figure in this chapter as an example for new princes to follow. However, a careful examination of the history Machiavelli tells of the French forces in the *Prince* reveals that there was a deeper cause for Louis' failure to mesh his Italian gains with the French state. He invaded Italy with mixed forces.

In the discussion of auxiliary arms in Chapter 13, Machiavelli refers indirectly to the forces of Louis XII in the opening where he discusses the dangers involved in the use of auxiliary forces. He does this by citing the Florentine use of French auxiliaries in laying siege to Pisa in 1500 and Cesare Borgia's use of French auxiliaries during his campaigns in the Romagna. After discussing the dangers they incurred by employing French troops, Machiavelli goes on to explain that by the time Louis XII invaded Italy, the French military was in decline due to the changes initiated by his predecessor, Louis XI. Louis XI had changed the ordinances governing French infantry set down by Charles VII. According to Machiavelli, Charles' original infantry ordinances produced for him a force of arms of his own that would have made French armies unconquerable if they had been preserved.[15] Instead, the changes initiated by Louis XI made French men-at-arms dependent on Swiss mercenaries, such that the French no longer believed they could win unless supported by the Swiss.[16]

Machiavelli's history implies that the French troops employed by Louis XII were no longer the *arma propriis* enjoyed by Charles VII. They had become mixed Swiss/French forces. He also implies that the setbacks Louis XII experienced during his Italian campaign were not only due to his poor judgment but also to the declining effectiveness of the French military forces as a mixed body of part mercenary and part *arma propriis*.

In a sense, the poor decision-making of Louis XII was forced upon him by the declining state of his military forces, a decline Louis XI had initiated. Machiavelli strengthens this inference in Chapter 13 by discussing the causes for the decline of the armies of Rome. In Chapter 3, Rome's republican armies acted as a counterpoint to the failures of Louis XII where they served as an example for new princes to emulate. The Romans were successful because they were not only concerned with present troubles but kept an eye out for future ones as well. In doing so, they were like competent physicians who detected consumptive fevers early on when they were still easy to cure. In Chapter 13, Machiavelli returns to the notion of the consumptive fever after describing the changes Louis XI made to the militia ordonnances set down by Charles. His decision to change the modes governing French infantry was like drinking good-tasting poison whose pleasant taste disguises its harm. Machiavelli then refers to his Chapter 3 discussion of the Romans who distinguished themselves as good "doctors of state." He contrasts the military decision-making of the Roman Republicans to the policies of the Roman Empire, which mixed Roman forces with those of Goth mercenaries. From this beginning, "the forces of the Roman Empire began to enervate and all that virtue that was taken from it was given to them."[17]

By making these parallels, Machiavelli contrasts two approaches to the production of military force—one based on the image of the competent doctor who detects sickness and applies remedies early on and the other that of the patient who makes himself ill by drinking good-tasting poison. He contrasts the French armies under Charles VII with the mixed armies of Louis XII, the Roman republican armies with the mixed armies of the later Empire. On the basis of these parallels, Machiavelli's message is clear: the lasting success or eventual failure of mixed principalities stems in part from the quality of the forces engaged in the conquest. Machiavelli's category of mixed forces is not a static category of military force but one that refers to forces undergoing change. It can indicate the progressive weakening of forces as their strength is sapped by the bodies with which they are compounded, the Swiss for the French and the Germans for the Romans. However, as we will see in the case of Hannibal, it can also indicate that a force has leapt its categorical limitations and begun to intensify and grow in strength.

In Chapter 3 of this study, we investigated the influence of the second-century Greek mathematician/tactician, Aelianus Tacticus, on Machiavelli. There it was seen that differences between military forces stem from their practices and equipment types, their degree of responsiveness to the semiotic associations constructed through flag position and variations in music, and the continuity—or lack of continuity—of the different officer grades. The discussions carried out by Aelianus and Machiavelli about those subjects concentrate intently on the minutiae that must be coordinated to make the militia's disciplinary regime a reality. Conjoining mercenary and auxiliary forces with arms of one's own initiates a complex problematics of types of bodies and conditionings compounded by a spectrum of insoluble differences ranging from language, uniform, and styles of equipment to animating principles, values, and organizational structures. While Machiavelli's categories of armed force on the one hand qualify as mixed bodies in a Lucretian sense, on the other hand they exceed explanation on the basis of a purely atomic physics. Machiavelli consistently emphasizes another element important to the cohesion of his kind of mixed body—historical analyses detailing the conditions of their emergence that include the probable causes behind shifts in their governing practices and institutions.[18]

In doing so, Machiavelli's notion of mixed force maintains a relationship with the Lucretian notion of mixed bodies but also contains important areas of flexibility that the Roman poet's account of nature does not explore. Lucretius defines the identity of a composite body as a function of the continuity of its memory, which is itself a function of the regularity of the motions forming the individual composite. Machiavelli's category of mixed force invokes Lucretius' notion of identity but from two angles. On the one hand, military bodies form a composite by establishing continuous circuits through discrete sets of practices conjoined by coordinating points of communication and stabilizing points of tension to achieve some degree of regularity. On the other hand, Machiavelli's introduction of the category of *arma mixta* subverts the presentation of force categories as relatively stable subjects possessing distinct and at least semi-permanent sets of traits. Machiavelli's analyses of mixed forces hint at how compounding quantities of force incites changes to the bodies thus compounded. His analyses of mixed forces involve identifying those factors that allow a unit of force to remain the same with itself over time while emphasizing the factors that propel it to cross thresholds between categories, as when *arma propriis* shifts into either mercenary or auxiliary status either in whole or in part. In doing so, Machiavelli forefronts the discontinuities and breaks in the circuits of composites that usually remain suppressed by the insistence of routine and the expectations of regularity.[19]

4. Mixed Forces in the *Discourses*

Machiavelli's approach to the subject of mixed forces in the *Prince* underlines the importance of assessing the quality of a force both from the standpoint of the quality of the arms and the performance of its leadership. For instance, in Chapter 17 of the *Prince*, Machiavelli cites the example of Hannibal during his discussion of the consequences a reputation for cruelty and mercy can have for princes. Machiavelli describes Hannibal's forces as, "mixed (*misto*) of endless generations of men led to serve in foreign (*aliena*) lands."[20] Hannibal's troops were a composite formed from a Carthaginian infantry core compounded with mercenaries of different nationalities ranging from across the Mediterranean.[21] Machiavelli argues that the effectiveness of Hannibal's mixed troops against the very Republican Roman armies he held up earlier in the *Prince* as a model to new princes was due to the cruelty of their captain. Even though Machiavelli suggests that Hannibal possessed "infinite other virtues," without his "inhuman cruelty" (*inumana crudeltà*) his other virtues would not have brought him the success he experienced, "*in terra aliena*."[22] Through the use of the Latin *alienus* here instead of the Italian *straniera* to describe the lands invaded by Hannibal, Machiavelli sharply emphasizes that the success Hannibal enjoyed occurred with his mixed army of mostly mercenary troops—i.e., *arma alienis*—against the Roman Republican armies composed of *arma propriis*.

He follows this discussion by contrasting the success of Hannibal with the success of Scipio. On Machiavelli's analysis, the two captains shared all virtues except a reputation for cruelty. Scipio's "*troppa pietà*" allowed his soldiers, "more license than was suitable to military discipline"[23] and caused the legions to rebel in Spain. Machiavelli adds that Scipio's failure in leadership on this point was such that Fabius Maximus termed him, "corruptor of the Roman military." Livy goes further and has Fabius claim that Scipio *was born* to corrupt the Roman military.[24] Machiavelli concludes the discussion of Scipio by attributing the cause for his exemplary reputation as a Roman captain to the Roman Senate. The Senate governed their captain such that, "this damaging quality of his not only was hidden, but contributed to his memory."[25]

Two issues emerge from Machiavelli's discussion of Hannibal's leadership of mixed forces and the contrast he sets up with the example of Scipio. Hannibalian cruelty factored decisively in the success of the Cathaginian mixed troops against the Roman republican armies, showing that mixed forces can be effective against even exemplary instances of arms of one's own. His analyses show that the quality of the commander adds a decisive component to the quality of the force. Hannibal's reputation for cruelty catalyzed the mixed troops he led who exceeded the limitations generally exhibited by troops compounded of mercenaries and auxiliaries. On the other hand, Scipio's mercy alienated his troops and turned them to open rebellion.

5. Hannibal, Scipio, Manlius Torquatus, Valerius Corvinus

Machiavelli discusses the case of Hannibal at even greater length in the *Discourses* at 3.21 where he implies that, despite his success, even Hannibal was unable to evade the consequences of those who make use of mixed forces. Hannibal dies by drinking poison, having been driven from Carthage by domestic political enemies to the court of King Prusias of Bithynia, pressed hard by the Romans. Machiavelli describes the experiences Hannibal had following his defeat as a consequence of his, "mode of impious living" (*modo di vivere impio*). He then explains that the Roman people could never pardon him, and so even after he had been disarmed and dispersed, they had him killed.[26] Machiavelli here continues the association of the use of mixed forces and drinking poison made in the *Prince*, though according to the account given in Livy, Hannibal himself took the poison he had saved for the possibility the Romans might capture him.[27] The chapter ends by returning to Machiavelli's praise of Hannibal as a captain whose virtues—principally his cruelty—made it possible for him to lead a mixed army in which differences among the soldiers neither generated internal dissension nor dissension against Hannibal. Machiavelli then adds that the cause for this was the "terror" Hannibal's person inspired among his soldiers.

As he did in the *Prince*, Machiavelli in the *Discourses* also contrasts the careers of Hannibal and Scipio. Machiavelli connects the effectiveness of mixed forces with the quality of the leader and, as he found in the *Prince*, so also in the *Discourses* he finds that Hannibal's cruelty inspired such terror among the forces he led that he made mercenaries and auxiliaries operate beyond their categorical limitations. The *crudeltà* of Hannibal effectively united "infinite kinds of mixed forces"—from Numidian cavalry to Gallic infantry. This patchwork army lacked a common disciplinary basis, but Hannibal's reputation for cruelty entered the associative play of signs and acted as a substitute for a shared disciplinary framework. To further emphasize this, Machiavelli compares the characters of Scipio and Hannibal at the close of the chapter: "...Hannibal and Scipio produced the same effect – one with praiseworthy (*laudibili*) things and the other with detestable (*detestabili*)." While giving the impression early in the chapter of endorsing Scipio's more humane modes of proceeding, Machiavelli closes noting that Scipio was "constrained to use part of that cruelty that he had fled."[28] Of the two modes of proceeding, Machiavelli assesses the two captains on the basis of their effects and subtly affirms Hannibal's cruelty and the terror he inspired as the more praiseworthy manner of leadership.

However, after comparing the glory of the Carthaginian and Roman leaders, Machiavelli moves on to discuss another pair of captains—the Roman consuls, Manlius Torquatus and Valerius Corvinus. Far from differentiating the two Roman captains from Hannibal and Scipio, Machiavelli reviews their careers and deepens the discussion of the effects captains can produce in the forces they lead. As he does so, it becomes evident that where the cruelty of Hannibal united mixed forces that should not have been effective given their qualities, the harshness of Torquatus also had an ameliatory effect on Rome's forces by returning them to the strict tradition of military discipline during a period when those very orders were changing.

However, at 3.22 Machiavelli does not explicitly compare Hannibal with Torquatus but with Valerius Corvinus. As it turns out, Machiavelli's analyses of Torquatus and Corvinus share a prominent feature. The diverse ways of proceeding of these two Roman captains may have brought both of them success, but their leadership styles also offer yet another way of thinking about the notion of mixed forces in Machiavelli. The different performances of Torquatus and Corvinus had the effect of setting in motion a re-evaluation of political conditions within the militia itself by the style of relationship the rank and file had to these two captains. This caused either the intensification or the alteration of the disciplinary fabric of the militia. In doing so, the comparison of the captains' styles of command from the standpoint of their effects gestures toward another way forces can be considered *mixed*.

Machiavelli prepares the contrast he will draw between the two captains by first connecting the notions of *proporzione* and *disproporzione* with the topic of force in the course of discussing how values conducive to liberty followed from the harshness with which Manlius Torquatus enforced military discipline; as he states:

> Where it has to be noted that, wanting to be obeyed, it is necessary to know how to command; and those know how to command who make a comparison from their qualities to those who are to obey, and when they see proportion there then they command; when disproportion, they abstain.[29]

Immediately following this observation, Machiavelli extends the notion beyond the sphere of military activity and connects the theme of a shift in political form with the success or failure of establishing proportionality of violence between political actors:

> a prudent man used to say that to hold a republic with violence, proportion from him who forced to him who was forced was fitting. And whenever this proportion existed, one could believe that the violence was durable. But when those to whom violence was done were stronger than those doing violence, one could doubt that any day that violence would cease.[30]

This is not a new theme, and Machiavelli first raises it at *Discourses* 1.55, where the term *proporzione* first appears in the text during a very similar discussion.

Here Machiavelli takes up the subject of the obstacles confronting anyone wishing to create a principality where political equality and a republican political community already exist. Conversely, nearly insuperable difficulties confront any innovator desiring to create conditions of freedom and a republican political space where a principality and conditions of extreme political inequality exist. The distinction Machiavelli draws here between conditions of political equality and inequality depends on one distinctive factor—whether or not the province in question contains gentlemen (*gentiluomini*), but qualifying as "a gentleman" depends on more than the possession of a title. As he states:

> He who is where there is very much equality and wants to make a kingdom or principality will never be able to do it if he does not draw from that equality many of ambitious and unquiet spirit (*animo ambizioso e inquieto*) and makes them gentlemen *in fact, and not in name*, granting them favor of substances (*sustanze*) and men.[31]

Gentlemen are those who live off their substances without "any care for cultivation or for other necessary trouble in living." The presence of many of these gentlemen in a province makes it nearly impossible to generate conditions conducive to maintaining political equality.

During the same discussion Machiavelli also affirms that where conditions of political equality already exist, it is just as difficult for a political innovator to force a change of political form. Machiavelli identifies here two main characteristics of republican political dimensions that make them resistant to change. The first involves the infrequency with which citizens of such communities interact with neighboring towns, cities, and provinces. Machiavelli here takes as his paradigm the example of the Swiss. By rarely having intercourse with their neighbors, communities like the Swiss avoid contracting corrupt customs, like those displayed by the French, Spanish, and Italians whom he claims are the cause of "the corruption of the whole world." The second factor in their resistance to change stems from the extreme antipathy citizens of republics have to those who live as gentlemen:

> Those republics that maintain a political and incorrupt life do not support that some of their citizens either are or live in the usage of a gentleman.[32]

Machiavelli indicates that should one of these fall into the hands of the citizens, the gentlemen are killed to forestall the beginnings of political corruption. According to the logic of 1.55, the material wealth of these new gentlemen gives them the force but, more importantly, ignites in them the desires necessary to seek to extend their stations. This dynamic, once in motion, perpetuates conditions of inequality. As Machiavelli continues: "The others are constrained [by the gentlemen] to endure the yoke that force, and nothing else, can never make them endure. Since there is proportion by this way from whomever forces to whoever is forced, men stand firm, each in his orders."[33]

6. Command Performance and the Valence of Leadership

Returning to 3.22, Machiavelli discusses the very different commands of the two consuls, Manlius Torquatus and Valerius Corvinus. On his first estimation, both were excellent and successful captains. Torquatus commanded his soldiers with severity and harshness, imposing extreme punishments. Machiavelli cites Torquatus' harsh nature as a reason why the Romans defeated the Latins, who were otherwise in all respects their military equals. In Machiavelli's estimation, the severity of Torquatus was such that it revived the spirit of military discipline in Rome when this had begun to wane.

Torquatus owes his reputation for excessive harshness in part to his execution of his own son, which occurred just prior to a battle between the Romans and the Latins at the outbreak of the Latin War (340 BC). Livy narrates that this war occurred between two nearly equal peoples.[34] Because of the great similarity between them, the Roman consuls proclaimed it forbidden for a Roman soldier to attack the Latins pre-emptively. Despite this edict, the consul's son engaged and killed a Latin cavalryman who had challenged him. Learning of his son's actions, Torquatus promptly assembled the soldiers, condemned his son and had him executed. He claimed his decision was made necessary because his son's break with military discipline threatened the republic itself.

The son's execution struck fear in the soldiers,[35] and the event itself is the origin of the phrase, *Manlian commands* (*Manliana imperia*). The episode is even cited by Livy as a reason for the subsequent Roman victory over the Latins, together with the suicide of the consul, Decius, who killed himself during a reversal in battle to motivate the troops. However, Livy's final analysis finds that the victory of the Romans was due less to these extreme spectacles of self-sacrifice on the part of the two consuls than to Torquatus himself, who tactically used his reserves during the battle to disorder the Latin army. For Livy, the Romans defeat the Latins because of Torquatus' superior strategy, not because he executes his son.[36] Livy himself stipulates that, because the armies were so evenly matched, whichever of the two armies—Roman or Latin —that had Torquatus as its *tactician* would have carried the battle. Machiavelli concludes that if a republic were fortunate enough to have the example of a Torquatus often reduce it to its beginnings ("*riducono gli ordini di quella verso il principio loro*"), it would be perpetual.[37]

On the other hand, Valerius Corvinus proceeded very differently. He commanded the troops humanely and with equanimity. At sports Corvinus competed with the rest of the soldiers as an equal and won or lost courteously. Those who were not his equals he treated as if they were even, according to Livy, undertaking "all obligations ungrudgingly among the meanest of soldiers."[38]

On Machiavelli's estimation, where the harshness of Torquatus with his soldiers undercut any private political ambitions he might have had, the behavior of Corvinus had a very different effect. Corvinus was free to "observe the customary things" (*cose consuete*). Because the military custom (*consuetudine*) was good, it took little effort to observe, and the need for punishments was imputed to upholding custom and not to Corvinus. Following custom allowed him to operate humanely and still earn honor. The soldiers of Corvinus became his friends and *partigiani*, an effect, Machiavelli notes, that could have been disastrous for freedom in the republic. Machiavelli then ends his discussion of the two consuls with a warning about the "bad effects on liberty of a long command."[39] With this conclusion, Machiavelli emphasizes that negative consequences did not follow from the command of Corvinus both because the Romans were not yet corrupt and Corvinus's command was short.[40]

Where the actions of Torquatus exacted obedience, they did not win him partisans. On the other hand, the behavior of Corvinus did have the effect of acquiring friends who were attached specifically to him and not to the common good. The relationship between Corvinus and his troops resembles the attachment sought by a prince of his or her subjects. In his final evaluation of the two captains, Machiavelli even overlaps the behavior of Corvinus with that of Xenophon's Cyrus, who received obedience from his soldiers and love from citizens *and* soldiers by treating them humanely. In 3.22, Machiavelli concludes that someone desiring to be prince needs to follow the example of Corvinus,[41] while a republic that wants to live freely wants a Torquatus for its captain.

'Machiavelli's discussion of the differences in the performances of Manlius Torquatus and Valerius Corvinus gestures towards the ease with which republican freedom can be compromised, but it does something further. It suggests that even where conditions of extreme equality exist spaces of princely inequality can spring up virtually within it. Thus, the partisan political relationships Corvinus developed with his troops were such that partisan relations existed but did not achieve the force needed to affect the ranks or military discipline in a lasting way.

As seen in Chapter 1, distributions of rank generate a field of values that activate and lock desire within progressively normalized, disciplinary circuits. Where the discussion of chapter 1 focused mainly on how the militia's disciplinary regime generated semi-autonomous soldiers through internalization of the values embedded in practices, Machiavelli's analyses of the behavior of captains discusses how the performance of leadership affects those concretized values. Machiavelli's discussions of mixed bodies and mixed forces underline how the qualities of captains like Hannibal, Scipio, Torquatus, and Corvinus can shift the valence of the forces they lead, intensifying or re-distributing fields of values in the process. Recalling the importance of continuity of memories to Lucretius' notion of identity, the performance of a captain can cause those who follow them to "forget themselves," disrupting associative chains and causing a new identity to emerge. This happens as a process of disruption of the associative circuits that connect up the disparate bodies that shape the force. This disruption can occur as a shock to those circuits or as their fraying, as closure and completion of them or as points of opening that generate increasing resistance to the communication of flow.

For Machiavelli, a captain's performance operates as a terminal for the circuits that unite the bodies of a composite force. This is why a captain's performance can shift the valence of a force to the point of its leaping categorical limits. Hannibal's mainly mercenary forces were united by his *reputation* for cruelty; Scipio's forces were *alienated* by his appearance of humanity to the point of rebellion.[42] On the other hand, Torquatus' hardness (*durezza*), severity (*severità*), and harshness (*asprezza*) deepened the connection between the discipline of his soldiers and the good of the republic by menacing private spaces of desire and exceptionalist reasoning. The *asprezza* of Manlius Torquatus shares a family resemblance with Hannibalian cruelty. The principal difference between the cases is the different context in which the two commanders operated. Torquatus employed the logic of *asprezza* in troops who already possessed a common subjective framework generated by similar military practices and shared semiotic and historical horizons.[43] Torquatus could expect his soldiers to be "like himself" because the disciplinary logics within which he operated supported those expectations even though they approached and exceeded the experiential thresholds to which his troops were accustomed. Torquatus' style of command affirmed conditions of equality with respect to distributions of rank. On the other hand, a captain like Hannibal had only a *reputation* for cruelty to hold together infinite generations of men.[44] Where Hannibal ultimately failed, Torquatus succeeded, and as Machiavelli notes about him:

> Therefore, when a man comes to a rank that commands, he desires to find all men similar to himself, and his strong spirit (*animo*) makes him command strong things; and that same one, as they are commanded, wants them observed.[45]

Here equality refers in part to the equal application of severe measures ("*fatica o pena*") that exclude no one, applying equally the expectations of rank and the consequences of command across the fabric of the militia. On the other hand, the actions of Corvinus in treating the unequal as equal affected the desires of his troops and began to warp the republican weave. Corvinus *virtualized* the significance of military rank for a time by behaving with his soldiers as an equal and, by doing so, initiated a process that generated *partigiani* from among his soldiers. Intentionally or not, Corvinus generated within his ranks relationships that resembled more princely than republican relations.

Where the affection the soldiers had for Corvinus did not ultimately express their potential negative consequences, Machiavelli does cite (or invent) a context in which a similar relationship between leader and troops did so. In both Chapters 1.55 and 3.22, Machiavelli refers to Venetian political conditions. The examples he uses affirm that two incommensurable political dimensions can co-exist. At 1.55, he argues that the example of the Venetian republic does not act as a counter-example to his claim that a class of gentlemen makes it impossible to sustain conditions of equality. In Venice, the class of gentlemen possessed neither castles nor jurisdiction over men. Thus the rank of "gentleman" existed there in name but not in fact, and as a name it operated mainly as a designation of dignity and reputation.

At the end of 3.22—after discussing the case of Corvinus—Machiavelli then describes an episode in which a gentleman *did* menace the Venetian republic. As Machiavelli tells it, once, when the galleys of Venice had returned from war, conflicts broke out among the sailors. The conflicts between the mariners could not be resolved by "the force of the ministers, the reverence of the citizens or [even] by fear of the magistrates." However, the tumults *did* quiet down when, "to those mariners appeared before them a gentleman who had been their captain the year before."[46] For love of *him* the mariners withdrew. Following the resolution of the tumults, the Venetian Senate remained suspicious of this unnamed gentleman and contrived circumstances to have him killed.

The event of the conflict is not recorded outside of Machiavelli's mention of it here, giving it the appearance of an episode made up by him to emphasize the distinctions he draws in 3.22 between Torquatus and Corvinus. By including the story, Machiavelli points to another way troops can be considered mixed. When the French compounded their men at arms with Swiss infantry, they not only combined two quantities of force but initiated a process of change at the end of which French men-at-arms no longer "felt confident" to take the field unless accompanied by Swiss pike. The objective compounding of different troop qualities changed the subjective conditioning of the French troops.

By analyzing the cases of Corvinus and the unnamed Venetian commander, Machiavelli indicates another way the performance of captains can change subjective conditions in those they lead. Even though the love the mariners had for him remained hidden for a year, when the disputes broke out the virtualized princely proportions that existed between the unnamed Venetian gentleman and the mariners suddenly materialized. By fabricating this example Machiavelli suggests that far from constituting mutually exclusive political spaces, relations of princely inequality and republican political freedom can co-exist. This is possible because forces qualify as being *mixed* not only due to their external organization but also due to their subjective ordering. The category applies not only to differently organized quantities of force—like mercenaries, auxiliaries, and one's own troops—but extends also to a redistribution of the subjective valuations of the soldiers themselves who form the building blocks of those larger composites.[47] The attachment the sailors developed for the Venetian galley captain—like the loyalty Corvinus' soldiers developed for him—occurred through a re-ordering of their subjectivity. Machiavelli highlights here how the relationship between captain and troops can initiate a process that incites changes in those who follow, whether from valuations of partisan affection to republican equality or vice versa.

7. Appius Claudius and Intrinsic Forces

In Chapters 1.40 and 1.43, Machiavelli addresses another case that exhibits many of the themes found in his analyses of the careers of Hannibal, Scipio, Torquatus, and Corvinus when he discusses the career of Appius Claudius and the decemvirate. Machiavelli's analysis of this case again reveals the plasticity of subjective conditioning and its effects on the quality of a force. In 1.43, Machiavelli first notes that "under the consuls Roman armies were always accustomed to be victorious, under the decemvirs they always lost."[48] He analyzes the character of Rome's armies under the rule of the decemvirs and concludes that during their reign, Rome's armies performed like mercenaries. When the decemvirs were eliminated, the soldiers again served as free persons and their spirit (*animo*) returned.

In telling the story of the decemvirs, Machiavelli reveals that the cause for the shift in the quality of the armies was due to the tyranny of Appius Claudius, who failed to secure himself with "intrinsic forces." In order to become decemvir, the formerly arrogant Claudius "used so much humanity toward the plebs" that he was appointed decemvir not once, but twice. During his second appointment, he reverted to showing his contempt for the plebs.[49] Appius infected his colleagues with his customs, favoring the nobles and beating down the people. These conditions continued until the Sabini and Volsci moved against the Romans. The Senate led the armies to meet them, but Claudius's attempt to force Verginia—the daughter of the centurion, Lucius Verginius—led to the secession of the armies and Claudius' downfall.

Machiavelli concludes from this that Claudius made a serious error when he favored the nobles and beat down the people because the ambition and avarice of the nobles is so great that inevitably some part of the them remain "outside the tyranny." This unavoidable consequence causes the excluded group to become the tyrant's enemy. Machiavelli then introduces a variant of the maxim on force that occurred at 1.55 and 3.22:

> ... to want to hold a thing with violence it is necessary that who forces is more powerful than who is forced. From this it arises that those tyrants that have the universal as friend (*che hanno amico lo universale*) and the *grandi* as enemies are more secure. Their violence is sustained by greater force than that one who has the people for an enemy and the nobility for a friend ...[50]

The reason he gives for this is that under these circumstances, the one with the people as a friend secures himself on "intrinsic forces."[51] In 1.40, Machiavelli reasons at length on the roles played by the people and the nobles in the emergence of the decemvirs' temporary tyranny. Subjective conditions made each class vulnerable to the false favorable persona ("*aliena persona*") Claudius adopted to win their support. It was the people's overly strong desire ("*troppo desiderio*") and excessive wish ("*eccessiva voglia*") to be free of the consuls, as well as the excessive desire of the nobles to be free of the tribunes, that disposed both groups to support the decemvirate and gave Claudius the opening he needed to assume power.[52]

As another perspective on the category of mixed forces in Machiavelli, the episode is key to showing the decisive role the quality of the *capo* plays in the quality of the forces he or she leads. It also importantly suggests the influence political leadership can exercise on the military, even shifting its quality. The change in the quality of the Roman troops does not occur due to policy changes concerning how they were organized. Where French forces became mixed both objectively and then, later, subjectively as a consequence of the policy decisions of Louis XI, Machiavelli emphasizes that the Roman troops under the decemvirate changed their "disposition" (*disposizione*) but retained their *virtù*. They functioned like mercenaries but only until the decemvirate ended.[53] With the election of new consuls, the troops returned to the "same spirit," (*medesimo animo*) and carried out campaigns, "according to their ancient customs." The analysis Machiavelli undertakes of Appius Claudius and the decemvirate in *Discourses* 1.40 to 1.43 suggest how the performance of political leadership can trigger a shift in the subjective conditions of troop discipline. In Rome, the decemvirate affected Rome's forces such that *arms of one's own* shifted quality and temporarily performed as *arma alienis*.[54]

8. Conclusion

Machiavelli's discussions of mixed forces in the *Prince* and the *Discourses* differs from his discussions of other force categories like those of mercenary or auxiliary forces. Machiavelli's category of mixed forces extends and elaborates on the Lucretian notion of mixed bodies. For Lucretius, the soul and body occur as networks of intra-dependent composites exchanging motions distinguished by degrees of velocity and density. The individual human body performs as an assemblage of such mixed bodies whose restless weaves of *primordia* carry implications for Lucretian notions of identity. Ultimately for Lucretius the human experience of identity depends on the continuity of memory's associations, itself an effect of specific arrangements of composite bodies.

Machiavelli's analyses of mixed forces both reflect this Lucretian reality and exceed it. Machiavelli shows how forces of different qualities reorganize internally when compounded. For this reason, he generally finds that mixed forces are superior to mercenary and auxiliary troops. However, the category of mixed forces differs from these other two categories because it describes forces without a fixed character or single governing logic. Machiavelli's analyses of specific cases of mixed forces reveal a category that describes forces undergoing qualitative change. It may be a sign that poorly disciplined troops have strengthened due to their association with better organized forces; it may also be an indication that more optimally organized troops have undergone a dilation of disciplinary practices and are declining in intensity. Either way, the category of mixed forces in Machiavelli describes forces in the process of alteration.

These alterations themselves assume different characters. Mixed troops not only undergo change and reorganization by being compounded with different forces, but factors like leadership can cause forces to undergo category shifts. Machiavelli's analyses of the careers of Hannibal, Scipio, Torquatus, Corvinus, and even Appius Claudius emphasize how a quantity of force can shift valence on the basis of the performance of its leadership. Hannibal's style of command made vastly more effective an otherwise motley collection of mercenary and auxiliary troops, while Corvinus' behavior—like the unnamed Venetian gentleman—generated princely relations of affection amidst republican ranks. By focusing on the effects of the performance of captains, Machiavelli shows how their spectacles can "re-interpret" the valence of the forces they lead, intensifying or re-distributing fields of values, even to the point where these forces disassociate from what they were and "forget themselves" by becoming something new. Machiavelli's discussions of the effects captains can have on the forces they lead suggests how a new force may emerge on the basis of a reorganization of the subjective conditions active in those bodies which compose it. Further, Machiavelli's analysis of the case of Appius Claudius demonstrates that factors capable of triggering a shift in the quality of a force connect the militia with institutions, processes, and offices that exceed it.

Conclusion: Captains of Critique

This study has investigated Machiavelli's application of categories of armed force and focused on the implications arising from Machiavelli's tendency to complicate his employment of them. Under certain circumstances, Machiavelli's discussions show mercenary and auxiliary arms performing as effectively as seasoned, well-trained citizen troops fighting for their prince, while under other circumstances republican forces exhibit the qualities of soldiers of fortune.

The complexity in Machiavelli's presentation of categories of armed force stems in part from the importance the Lucretian account of nature had for him. Lucretian influence appears in Machiavelli's understanding of the militia as a mixed body where differently equipped and trained human bodies occupy the position of Lucretian *primordia*. The two thinkers also overlap in how they distinguish soul and spirit (*animus* and *anima* in Lucretius, or *anima* and *animo* in Machiavelli), and the function this distinction plays in their accounts of human behavior. Finally, elements of the Lucretian account of the *umori* can be detected in Machiavelli's discussions of the conflict of *grandi* and *popolo*, and in the factors that explain why military forces change in quality.

This study also argues that Machiavelli accomplishes an intervention in the history of military tactics by adopting military and textual strategies presented by Aelianus Tacticus in *De instruendis aciebus.* Like Aelianus, Machiavelli resists tradition and shifts the focus of his discussions of military strategy and tactics from the upper level officers and the actions of the army's main principal divisions. He focuses, instead, on the behavior of the individual soldier and the lower level officers, making detailed representations of small unit actions in both narrative and diagram. Also like Aelianus, Machiavelli's reliance on diagrams to represent the placement of differently equipped soldiers and the maneuvers they execute opens up the topic of military strategy and tactics to potential audiences who may lack practical experience in the field. Finally, on the basis of his critique of the phalanx tactics presented by Aelianus, Machiavelli develops a regime of military discipline whose objective is the internalization of signs and practices on the part of the individual soldiers, through which they become self-regulating.

The analyses of Machiavelli's two principal forms of the "arms of others"—mercenaries and auxiliaries—showed the flexibility with which Machiavelli applies these force categories. At times, Machiavelli's categorical flexibility communicated ways in which the apparent dangers these kinds of troops posed could be managed and their defects suppressed. For commanders like Francesco Sforza or Hannibal, mercenary and auxiliary troops could be made to function as "arms of one's own." However, under certain conditions, "arms of one's own" were seen to shift category, as in the case of the Roman legions stationed at Capua where economic factors like heavy indebtedness caused *arma propriis* to behave like auxiliaries.

Finally Machiavelli's treatment of the topic of mixed forces forefronts the notion that forces of different qualities can incite changes in one another. In discussing these kinds of changes, Machiavelli highlights how captains can play a prominent role in effecting such quality shifts. When Machiavelli contrasts the effects of the performance of Valerius Corvinus and Manlius Torquatus, or Hannibal with Scipio and Appius Claudius, he suggests in the process that princely relations can spring up within republican distributions of rank and how extreme discipline enforces equal distribution of honors by suppressing spaces of private desire. The different performance styles of these captains caused the forces they led to shift their quality.

This study examined closely the relationship between rank-and-file soldiers and the lower, intermediate, and upper level officers for the factors that generate and disrupt the conditions of their association. It did this to better understand the circuits of signs and associations at the heart of Machiavelli's disciplinary regime as immanent to the associations they make possible. But this also suggests that the different degrees of rank that concretely distribute the militia's institutional values can be viewed as layers of strata within a composite body where the intensity of the organization of the lower strata generate the functionality of those that organize upon them.[1] Stefano Visentin describes this process when he explains Machiavelli's conception of the relationship of *moltitudine* to *capo* as a kind of paradoxical emanation of the former's fractured humoral conflictedness:

> The paradoxical aspect of the relationship between the prince and the multitude consists then in the necessity of a separation, of a rupture that the first completes in confronting the passions and the desires of the second that must know how to grow estranged from and, in fact, oppose itself.[2]

Machiavelli anchors the disciplinary mechanics of his militia in a continuity of leadership, starting from the *capidieci* and *centurioni* who serve as relays from rank-and-file soldiers to the roles of constables, brigade heads, and captain. Promotion of rank in Machiavelli's brigade depends on *capi* who have performed excessively well. Machiavelli's *capi* are then *of* the milita in two senses: they have internalized the disciplinary conditioning and experience which generates the militia as a composite body; and, as they have done so and only to the extent they have done so, those circuits of practices and signs have mapped out a subjective associative horizon which all the troops share in common.

However, Machiavelli notes that *capi* differ from the rank and file on the basis of the strength of their *animi*. Through an excess of *animi* they have evaded, shed, and suppressed objective and subjective barriers that would otherwise have captivated and captured them. Or, as Visentin puts this, they find themselves positioned as heads of lines, centurions anchoring formations, constables, heads of brigades, and even captains due in large part to their "surplus of subjectivity."[3] For Machiavelli, what then are the implications and possibilities of this "subjective surplus"?

Machiavelli clearly assigns to his captains the role of readers and interpreters of signs. Sections of Books 4, 5, and 6 of the *Art of War* provide guidance to captains on, for instance, interpreting correctly the signs presented by disrupted bird movements or dust clouds or discarded spoils. They explain to potential captains how to recognize the phenomena as signs and then to read in them an unseen enemy's intentions.[4] In other passages, Machiavelli has Colonna describe the importance of a captain learning to read accurately and influence the affective conditions of his or her troops, as he does when at the end of Book 4 he explains that to remove an *opinione sinistra* from a multitude, a captain must be an accomplished orator in order to do "all those things by which the human passions are extinguished or inflamed."[5]

Machiavelli also shows that a captain's interpretive exertions have effects that extend beyond the militia. For instance, at *Discourses* 3.34 Machiavelli argues that the people commit fewer errors than do princes in deciding appointments to prominent positions. He identifies the reason behind the people's better decision-making in how well-ordered republics create assemblies that mimic the relationship a prince has to his or her counselors. In these assemblies a candidate's defects are presented, and this positions the people to choose the more appropriate candidate. Machiavelli then cites the example of Quintus Fabius, who opposed the election of Titus Ottacilius to the position of Roman consul during the Second Punic War. On Machiavelli's reading, Fabius criticized Ottacilius, channeling the people's favor toward a different candidate. Machiavelli concludes:

> Therefore, the people, judging in the election of magistrates according to those counter-signs [*contrassegni*], were able to possess much truth, and when they can be advised like princes are, they make errors less than princes do.[6]

In Machiavelli's version of the episode, Fabius engages in a conflict of interpretation around the traits that supported Ottacilius' candidacy for the position of consul. By issuing *contrassegni*, Fabius weakened the assembly's impression of Ottacilius' suitability, so that the assembly made a different choice.

Examining the episode in Livy underscores how Quintus Fabius intentionally invoked the shared framework of military service as a platform for the unfolding of the battle of signs and counter-signs. As Livy recounts, when Fabius returned from the war to hold the elections, he proceeded directly to the Campus Martius without entering the city. This move allowed him to retain full military authority during his appeal to the people. During his speech, Fabius first invoked the dangers to Rome posed by Hannibal and then asked the electors to choose a consul with the "same seriousness with which you go into battle-line under arms."[7] Speaking against Ottacilius, Fabius even identifies his opponent as a member of his family in a way that strengthens his case against him before further citing Ottacilius' failures in his role as captain of Rome's fleet to cut off Hannibal's supply lines and protect the Italian coast. Fabius recounts Ottacilius' military failures as the principal reason for why Ottacilius should not be elected consul.

Fabius then closes his speech by again asking the assembly to consider their choice as if they were armed soldiers arrayed for battle with a choice between two generals. As he does so, he recalls the military disasters at Trasumennus and Cannae. At no point during his speech does Fabius relax the military associations that frame the choice he presents. Even when Ottacilius shouts against him, Fabius summons the lictors and reminds his opponent that, since he did not lay down his military authority on entering the city, any sentence Fabius pronounced against him during these proceedings would have no right of appeal.

The revote results in the prolongation of Quintus Fabius' consulship. Livy indicates the overall strategy behind Fabius' performance when he notes further on that Ottacilius is subsequently ordered by the two consuls, Quintus Fabius and Marcus Marcellus, to remain captain of Rome's fleet. This decision raises the suspicion that Ottacilius' failures were the best anyone could have done given the mediocrity of Rome's sea forces.[8]

Machiavelli's use of this episode highlights features of the military service shared by the assembly relied on by Fabius to shift the people's decision. The episode as a whole shows how military practices and associations performed as a shared interpretive framework within which the critic, Fabius, outmaneuvered his opponent. The success of Fabius' *contrassegni* curated the decision of the people's assembly toward the appointment of the next counsel—himself.

This episode from *Discourses* 3.34 furnishes a clear example of an interpretive battle whose outcome depended on the effectiveness with which the two captains—Fabius and Ottacilius—maneuvered the historical and practical associations of the militia's disciplinary regime in their appeals to the people's assembly.

(Beyond the Militia)—Armed and Unarmed Prophets

Clearly religion plays an energetic, if complicated, role in the function of the disciplinary regime that organizes military force. In the *Art of War* at the close of Book 4, Machiavelli emphasizes the importance of captains to master oratory. In the same passage he also emphasizes the importance for captains to follow the example of the ancients and reinvent tactics for mixing religion and the fear of God into their orders.[9] As he does so, he refers to the Roman general Sertorius, who sustained his rebellion against Sulla by successfully convincing the local tribes in Spain that the goddess Diana promised him victory by speaking to him through a white faun. Machiavelli includes as well the performance of Sulla, who claimed to speak with an image from the temple of Apollo, before closing Book 4 with the example of Charles VII who allowed it to be known that he took counsel from a young girl sent by God.[10] These examples clearly recall other prophetic performances Machiavelli discusses in both the *Prince* and the *Discourses*, like those of Numa Pompilius, Moses, and Savonarola. Each of these leaders excited belief in their projects at least in part through skillful use of religion.

Further, Machiavelli frequently deploys the distinction between arms of one's own and the arms of others when he discusses the success and failure of a certain type of captain clearly linked to religion—the armed prophet. In Chapter 6 of the *Prince*, he judges the career of Moses successful and that of Girolamo Savonarola a failure because Moses possessed his own arms and Savonarola did not.[11] As Machiavelli states: "and yet things should be ordered in a way that when they [the people] no longer believe, one can make them believe by force."[12] Possessing arms of one's own produced a positive outcome for the prophetic captain, Moses, because arms generated a relationship between force and belief which sustained support for his project in those whom he led. Maintaining the people in a new persuasion requires the kind of force that can adjust a multitude's beliefs even when they begin to doubt that the innovator can make good on the promise that originally earned their enthusiasm.

Machiavelli notes that Savonarola resembled Moses when he successfully convinced the Florentines that he directly communicated with God. Machiavelli relates Savonarola's claim at *Discourses* 1.11, where he discusses how easily an ignorant and coarse people can be persuaded to adopt "a new order." He then states:

> To the people of Florence it does not appear that they are ignorant nor crude. Nevertheless they were persuaded by Father Girolamo Savonarola that he conversed with God.[13]

Further in the passage he adds:

> I do not wish to judge whether it was true or not because of such a man one ought to speak with reverence. But I do say rightly that an infinite number believed him without having seen anything extraordinary to make them believe him.[14]

In both the *Prince* and the *Discourses*, Machiavelli presents Savonarola as a leader who attempted to follow the example laid out by Moses.[15] Machiavelli telegraphs the degree to which Savonarola would have liked to have imitated Moses at *Discourses* 3.30. Here he links Moses and Savonarola directly when he speaks of how the envy of others can pose a great obstacle to anyone who would introduce new things. The only way to avoid the difficulties that follow from this envy is to follow the example of Moses: '

> And anyone who reads the Bible sensibly [*sensatamente*] will see that Moses, who wanted that his laws and his orders would go forward, was forced to kill infinite men who, moved by nothing other than envy [*nvidia*], opposed his plans. Friar Girolamo Savonarola knew this necessity very well...[16]

However, in this respect the friar could not follow the path of Moses because he lacked the "authority" to pursue this path.[17] Possessing arms of his own gave Moses the authority that Savonarola—hopelessly hobbled by the Florentine economy dependent on mercenary force—could not assemble. Still, as John Najemy underlines, the example of Savonarola was important to Machiavelli because the friar successfully convinced the Florentines to follow him for a considerable time *despite* lacking his own arms. For Najemy:

> Belief in supernatural or divine power can perhaps instill confidence and boldness, but victory goes to those who understand the power of such belief and how it works to shape the behavior of people.[18]

However, belief in a supernatural power does not simply provide the captain a neutral tool for shepherding the many. For Najemy, whether a captain was successful or not in their invocation of religious tropes, ceremonies, or practices depended on whether they successfully convinced others that they knew the truth of religion and were positioned to speak for the heavens. The successful use the Romans made of religion resulted both from the devotion to religion as practiced by the soldiers, but also "because they received and experienced that religion through the skillful interpretations of their political and military leaders."[19]

Machiavelli's preoccupation with the power of religion recalls Lucretius' insistence on the persistence of the fear of death. Lucretius identifies the tendency to return to superstitious thinking that can erupt in even those who have accepted the Epicurean arguments about the annihilation of the soul.[20] The ontological status of the fear of death makes it a potential obstacle to all human beings regardless of their rank, training, experience, function, or office. Machiavelli configures his militia to include at least two ways of responding to this fear—devotion and ceremony, on the one hand, and reading and interpretation, on the other.

This study then concludes by gesturing toward the importance of articulating further how Machiavelli understands the *animo*-energized process of estrangement and distancing as described by Visentin above that drives the formation and promotion of officers, and the role that the mechanics of interpretation plays within that process. It also suggests that Machiavelli has conceived his militia in advance as captured within an open-ended project. In this project, the prospect of possessing *arms of one's own* proceeds through ever greater intensifications of the subjective domain that in turn channel, *or* promote, individuals of exceptional *animi* to sustain it. Whether these captains, princes, armed prophets (or something other and somehow more)[21] experience success depends on how well those who occupy these roles calibrate their response to the conflict-charged imperatives for (re)-interpretation posed by the militia's organizing values whose drift and unpredicted shifts call not only for re-assessment but also erasure and even being made anew.

Notes

Introduction

1. King of Syracuse from 308 to 215 BC. See Polybius, *Histories* 1.9.
2. See John Najemy, "Machiavelli and Cesare Borgia: A Reconsideration of Chapter 7 of 'The Prince,'" *The Review of Politics* 75, no. 4 (2013): 543–9.
3. See Chapter 1, section 3.
4. "... a Ierone ad essere principe non mancava altro che il principato."
5. See *Discourses* 1.58, 2.1, and 2.30.
6. *Prince,* Chapter 5; also *Florentine Histories*, particularly Books 4–6.
7. Yves Winter, "The Prince and His Art of War: Machiavelli's Military Populism," *Social Research* 81, no. 1 (Spring, 2014): 164.
8. See Winter, "The Prince and His Art of War," 164.
9. Felix Gilbert, "Machiavelli and the Renaissance of the *Art of* War," in *Makers of Modern Strategy: from Machiavelli to the Nuclear Age*, ed. P. Paret (Princeton: Princeton University Press, 1986), 29.
10. Louis Althusser, *Machiavel et nous* (Paris: Éditions Tallandier, 2009), 147–50.
11. Harvey Mansfield, *Machiavelli's Virtue* (Chicago: University of Chicago Press, 1996), 204–05.
12. John McCormick, *Machiavellian Democracy* (Cambridge: Cambridge University Press, 2011), 34.
13. Christopher Lynch argues this in his commentary on the *Art of War*, trans. and ed. by Christopher Lynch (Chicago: University of Chicago Press, 2003), xiv.
14. See Mikael Hörnquist, "Perché non si usa allegare I Romani: Machiavelli and the Florentine Militia of 1506," *Renaissance Quarterly* v. 55 (2002): 148–91.
15. See John Najemy, "Machiavelli, the Militia, and Guicciardini's Accusation of Tyranny," in *Della tirannia: Machiavelli con Bartolo*, ed. Jérémie Barthas (Florence: Leo S. Olschki, 2007): see especially 79–80 and 85–9.
16. John Najemy, "Machiavelli, the Militia, and Guicciardini's Accusation of Tyranny," 93–6 and 98. As Winter argues in *Machiavelli and the Orders of Violence* (Cambridge: Cambridge University Press, 2018), Machiavelli's militia is composed of citizens and *sudditi* (subjects). Subjects are often exposed to a very different set of economic, biomedical, legal, and political circumstances than citizens would be. For these reasons, Winter concludes, "incorporating subject populations poses the

non-negligible risk that subject-soldiers may turn their weapons against their masters", 180.

17 See Robert Black in "Machiavelli and the Militia," *Italian Studies* 69, no. 1 (2014): 41–50.

18 Michael Mallett, "The Theory and Practice of Warfare in Machiavelli's Republic," in *Machiavelli and Republicanism*, ed. G. Bock, Q. Skinner, and M. Viroli (Cambridge: Cambridge University Press, 1990), describes the Florentine position during the fifteenth century as "the gullible paymaster of other people's troops" (177). Felix Gilbert, in "Machiavelli and the Renaissance of the *Art of* War," 18–19, also outlines the circumstances surrounding the militia ordinance and its implementation. See, too, Piero Pieri, *La crisi militare italiana nel rinascimento* (Naples: Riccardo Ricciardi Editore, 1934), especially Part II, Chapters 4–5.

19 Jean-Louis Fournel, "Il genere e il tempo delle parole: dire la guerra nei testi machiavelliani," in *The Radical Machiavelli*, ed. F. Lucchese, F. Frosini, and V. Morfino (Leiden: Brill, 2015), especially 34–6.

20 Machiavelli, *Art of War*, Book 2, 565.

21 Ibid., 35–6.

22 Bernard Wicht, "Les suisses comme révélateur du project Machiavélien du milice," in *Niccolò Machiavelli: politico storico letterato*, ed. Jean-Jacques Marchand (Rome: Salerno Editrice, 1996), 244.

23 Gabriele Pedullà, "Machiavelli the Tactician: Math, Graphs, and Knots in *The Art of War*," in *The Radical Machiavelli*, ed. F. De Lucchese, F. Frosini, and V. Morfino (Leiden: Brill, 2015), 83.

24 Marcia Colish, "Machiavelli's Art of War: A Reconsideration," *Renaissance Quarterly* (1998) v. 51: 1151–68. See, also, Harvey Mansfield, *Machiavelli's Virtue*, especially 202, for a different take on Machiavelli's reading of Colonna.

25 See Yves Winter, "The Prince and His Art of War," 185.

26 Frédérique Verrier, "Machiavelli and Fabrizio Colonna nell'Arte della guerra,': il polemologo sdoppiato," in *Niccolò Machiavelli: politico storico letterato*, ed. Jean-Jacques Marchand (Rome: Salerno Editrice, 1996), 178–9.

27 See the introduction of Chapter 1.

28 See, for instance, Chapter 1, section 4.

Chapter 1

1 See Sergio Bertelli, "Noterelle machiavelliane: Un codice di Lucrezio e di Terenzio," *Rivista storica italiana* 73 (1961): 544–55. However, the first to attribute this copy of the *De rerum natura* to Machiavelli was Chauncey Finch in "Machiavelli's Copy of Lucretius," *Classical Journal* 56 (1960): 29–32.

2 See Paul Rahe in *Against Throne and Altar* (Cambridge, MA: Cambridge University Press, 2008): 41, note 39. Also, Ada Palmer in *Reading Lucretius in the Renaissance* (Cambridge, MA: Harvard University Press, 2014), especially 79–81, and Alison Brown, Chapters 4 and 5, in *The Return of Lucretius to Renaissance Florence* (Cambridge, MA: Harvard University Press, 2010).

3 Alison Brown, *The Return of Lucretius to Renaissance Florence* (69), dates his transcription to 1497 while Rahe in *Against Throne and Altar* (34) hypothesizes the transcription occurred from the mid to late 1490s, the same range given by Robert Roecklin, *Machiavelli and Epicureanism* (Lanham, MD: Lexington Press, 2012), 6. On the other hand, Ada Palmer in *Reading Lucretius in the Renaissance* (81) points to the lack of hard evidence for the history of Machiavelli's copy and argues that Machiavelli may have transcribed his copy by 1500 but may not have completed it until 1512.

4 See, for instance, Brown, *The Return of Lucretius to Renaissance Florence*, 85. Brown argues that through Lucretius' influence Machiavelli's thought on these topics places him closer to the early modern outlook than traditional creationism or Aristotelian teleology. She contends that considerable benefits accrue to such a reading, since it links Machiavelli's interest in the Lucretian swerve expressed in the manuscript's marginalia to a notion of free will. For Brown, a reading which recognizes Lucretius' influence on Machiavelli on these points escapes the usual freedom versus determinism stalemate that generally frames interpretation of his texts. See also Brown in "Prefazione alla edizione italiana," trans. Andrea Asioli, in *Machiavello e Lucrezio* (Rome: Carocci editore S.p.A., 2013), 8–11, and "Lucretian Naturalism and the Evolution of Machiavelli's Ethics," in *The Radical Machiavelli*, ed. F. Lucchese, F. Frosini, and V. Morfino (Leiden: Brill, 2015).

5 See Chapter 3 in *The Return of Lucretius to Renaissance Florence*, where Brown emphasizes how Machiavelli borrowed from Marcello Adriani's 1497 inaugural lecture, *Nil admirari*.

6 Ibid., 85 and Alison Brown, "Prefazione alla edizione italiana."

7 Paul Rahe in *Against Throne and Altar* claims that Machiavelli follows the arguments Lucretius makes on these subjects in *De rerum natura*, book 5. See *De rerum natura*, 5.195–234, 5.223–7, 5.953–7, and 5.990–1. See also Rahe, *Against Throne and* Altar, 44, note 47.

8 See Paul Rahe, *Against Throne and Altar,* 32–45.

9 As Rahe concludes in *Against Throne and Altar*: "he regarded Epicurus' attempt to reconcile the physics of Democritus with human freedom as little more than a dodge" (41). See also Robert Black, *Machiavelli* (London: Routledge, 2013), 162.

10 See Ada Palmer, *Reading Lucretius in the Renaissance*, 81–8.

11 See Chapters 4 and 5 in Robert Roecklin, *Machiavelli and Epicureanism* (Lanham, MD: Lexington Books, 2012).

12 Ibid., 7.
13 Ibid., 25.
14 Vittorio Morfino, "Tra Lucrezio e Spinoza: la 'filosofia' di Machiavelli," in *Machiavelli immaginazaione e contingenza*, ed. F. Del Lucchese, L. Sartorello, and S. Visentin (Pisa: Edizioni ETS, 2006), 67–110, notes the frequent occurrence of the term *textura* in the *De rerum natura* and identifies it as a key to discovering this physics in Lucretius. As Lucretius employs it, *textura* refers to reality as a complex interweaving of bodies. See Morfino "Tra Lucrezio e Spinoza," 84–9, and "Lucrezio e la corrente sotterranea del materialismo," in *Lucrezio e la modernità, I secoli XV–XVI*, ed. F. Lucchese, V. Morfino, and G. Mormino (Naples: Bibliopolis, 2011), 33–59.
15 On a Lucretian reading of Borgia's downfall, see Sean Erwin, "Mixed Bodies, Agency and Narrative in Lucretius and Machiavelli," *Époché* 24, vol. 2 (Spring 2020), section 4.
16 Gabriele Pedullà, "Machiavelli the Tactician: Math, Graphs, and Knots in *The Art of War*," in *The Radical Machiavelli*, ed. F. De Lucchese, F. Frosini, and V. Morfino (Brill: Leiden, 2015), 81–101.
17 Ibid., 85; see also Michel Foucault, *Surveiller et punir: Naissance de la prison* (Paris: Gallimard, 1975), 3.1, "Les corps dociles," 163.
18 The principal anchor for Pedullà's reading is not Lucretius and Machiavelli's transcription of *De rerum natura*—which he does not mention—but the second-century AD Greek author Aelianus Tacticus, whose text, *De instruendis aciebus*, was available in Rome in a Latin edition produced by Eucharius Silber after 1487 in a volume that bound the brief Aelianus text with works by Vegetius, Frontinus, Modestus, and Onasander. This text was subject to numerous reprintings from 1490 onward and was widely disseminated; it will be discussed at length in the next chapter.
19 See Michel Foucault, *Il faut défendre la société* (Paris: Gallimard/Seuil, 1997) and *Sécurité, territoire, population* (Paris: Gallimard/Seuil, 2004). The omission of meaningful mention of Machiavelli's discussions of the discipline of war or *The Art of War* from Foucault's lectures of these years is puzzling given the central role Machiavelli plays in these Collège de France lectures of 1976–7 and 1978–9.
20 See, for instance, Lucretius, *De rerum natura* 1.29–1.40, 2.1–2.13, 2.35, 2.315–2.332, 5.1241–5.1330, 5.1308.
21 This is not the only form of naturalism at work. It is also possible to discern the workings of astrological determinism in Machiavelli's descriptions of natural dynamics. Anthony Parel develops the implications of this influence in *The Machiavellian Cosmos* (New Haven, CT: Yale University Press, 1992). Given that Machiavelli changes and adapts Lucretian physical dynamics to fit his purposes he may also have adapted the mechanics of astrological determinism, too. Astrological

determinism allows for explanations of natural phenomenon that both parallel religious explanations but do so without requiring actual divine agency. For this reason, both Epicurean atomism and astrological determinism could have proved useful to Machiavelli.

22 Machiavelli, *Discourses* 2.5, 341–3.
23 Ibid., 3.1, 416–20.
24 Palmer, *Reading Lucretius in the Renaissance*, 84.
25 Ibid., 86.
26 Palmer compares Machiavelli's version of the *De rerum natura* with the other fifty-four manuscripts of the work that survive from the period after 1417. Machiavelli's extensive marginalia runs throughout Book 2, beginning with line 10 and continuing to line 657. As Palmer infers: "These notes indicate that, unique among our annotators, Machiavelli had the technical details of Epicurean physics as a special interest when approaching the text." Ibid., 47–50 and 81–3.
27 Rahe, *Against Throne and Altar*, notes the Lucretian language of *Discourses* 3.1 but does not expand on the implications of the reference.
28 Machiavelli *Discourses* 3.1, 416–17.
29 Machiavelli, ibid., 426. The passage has attracted diverse attributions by scholars but for most, Lucretius figures prominently as a probable source. Francesco Bausi (ed.), *Discorsi sopra la prima deca di Tito Livio* (Rome: Salerno Editrice, 2001), Corrado Vivanti (ed.), *Discorsi sopra la prima deca di Tito Livio* (Turin: Einaudi, 2000), and Giorgio Inglese (ed.), *Discorsi sopra la prima deca di Tito Livio* (Milan: Rizzole Editore, 1984) find the roots of this passage in Sallust, Lucretius, and even Galen and Dante. The passages they suggest as the origin for the theme of return in *Discourses* 3.1 discuss for the most part the birth and decay of bodies. None of the proposed source passages mentions a return to beginnings, mixed bodies, or the notion of a limit to the existence of mixed bodies ordered by heaven. For instance, Bausi attributes the passage to a number of sources, among them Galen, *De sanitate tuenda*, and Ugo Benzi's commentary on Avicenna. In the end, Bausi attributes the passage to Machiavelli's tendency to relay sayings which he rewords in the process. Similarly, Vivanti (566, n.1) sees in the passage an allusion to Sallust's *The War with Jugurtha*, 1.2, which only mentions the rise and fall of the goods of both body and fortune ("*corporis et fortunae bonorum ut initia sic finis est, omniaque orta occidunt et aucta senescunt*"). On the other hand, Vivanti connects the passage with Lucretius, *De rerum natura* 2.1173–2.1174 where the cultivator of the vine complains, "*nec tenet omnia paulatim tabescere et ire ad scopulum, spatio aetatis defessa vetusto.*" Inglese cites this passage as well as Book 5, 92–6, where Lucretius describes heaven and the earth as subject to destruction, offering with this citation the only passage suggesting the theme of return to beginnings. The other passage suggested by Inglese is *De rerum natura* 5, 306–15, which describes how all things die and are

received back into body: "*si procreat ex se omnia, quod quidam memorant, recipitque perempta, totum nativo ac mortali corpore constant.*" Finally, Inglese also detects an echo of Dante, *Paradiso,* Canto 16, 76–80, where Dante's ancestor, Cacciaguida, states: "All mankind's institutions of every sort/ have their own death though in what long endures /it is hidden from you, your own lives being short," though this link is weaker than the connections he makes with Lucretius.

30 See *Discourses* 2.1 and *Florentine Histories* 5.1.
31 See Pedullà, "Machiavelli the Tactician: Math, Graphs, Knots in *The Art of War*," 83–7.
32 Palmer, *Reading Lucretius in the Renaissance*, 37.
33 Machiavelli, *Art of War,* Book 2, 560.
34 Livy, *From the Founding of the City,* book 8.8, 29–35.
35 See Clifford Rogers, "Tactics and the Face of Battle," in *European Warfare: 1350–1750*, ed. Frank Tallett and D. J. B. Trim (Cambridge: Cambridge University Press, 2010), 203–35.
36 Machiavelli, *Art of War*, Book 3, 591.
37 Ibid., Book 2, 584.
38 "Because a great multitude cannot be received like a small body, and therefore the small and distinct bodies that were in a Roman legion could be positioned so that they could be received within each other and help one another with ease" (ibid., Book 3, 593).
39 "*Però è necessario in uno esecito che vi sia assai corpi, e ogni corpo abbia la sua bandiera e la sua guida; perché, avendo questo, conviene che égli abbia assai anime e, per consequente, assai vita*" (ibid., Book 2, 584).
40 Ibid., Book 3, 592.
41 "*Il medesimo ne interviene delle bandiere, perché si tengono piuttosto per fare bella una mostra, che per altro militare uso*" (ibid., Book 2, 84).
42 Ibid., Book 2, 584
43 "*Perché, ferma che è la bandiera, i centurioni e i capidieci possono giudicare a occhio il luogo loro, e, ridotisi i sinistri da sinistra, i destri da destra con le distanze loro consuete, i fanti guidati dalla regola loro e dalle differenze de'contrassegni, possono essere subito ne'luoghi propri*" (ibid., Book 2, 579).
44 "*Ma noi hoggi non ce ne serviamo ad altro, che à dare loro piu soldo che à gli altri, & à fare che facciano qualche factione particolare*" (ibid., Book 2, 562). The third appearance of *anima* occurs at the start of Book 1, when Machiavelli as narrator discusses the untimely death of Cosimo Rucellai and, in the course of noting him as a good friend and citizen, observes in a parenthetical: "For I do not know what was so much his (not even excepting his soul [*anima*]) that it would not have been willingly spent by him for his friends" (ibid., Book 1, 532). On its own, this parenthetical could be dismissed as rhetorical flourish. However, if considered beside the other two occurrences of *anima* it contrasts a traditional concept of soul

with the materialist notion of *anima* that emerges later and which is compatible with Lucretius' notion of *animus* in Books 2 and 3 of *De rerum natura*.

45 "... *il quale con lo animo, con le parole, con lo esemplo, tenga gli altri fermi & disposti al combattere*" (ibid., Book 2, 584).

46 Ibid., Book 2, 584.

47 Ibid., Book 2, 574.

48 Ibid., Book 2, 574.

49 Ibid., Book 2, 572.

50 Chapter 3 below discusses in depth the function of music as an anchoring principle of the militia's discipline.

51 Ibid., Book 3, 593.

52 Ibid., Book 2, 573.

53 See Pedullà, "Machiavelli the Tactician: Math, Graphs, Knots in *The Art of War*," 85.

54 "*Haec eadem ratio naturam animi atque animai corpoream docet esse; ubi enim propellere membra, corripere ex somno corpus mutareque vultum atque hominem totum regere ac versare videtur, quorum nil fiere sine tactu posse videmus nec tactum porro sino corpore, none fatendumst corporea natura animum constare animamque*" (Lucretius, *De rerum natura* 3.160–165).

55 "*constare rotundis perquam seminibus debet perquamque minutis*" (Ibid., 3.186–187).

56 "*prima cietur enim, parvis perfecta figuris; inde calor motus et venti caeca potestas accipit, inde aer; inde omnia mobilitantur: concutitur sanguis, tum viscera persentiscunt omnia, postremis datur ossibus atque medullis*" (ibid., 3.245–3.260).

57 Ibid., 3.177–3.258.

58 Ibid., 3.276–3.281. See also Pierre-François Moreau, *Lucrèce. L'âme* (Paris: Presses Universitaires de France, 2002), 39.

59 Lucretius, *De rerum natura* 3.231–3.322; also, Moreau, *Lucrèce. L'âme*, 31; and Vittorio Morfino on the implications of Lucretian fibrous temporalities in "Tra Lucrezio e Spinoza: la 'filosofia' di Machiavelli," in *Machiavelli: immaginazione e contingenza*, ed. Filippo del Lucchese, Luca Sartorello, and Stefano Visentin (Pisa: Edizioni ETS, 2006), 90–1.

60 Lucretius describes this nature as "swift" (*celeris*) even when comparing it to the other constituents of soul—*heat (calor), air (aer), and wind (ventus)*—all of which are superlatively fast. At one point in Book 3 (*De rerum natura* 3.279–3.281), he names it the "force of motion" (*vis mobilis*) in the mixed soul which distributes motion to the other three: "*sic calor atque aer et venti caeca potestas mixta creant unam naturam et mobilis illa vis, initum motus ab se quae dividit ollis, sensifer unde oritur primum per viscera motus*" (Ibid., 3.269–3.272)

61 See ibid., 3.231–3.257, 3.345–3.366, and 3.270–3.275.

62 "*il n'y a pas ici une théorie de la sensation. Il y a une théorie de l'unité de la sensation et de l'excitation*" (Pierre-François Moreau, *Lucrèce. L'âme*, 36).

63 Machiavelli, *Art of War*, Book 2.
64 Machiavelli does allow that at the militia's inception, prior civilian occupations and social class exercised an influence on the roles assigned to draftees. For instance, the initial distinction between those enrolled into the infantry and those enrolled as cavalry operates from the distinction between the rural peasantry and urban aristocracy. However, since Colonna stipulates that for reasons of utility all soldiers will learn to ride horses as well as swim, he sets in motion the potential for a progressive redistribution of postings, since surely peasants discovered to be consummate horsemen will be placed in that part of the militia where their strengths are of most use. See, ibid., Book 2, 566–70.
65 *Animo* occurs twenty-eight times. The adjective *animoso* occurs another seven.
66 Machiavelli, *Art of War*, Book 1, 545.
67 Ibid., Book 4, 619.
68 Ibid., Book 2, 584.
69 Ibid., Book 1, 533.
70 Ibid., Book 1, 534.
71 Ibid., Book 1, 542.
72 Ibid., Book 4, 626.
73 Ibid., Book 3, 611.
74 Machiavelli, *Art of War*, Book 7, 675.
75 Ibid., Book 1, 532.
76 Ibid., Book 1, 551.
77 Ibid., Book 7, 688.
78 "...*che uno uomo animoso sarà sopra uno cavallo vile e uno vile sopra uno animoso*" (Ibid., Book 2, 567). See also Machiavelli, *Discourses,* Book 2, Chapter 18, where Machiavelli describes the critique of cavalry in the same terms but adds that the Parthian style of combat outdid the Romans by deception rather than force (*"ingannato che sforzato"*). See also the comments by Christopher Lynch (xxxii–xxxiii) on Machiavelli's intent to combine Eastern and Western modes of combat in Niccolo Machiavelli, *Art of War*, trans. and ed. by Christopher Lynch (Chicago: University of Chicago Press, 2003).
79 "*donde conviene che queste disparitadi d'animo facciano disordine,*" Machiavelli, *Art of War,* Book 2.
80 For Lucretius' most extensive discussion of the *clinamen*, see *De rerum natura* 2.216–2.293.
81 Ibid., 2.216–2.220 and 2.290–2.293. Also, see Cicero, *De natura deorum*, 1.69 and *De finibus*, 1.18–20.
82 Palmer's analysis supports Machiavelli's interest in this aspect of atomic physics. Out of twenty-two marginal comments on Book 2, three focus on precisely Lucretius'

discussion of the swerve in his copy of the *De rerum natura*. See *Reading Lucretius in the Renaissance,* 82.

83 "non posse tamen prorumpere equorum vim cupidam tam de subitoquam mens avet ipsa," ibid., 2.264–2.265.

84 For Colonna's discussions of the Parthian problem, see Machiavelli, *Art of War,* Books 2 and 3 and also Machiavelli, *Discourses,* Book 2, Chapter 18, where Machiavelli notes as well the success of the Parthians over the Romans.

85 Ibid., Book 2, 566.

86 This raises the suggestion that Machiavelli acknowledges two different horizons of warfare based on two different aspects of Lucretian physics, i.e., the immanent connection of cause and effect and spontaneous declination from projected trajectories.

87 Ibid., Book 5, 641–2.

88 However, it would appear to be only the beginning of the critique, since not only does Machiavelli divide the world in half by distinguishing between the Roman and Parthian modes of combat, but he also appears to leave out entirely combat by sea. He does, however, return in Book 1 to fault the Venetians for hiring a mercenary captain to defend Vicenza instead of employing their own sea captains in land combat, since "even more easily would a sea captain—who is used to combat with sea, winds and men—become a land captain, where one fights only with men, than would a land captain become a sea captain" (Ibid., Book 1, 549–55). Machiavelli even has Colonna remind the reader of the limitations of his treatment of warfare when, at the end of Book 7, Colonna emphasizes the importance of sea warfare and his lack of experience with it: "*Di quello di mare io non presumerei parlare, per non ne avere alcuna notizia; ma lascieronne parlare a' genovesi e a' viniziani, i quali con simili studi hanno per lo addietro fatto gran cose*" (Ibid., Book 7, 684). As will be seen in the next chapter, Machiavelli's restriction of his reasoning to a certain form of land combat would not be so troubling were it not for the influence of the second-century Greek author, Aelianus Tacticus, on Machiavelli's account of warfare in the *Art of War*. For instance, at the start of Chapter 2 of his *Tactica Theoria*, Aelianus clearly distinguishes between modes of combat according to those fought πεζική and those fought ναυτική, i.e., by infantry or by navy, and even a superficial examination demonstrates that Aelianus does not share Colonna's (or Machiavelli's) apparent reservations with combat on horseback. See Filippo Di Cataldo, "*Eliano—La 'Tactica Theoria*'," (Ph.D. diss., Università degli studi di Catania, 2009–10), 34–5.

Chapter 2

1 Maurice of Nassau and Gustavus Adolphus of Sweden—among others—found it influential precisely on the basis of its extended discussions of small unit tactics,

description of the intermediate officer structure, and its reliance on tactical diagrams to add precision to accounts of troop formations and movements. Even when Machiavelli scholars acknowledge these features of the text, they see the text's plethora of technical details as a critical limitation of it that narrows the scope of its importance, especially when compared to Machiavelli's other works where his timeless political philosophy seems to them more clearly spelled out. For approaches that acknowledge the importance of the *Art of War* in Machiavelli's transmission history, see Ioannis Evrigenis, *Fear of Enemies and Collective Action* (Cambridge: Cambridge University Press, 2008), Chapter 4, especially 72–6; Gabriele Pedullà, "Machiavelli the Tactician: Math, Graphs, and Knots in *The Art of War*," in *The Radical Machiavelli*, ed. Filippo Del Lucchese, Fabio Frosini, and Vittorio Morfino (Leiden: Brill, 2015), 81–5; and Clifford Rogers, "Tactics and the Face of Battle," in *European Warfare: 1350–1750*, ed. Frank Tallett and D. J .B. Trim (Cambridge: Cambridge University Press, 2010), 220.

2 On the very different careers the manuscript of Aelianus had in the Byzantine and Latin traditions, see Eliano in *La "Tactica Theoria,"* 2–3.

3 The shift to the Swiss pike square was reinforced by developments in steel technology. At the turn of the fifteenth century, Milanese smiths perfected new techniques that greatly strengthened the steel used in armor. Crossbows and longbows could not reliably penetrate quenched high-carbon steel, making the shift to the relatively inaccurate and slower handgun necessary. As Rogers explains in "Tactics and the Face of Battle," 210–11, a longbow or a steel-bowed crossbow could produce a maximum of 130 to 200 joules of kinetic energy. On the other hand, a well-charged musket ball left the barrel with over 2,700 joules of energy and even a cavalryman's pistol packed a thump of over 1,000 joules.

4 An archer could shoot nine or ten arrows a minute, whereas a fifteenth- and sixteenth-century arquebusier would be lucky to get off ten shots an hour; see ibid., 210–17.

5 At the battle of Agincourt in 1415, the English deployed only two types of soldier—archers and dismounted men at arms. One hundred years later, armies included six types of footmen, up to six types of horsemen along with field artillery, organized into relatively independent units.

6 As Bert Hall states in *Weapons and Warfare in Renaissance Europe* (Baltimore: Johns Hopkins University Press, 1997): "Pikemen had to be prepared to sacrifice part of their formation in order to maintain the integrity of the whole, and any failure on their part usually resulted in the breaking up of the entire mass" (32).

7 See David Eltis, *The Military Revolution in Sixteenth Century Europe* (New York: Barnes & Noble, 1998), 111. Pike squares sixty or seventy-five ranks deep had a host of advantages over the shallow medieval style infantry line they displaced. The

formation possessed great mass and a potential to generate momentum that medieval infantry, arranged at a depth of one or two lines, could not match.

8 Two authors who reflect on the question of whether Aelianus rises to the level of serious tactician are Alphonse Dain in *Histoire du texte d'Élien le Tacticien des origines à la fin du Moyen Âge* (Paris: Société d'édition "Les Belles lettres," 1946) and Gabriele Pedullà, "Machiavelli the Tactician: Math, Graphs, and Knots in *The Art of War*." After considering the option that Aelianus was a dilettante playing at wargames in his text, Dain concludes: *"C'est par l'automatisme discipliné des petites unités qu'on forme une armée manoeuvrière"* (46). Both Dain and Pedullà agree that Aelianus's focus on the small unit and the individual soldier introduces something new to the history of war theory. For Pedullà: "The purely strategic level—that is the conducting of the battle or even of the entire campaign—is here superseded by a shift to individual units (in only one case a diagram of *De instruendis aciebus* shows more than 200 armed men, while in the majority of cases they are just a few dozen," (ibid., 88) and then later: "Between the general and the soldier there is a space to be filled; otherwise the phalanx will collapse" (ibid., 88). Both authors are in agreement that Aelianus's influence stems from the framework he created for tactically relating the actions of the individual soldier to the overall functioning of larger formations whether a battalion, legion or army as a whole.

9 Eliano, *Eliano—La "Tactica Theoria,"* 63–9.
10 Machiavelli, *Art of War*, 577.
11 *"… unum remedium est ut alam cornumque replices et rotundes, quatenus conversi tui sociorum terga defendant; sed in angulo ipsius extremitatis fortissimo collocentur, quia ibi impetus amplior fieri consuevit."* Vegetius, *Epitoma rei militaris*, 102–03.
12 At ibid., section 3.19, 102–03, and 3.14, 94–7.
13 For Dain, *Histoire du texte d'Élien le Tacticien des origines à la fin du Moyen Âge*, Aelianus plays a critical role in the history of war because, *"…il met en balance les théories purement rationnelles de la doctrine militaire des Grecs avec la pratique réelle des opérations qui ont rendu illustre le nom Romain. A ses yeux, les Romains savent faire la guerre, les Grecs savent comment en écrit et on en discute."* (43)
14 See Giovanni Battista Della Valle, *Vallo* (Venice: Nicolò d'Aristotile, 1529), especially Book 2.
15 Roberto Valturio, *De re militari* (Verona: Nicolai, 1472), especially Book 10.
16 See J. R. Hale, "A Humanistic Visual Aid. The Military Diagram in the Renaissance," *Renaissance Studies* 2, no. 2 (Oct. 1988): 280–98.
17 Pedullà, "Machiavelli the Tactician: Math, Graphs, and Knots in *The Art of War*," 88; and Eliano, *Eliano—La "Tactica Theoria."*
18 Machiavelli, *Art of War*, 690.

19 Yves Winter, in *Machiavelli and the Orders of Violence* (Cambridge: Cambridge University Press, 2018), importantly emphasizes Machiavelli's theatricality of violence and how, for Machiavelli, political violence generates an idiom of marks and signs. Though Winter briefly discusses the violence of warfare, his observations concerning the play of signs focus mainly on punishment and the inception of signs due to the shock of extraordinary violence (see especially 143–66).

20 Aelianus, *De instruendis aciebus*, 71.

21 Ibid., 71 and Eliano, *Eliano—La "Tactica Theoria,"* 32.

22 Eliano, *Eliano—La "Tactica Theoria,"* 32.

23 An important difference exists between the potential audiences of the two texts. Through his emphasis on definition and the consistent use of terms, Aelianus makes his text available to a potentially wider audience than does Machiavelli. It is clear in the exchanges between Colonna and Cosimo Rucellai, Zanobi Buondelmonti, Batista della Palla, and Luigi Alamanni that, at a minimum, Colonna's interlocutors are already well versed in contemporary styles of warfare and are acquainted with ancient sources on war.

24 Notice here the use of letters that, when combined, can form higher orders of meaning in a sense that parallels closely how Lucretius reasons about the *primordia* as building blocks of mixed bodies, which Lucretius also explains using the image of the alphabet as the basis of linguistic meaning construction in *De rerum natura*. Michael Mallett in *Mercenaries and their Masters* (Haverton: Pen and Sword, 2019) stipulates that upper level officers could be relied on to be literate and actively engaged with classical sources on war; as he states: "Both the fourteenth and fifteen centuries produced their share of military theorists and military treatises. How far were these, or the classical sources on which they relied heavily, read and studied by soldiers? That most of the leaders of Italian armies were literate can be taken for granted: that some of them...had important and established libraries was an established fact" (176). Machiavelli's diagrams present themselves as a kind of language whose *segni* and *caratteri* form building blocks that can be progressively combined in ways similar to the way sentences are generated through an alphabet and principles of grammar. See Lucretius, *De rerum natura*, 2.688–699 and 2.1012–1022; Barbara Spackman, "Politics on the Warpath: Machiavelli's *Art of War*," in *Machiavelli and the Discourse of Literature*, ed. Albert Russell Ascoli and Victoria Kahn (New York: Cornell University Press, 1993), 179–95, and Winter, *Machiavelli and the Orders of Violence*, 157.

25 Plato, *Laws*, 626a.

26 For Machiavelli, they serve an additional purpose—they act as an important medium through which the potential prince can ceaselessly practice war, since, as the *Prince*, Chapter 14, opens: *"Debbe dunque uno principe non avere altro*

obietto né altro pensiero né prendere cosa alcuna per sua arte, fuora della guerra e ordini e disciplina di essa: perché quella è sola arte che si aspetta a chi comanda, ed è di tanta virtù che non solamente mantiene quelli che sono nati principi, ma molte volte fa gli uomini di private fortuna salire a quello grado" (157). See also Harvey Mansfield, *Machiavelli's Virtue* (Chicago: University of Chicago Press, 1996), Chapter 8.

27 Or simply behave like wolves with them; see Plato, *Republic*, 395c and 414e–417b.
28 He employs *proporzione* rarely, but notably, in his other major works. *Proporzione* occurs five times in the *Discourses* at 1.55 and 3.22 where it contrasts the leadership styles of Manlius Torquatus, Appius Claudius, and Valerius Corvinus. In the *Prince* it occurs in Chapters 6 and 14. In Chapter 6, *proporzione* describes the relationship of Hiero to Moses, Cyrus, Romulus, and Theseus during a discussion of the theme of both *arma alienis* and *arma propriis* and armed and unarmed prophets. In Chapter 14, the term appears during a discussion of the same distinction where he states: "For there is no proportion between one who is armed and one who is unarmed (*"Perché da uno armato a uno disarmato non è proporzione alcuna"*), and it is not reasonable that whoever is armed obey willingly whoever is unarmed, and that someone unarmed be secure among armed servants." The term does not occur in the *Florentine Histories*. For discussion of *proporzione* in these contexts, see Chapter 5 below and the discussion of the category of mixed forces.
29 Machiavelli, *Art of War*, 537–9.
30 See Mansfield, *Machiavelli's Virtue*, 198–202.
31 *"Tal che, se uno re non si ordina in modo che i suoi fanti a tempo di pace stieno contenti tornarsi a casa e vivere delle loro arti, conviene di necessità che rovini; perché non si truova la più pericolosa fanteria che quella che è composta di coloro che fanno la guerra come per loro arte"* (Machiavelli, *Art of War*, 541). Though Machiavelli cautions against the practice of the art of war during peacetime, he is of an entirely different mind about the *study* of war. As he states (Machiavelli, *Art of War*, 540): *"Debbe adunque una città bene ordinate volere che questa studio di guerra si usi ne' tempi di pace per esercizio e ne' tempi di guerra per necessità e per gloria, e al publico solo lasciarla usare per arte, come fece Roma."*
32 However, Machiavelli shows how the strengths of the phalanx can be combined with the cohort tactics of the Romans in a way that allows the phalanx portion of Colonna's unit to reform the formation in a way the Greek phalanxes could not. Compare especially Colonna's examination of the phalanx in the *Art of War*, Book 3, 591–2, to his analysis of the combined legion/phalanx formation in Book 3, 596–7.
33 This order is based on the order they assume when practicing their most basic skills—what Machiavelli terms "the snails." Notice here Colonna indicates the limits of the dialogue format in referring to the practice of the snails (*"chiocciole"*), whose

description he postpones because it is easier for him to demonstrate that maneuver, "more with deeds than with words" ("*più con i fatti che con le parole*"); see Machiavelli, *Art of War*, 575.

34 Ibid., 577.

35 Doubling the flank is a tactic to outflank or to avoid being outflanked by the enemy. There are two ways to accomplish it—"deceptively," by placing the cavalry and the light-armed velites on the wings of the formation and, "genuinely," when those behind the front line move to occupy the empty spaces between the soldiers who form the front. Aelianus explains the value of the maneuver under circumstances when it could be useful to form a very narrow front and double or quadruple the depth of the phalanx to increase the pressure from the soldiers whose forward momentum helps to break through the enemy's line.

36 Ibid., 577.

37 The cavalry are also not placed among the hoplites but outside the formation.

38 And this is only the first difficulty, since Machiavelli adds as well extraordinary pikes to round out his formation of 600.

39 Eliano, *Eliano—La "Tactica Theoria*," Chapter 10.

40 Aelianus defines *virtus*/ἀρετὴ as a function of three factors: *magnitudo* (μεγέθος), *robore corporis* (ῥώμη), and *peritia militari* (ἐμπειρία). See, *Eliano—La "Tactica Theoria*," Chapter 13.

41 A main problem Machiavelli underlines is that doubling by file ("*raddoppiare le file*") will not allow for an odd-numbered line; see *Art of War*, 576.

42 On the other hand, Aelianus consistently champions mathematics, and especially principles of geometry over the concrete issues raised by deployment of troops in the field. See, for instance, *Eliano—La "Tactica Theoria*," "Proemio," 29.

43 See Eliano, *Eliano—La "Tactica Theoria*," Chapter 8, 43–5.

44 Barbara Spackman, in "Politics on the Warpath: Machiavelli's *Art of War*," emphasizes the semiotic force of tactical language in general and in Machiavelli's *Art of War* in particular when she argues, "warfare has little to do with brute force and much to do with brute semiosis; it aims not so much to destroy the enemy's physical resources as to construct a seemingly invincible discourse of power" (180). See also Vickie Sullivan on the unarmed prophet in "Patricide and the Plot of the Prince: Cesare Borgia and Machiavelli's Italy," *American Political Science Review* 88, no. 4 (1994): 887–900.

45 In an "open order," each soldier occupies four cubits. In a "close order," they occupy one cubit, which is to say that the shields of each soldier overlap and are contiguous with the other soldiers in the same rank. In the "compact order," soldiers are so close they are immobile, important in a formation used mainly to resist an enemy's charge.

46 "*È necessario pertanto fare due cose: prima, avere questa battaglia piena di contrassegni; l'altra, tenere sempre questo ordine: che quegli medesimi fanti stieno sempre in quelle medesime file*" (Machiavelli, *Art of War*, 578).

47 "*Perché i soldati chi sanno fare questo bene sono soldati pratichi e ancora che non avessero mai veduti nemeci in viso, si possono chiamare i soldati vecchi*" (ibid., 578).
48 As Machiavelli (ibid., 684) has Colonna explain to his interlocutors, his point is not to teach them about ancient modes, "*ma come in questi tempi si potesse ordinare una milizia che avesse piú virtú che quella che si usa.*"
49 Ibid., 541–2.
50 In fact, Colonna contends that with the adjustment of these term limits, the same men began to serve longer terms in the legions. As a consequence, the legions became increasingly autonomous and began to exercise the power to make and unmake the emperors.
51 In the case of the veterans, there just happened to be a lot more of them. Perhaps this is the reason behind Machiavelli retaining the error that shows up in successive editions of the *Art of War*. In tabulating the number of *capidieci* in the battalion, Colonna in Book 2 comes up with 1,500 for their overall number when the proper solution is closer to 600. In a battalion of 6,000 men, roughly one tenth of them figure as *capidieci*. However, this creates a problem. Unlike the *conestabili* and *capitano*, the *capidieci* and *centurioni* are part of their formations. They will see combat, and they will experience casualties, and in some confrontations those casualties may be severe. Given this inevitability, the legion always requires an excess of lower level officers, even if the soldiers in question do not formally occupy the role of the *capidieci*. Machiavelli retained the number 1,500 for the total number of *capidieci* in his legion in successive publications at Rome, Florence, Venice, and Geneva through the 1550s. Several of these editions appeared during his lifetime and, yet, the number remained unchanged despite the obvious calculation error. For this reason, when Christopher Lynch in his translation of the *Art of War* (Chicago: University of Chicago Press, 2003, "Interpretive Essay," 47, note 66) corrects the text to read 600 despite the occurrence of 1,500 in the original manuscript, this may obscure an important feature embedded in Machiavelli's disciplinary regime. The logic of the officer grades is clear. There must exist *capidieci* who have all the requisite skills of this lowest level officer grade even if they lack the title and the post that comes with the commission. Why the number 1,500? This approximates the number of veterans (*triarii*) Machiavelli postulates his legion will contain. They constitute one quarter of the 6,000 total number composing his *battaglione*. As Machiavelli describes the relationship between those who occupy the same rank in Book 4 of the *Art of War* when speaking of the grade of constable: "*né mi curerei che fussero sei uomini di pari grado, acciò che ciascuno di loro facesse a gara per essere promosso alla seconda battaglia*" (610). On the persistence of the error through successive editions, compare Niccolò Machiavelli, *Arte della guerra* (Florence: li Heredi di Philippo di Giunta, 1521), Book 2, page 33, with the Philippo di Giunta 1528 edition, Book 2, page 32, as well as with the same passage in Niccolò

Machiavelli, *I sette libri dell'arte della guerra di Nicolo Machiavelli, cittadino e segretario fiorentino* (Venice, 1550).

52 *"Ma per fuggire quel danno che poteva fare loro questo continuo esercizio, poiché il tempo non variava, ei variavano gli uomini, e andavano temporeggiando in modo con le loro legioni, che in quindici anni sempre l'avevano rinnovate"* (Machiavelli, *Art of War*, 541). As Yves Winter argues in "The Prince and His Art of War": "Warfare must be hemmed in by civil life, which is accomplished by turning citizens or subjects into soldiers and by returning them to be citizens or subjects in times of peace" (178).

53 See also Machiavelli, *Art of War*, Book 4, 591 and 606–07.

54 On some of the implications of these proportions, see Ugo Dotti, *Niccolò Machiavelli; La fenomenologia del potere* (Milan: Feltrinelli Editore, 1980), 71–83, on the element of "giacobinismo" in Machiavelli's military reasoning; also Louis Althusser, *Écrits philosophiques et politiques* (Paris: Éditions Stock/IMEC, 1995), 140–68; Jérémie Barthas, *L'argent n'est pas le nerf de la guerre: essai sur un prétendue erreur de Machiavel* (Rome: École Française de Rome, 2011), 15–16, and Antonio Gramsci, *Quaderni del carcere, v. 2*, ed. Valentino Gerratana (Turin: Guilio Einaudi, 1977), quaderno (section 162) 1038–39. Notably, for Barthas: "*Point de mystère dans son éviction de la chancellerie au moment du renversement de la république du Grand Conseil, si son activité pratique, et notamment le projet d'armer le peuple, n'est pas comprise comme celle d'un fonctionnaire neuter, mais bien comme celle d'un défenseur de l'État Populaire et d'un combattant pour la liberté*" (107–08).

55 Human beings are distributed on the basis of the quality of their experience and the physiological changes they undergo as they age. Colonna emphasizes this fact when he argues that term limits should extend from eighteen to thirty-five because it is the period when "the legs, the hands and the eyes respond to one another" (*"le gambe, le mani e l'occhio rispondevano l'uno all'altro"*); Machiavelli, *Art of War*, 541.

56 Colonna also adds later in Book 3 that the numbers that populate the battlefield correspond as well to grades of rank and a system of honor: "*Vuolsi ancora che questi numeri sieno scala a' gradi degli onori degli eserciti*" (Machiavelli, ibid., 609).

57 Machiavelli, ibid., 578–80.

58 Machiavelli, *Art of War*, 694–5.

59 "*. . . la prima et la più utile, è farla tutta massiccia, et darle la forma di due quadri.*"

60 In the first way of forming the square, the pike men simply double their lines and the rest of the troops form behind them. See Machiavelli, ibid., 692–3.

61 Machiavelli, ibid., 579.

62 In Book 5, Colonna equates the discipline necessary to transform the base square figure for that enemy which others do not see but that one fears ("*contro a nimico che altri non vede ma che si teme*", 633) with the possession of military

discipline ("*né è altro la disciplina militare che sapere bene comandare ed eseguire queste cose*," 633).

63 The need for considerable autonomy on the part of the soldiers stems from the human body itself. For instance, Machiavelli points out how the distance from shoulder to shoulder is greater than the distance from chest to back. If the unit needs to complete an about-face in order to engage the enemy, the spacing between the individual soldiers remains the same. However, whenever the unit faces left or right, the spacing between soldiers will be thrown out of whack, since the distance from one shoulder to the other is greater than the distance from the chest to the back. Colonna expects the soldiers to work out the spacing issues by themselves.

64 In the *Art of War*, Book 4, Machiavelli indicates how flexibly even the Romans employed these arrangements. At the battle of Zama (202 BC), Scipio Africanus combined *principes* and *triarii* into one line with intervals arranged, not for retreat, but to withstand the charge of Hannibal's elephants. Scipio placed the *hastati* on the wings of the formation. This formation does not permit retreat or renewal of the lines. Extending this line of tactical logic could see units depending less on geometrical formation like lines and squares and more on loosely organized hetereogeneous clouds of force values that make apparent disorganization—from the standpoint of Euclidean reasoning—into an overall strategy and tactical advantage. Consider also the discussion of the Parthian form of warfare in Section 8, Chapter 1 above.

65 See Markus Fischer, *Well Ordered License* (Boston: Lexington Books, 2000), Chapter 3.

66 How the apparently opposing requirements of autonomic spontaneity and machinic responsiveness could co-exist in one and the same individual would be difficult to resolve if Machiavelli did not rely on a Lucretian natural physics where mixed bodies exhibit behaviors attributable to both kinds of causality.

67 This raises an interesting issue concerning the progressive effects of Colonna's discipline on the soldiers. For Colonna, the effects of discipline include leveling out differences of ferocity, strength, and fearfulness naturally present among human beings. The ferocious Gauls can be successfully opposed by less ferocious troops with better discipline. Timid soldiers grow less fearful due to their being better ordered. Colonna even speaks about his troops fighting with *ozio* in the *Art of War*, Book 3: "*guardate con quanta virtú, sicurtà e ozio ammazzano il nimico*" (599). See also Michel Foucault, *Surveiller et punir: Naissance de la prison*, 159–99.

68 Machiavelli's reliance on distinctions involving number, figuration, and proportionality here raise an important question whether and how the Euclidean tradition may have influenced his reasoning. For instance, where Euclid Book 5 reasons about proportionality around magnitude, Book 7 reasons about proportionality and number. Euclid's use of a line segment in the diagrams of that book to signify a unit (and the controversy this engendered) bears a striking likeness

to how Machiavelli designates the individual soldier as his *primordia* anchoring the inquiry Colonna launches in the *Art of War*. See Euclid, *The Thirteen Books of the Elements, Volume 2*, trans. Thomas L. Heath (New York: Dover, 1956), 277–95.

69 As Mansfield argues in *Machiavelli's Virtue*: "For the expansion of the art of war to include all politics gives Machiavelli's doctrine a new psychology that frees it from tradition and morality" (199). For warfare as a battle of and for consciousness, see also Sullivan, "Patricide and the Plot of the Prince: Cesare Borgia and Machiavelli's Italy," on the unarmed prophet, 897–8.

70 "... *come chi balla procede con il tempo della musica e, andando con quella, non erra, così uno esercito, ubbidendo nel muoversi a quell suono, non si disordina. E però variavano il suono, secondo che volevano variare il moto e secondo che volevano accendere or quietare o fermare gli animi degli uomini*" (Machiavelli, *Art of War*, 584).

71 The theme of Chapter 1 resurfaces here along with Machiavelli's distinction between *anima* and *animo*: "*Perché è necessario in uno esercito che vi sia assai corpi, e ogni corpo abbia la sua bandiera e la sua guida; perché avendo questo, conviene che'egli abbia assai anime e, per consequente, assai vita. Deono adunque i fanti camminare secondo la bandiera, e la bandiera muoversi secondo il suono; il quale suono, bene ordinato, comanda allo esercito*" (ibid., 584).

72 See Dante, *Paradiso*, canto XXV, 133–5.

73 "... *sappiendo tenere bene le file, talmente che né luogo né moto le disordinino, intendo bene i comandamenti del capo mediante il suono e sappiendo di subito ritornare nel suo luogo, possono poi facilmente, come io dissi con l'altre battaglie, in un esercito giusto operare*" (Machiavelli, *Art of War*, 574). See also Machiavelli, ibid., 606–07, and Colonna's discussion of the four exercises fundamental to training the troops. In particular the fourth trains the soldiers to recognize the command of the captain, "*per virtú delle suono e delle bandiere*," and Colonna's preference for the Greek and Roman mode of employing horns and trumpets over flutes and cithers simply because these are the most likely to be heard whatever the noise level for an infantry that will fight in silence (see Machiavelli, ibid., 598 and 611).

74 See Mikael Hörnquist, "Machiavelli's Military Project and the *Art of War*," in *The Cambridge Companion to Machiavelli*, ed. John M. Najemy (Cambridge: Cambridge University Press, 2010), 115–17, for the obstacles Machiavelli experienced when he attempted to organize the Florentine militia.

Chapter 3

1 An earlier version of this chapter appeared as, "A War of One's Own: Mercenaries and the Theme of arma aliena in Machiavelli's, *il Principe*," in the *British Journal of the History of Philosophy* 18, no.4 (2010): 541–74.

2 For studies that approach the topic of Italian mercenaries in the fourteenth and fifteenth centuries as an increasingly organized market in contract force, see Daniel Waley, "The Army of the Florentine Republic from the Twelfth to the Fourteenth Century," in *Florentine Studies: Politics and Society in Renaissance Florence*, ed. Nicolai Rubinstein (Evanston: Northwestern University Press, 1968), 70–108. See also Eliot Cohen, "A Revolution in Warfare," *Foreign Affairs* 75, no. 2 (March/April, 1996): 37–54; Peter Warren Singer, *Corporate Warriors* (Ithaca, NY: Cornell University Press, 2003), 22–6; C. C. Bayley, *War and Society in Renaissance Florence* (Toronto: University of Toronto Press, 1961), especially Chapter 1; and Deborah Avant, *The Market for Force* (Cambridge: Cambridge University Press, 2005).

3 Auxiliary arms are soldiers loaned to some prince or republic by another prince or republic. Machiavelli describes them as being "more dangerous" than mercenary soldiers: "*In somma, nelle mercenarie è più pericolosa la ignavia, nelle ausiliare, la virtù.*" See *Prince* Chapter 13 and the discussion of auxiliaries in Chapter 4 below. All page references to Machiavelli refer to Machiavelli's, *Opere*, Volumes 1–3, ed. Corrado Vivanti (Turin: Einaudi-Gallimard, 1997).

4 Discussions of the theme of the "arms of others" in Machiavelli generally focus on how his negative critique of mercenaries functions as a plank of support for the militia project. For instance, Michael Mallet, "The Theory and Practice of Warfare," in *Machiavelli and Republicanism*, ed. Gisela Bock, Quentin Skinner, and Maurizio Viroli (Cambridge: Cambridge University Press, 1990), 173–80, argues that Machiavelli's critique of mercenaries is important not for his practical ideas about war but rather for his "concern to re-create the links between the civilian and military spheres, to draw the military world of war back into the heart of political and civic life, to use military training to encourage civic virtue and patriotism." Mallett argues that Machiavelli's critique aims to undercut the attractiveness of mercenaries by making the condottieri objects of ridicule and creating support for a citizen-based militia. For similar assessments of the function of Machiavelli's critique of the condottieri, see Louis Althusser, *Machiavelli and Us* (New York: Verso, 1999), 84–6; C. C. Bayley, *War and Society in Renaissance Florence*, Chapters 1, 2, and 5; Federico Chabod, *Machiavelli and the Renaissance* (London: Bowes and Bowes, 1958), especially Chapter II.4; Maury Feld, "Machiavelli's Militia and Machiavelli's Mercenaries," in *The Military, Militarism, and the Polity*, ed. Michel Martin and Ellen McCrate (New York: The Free Press, 1984), 72–92; Benedetto Fontana, *Hegemony and Power* (Minneapolis: University of Minnesota Press, 1993), 137; Ugo Dotti, *La fenomenologia del potere* (Milan: Feltrinelli Editore, 1980), 70–3; Felix Gilbert, *Machiavelli and Guicciardini* (Princeton: Princeton University Press, 1965), 131 & 163, and "Machiavelli: The Renaissance of the Art of War," in *Makers of Modern Strategy*, ed. Edward Earle (Princeton: Princeton University Press, 1944), 12–13; Mikael Hörnquist, *Machiavelli and Empire* (Cambridge: Cambridge University Press,

2004), esp. 86–92; also Hörnquist, "Machiavelli's Military Project and the *Art of War*," in *The Cambridge Companion to Machiavelli*, ed. John M. Najemy (Cambridge: Cambridge University Press, 2010), 112–27; Mark Hulliung, *Citizen Machiavelli* (Princeton: Princeton University Press, 1983), 39–40 and 93–4. J. G. A. Pocock, *The Machiavellian Moment* (Princeton: Princeton University Press, 1975), 200–04; Giuseppe Prezzolini, *Machiavelli*, trans. Gioconda Savini (Rome: Gherardo Casini Editore, 1967), 39–42 and 125–6; Quentin Skinner, *Machiavelli* (New York: Hill & Wang, 1981), 31–4, 75–7, and *The Foundations of Modern Political Thought*, Volume 1 (Cambridge: Cambridge University Press, 1978), Chapters 4 and 5; Claire Snyder, *Citizen Soldier and Manly Warriors* (Lanham, MD: Rowan & Littlefield, 1999), 20–2; Leo Strauss, *Thoughts on Machiavelli* (Chicago: University of Chicago Press, 1958), 63–4; Vickie Sullivan, *Machiavelli's Three Romes* (Dekalb: Northern Illinois University Press, 1996), 27–8 and 198–9, notes 22–4; Frederick Louis Taylor, *The Art of War in Italy, 1494–1529* (Cambridge: Cambridge University Press, 1921), 167–77; Miguel Vatter, *Between Form and Event: Machiavelli's Theory of Political Freedom* (Dordrecht: Kluwer, 2000), 111; Daniel Waley, "The Army of the Florentine Republic from the Twelfth to the Fourteenth Century", 108. Each of these commentators emphasizes Machiavelli's negative assessment of the condottieri. For treatments that recognize Machiavelli's nuanced treatment of mercenaries, see Claude Lefort, *Le travail de l'oeuvre Machiavel* (Paris: Gallimard, 1972), 562–3; Harvey Mansfield, *Machiavelli's Virtue* (Chicago: University of Chicago Press, 1996), especially 266–7, and Anthony Mockler, *The Mercenaries* (New York: Macmillan, 1969), 47–53.

5 In *Machiavelli*, Skinner argues that Machiavelli's attack on the mercenary system of his day was less an attack on that system than a critique of the failings of Florentine diplomacy. See also Quentin Skinner, "The Idea of Negative Liberty: Philosophical and Historical Perspectives," in *Philosophy in History*, ed. Richard Rorty, Jerome B. Schneewind, and Quentin Skinner (Cambridge: Cambridge University Press, 1980), 209–10.

6 Machiavelli dedicates the *Discourses* to Zanobi Buondelmonte and Cosimo Rucellai, both of whom he addresses as those who, like Hiero of Syracuse, deserve to be princes. By the time the first manuscript version of the *Discourses* was dedicated to them in 1521, Cosimo was dead and Zanobi in exile.

7 There are clearly at least two types of new princes, one necessarily dependent on the arms of others and the other potentially not so. A new prince like Louis XII of France, who acquires new territories could begin, as Louis did (at least in part), with their own arms. On the other hand, the new prince who is new both to their territory and to their regime would, at the outset, begin their career with the arms of others. The figures Machiavelli furnishes as examples of this type of new prince, such as Cesare Borgia and Hiero of Syracuse, are notable as examples of this kind because both began their careers by using the arms of others. However, the difficulties mount

the more these paradigmatic cases are scrutinized. For example, Machiavelli describes Hiero as transitioning to arms of his own. On the other hand, Polybius clearly recounts that Hiero stabilizes his regime by hiring *mercenaries of his own* after destroying his old, unruly mercenaries. See Polybius, *Histories*, trans. W. R. Paton (Cambridge, MA: Harvard University Press, 1922), 1.9; Machiavelli, *Prince*, Chapters 5–7 and 12. The case of Cesare Borgia is even more problematic. See especially John J. Najemy, "Machiavelli and Cesare Borgia: A Reconsideration of Chapter 7 of "The Prince"," *The Review of Politics* 75, no. 4 (2013): 543–9.

8 *Prince*, Chapter 1. See also *The Florentine Histories*, Books 4–6.

9 Thus, the principal interlocutor present throughout the *Art of War* is the *condottiere*, Fabrizio Colonna, who himself strongly opposes the use of mercenaries and expresses moral concerns about following the art of war as a profession. As Colonna states in his dialogue with Cosimo Rucellai in Book 1: "Being that this is an art by means of which men at all times cannot live honestly (*non possono vivere onestamente*). Only a republic or a kingdom can make use of this art and both of these, when well ordered, never allow any citizens or soldiers to use it as an art; nor has a good man (*alcuno uomo buono*) ever exercised it as his particular art" Opere 1, 543–4.

10 For treatments of republican civic humanism, see Hans Baron, *The Crisis of the Early Italian Renaissance* (Princeton: Princeton University Press, 1966); Mark Hulliung, *Citizen Machiavelli*; John M. Najemy, "Civic Humanism and Florentine Politics," in *Renaissance Civic Humanism*, ed. James Hankins (Cambridge: Cambridge University Press, 2000), 75–104; also, Jacob Buckhardt, *The Civilization of the Renaissance in Italy*, trans. S. G. C. Middlemore (Vienna: Phaidon Press, 1932). For a comparison of the treatments of this period by Bruni and Burckhardt, see Harvey Mansfield's "Bruni and Machiavelli on Civic Humanism," in *Renaissance Civic Humanism*, 223–46.

11 Hans Baron in *The Crisis of the Early Italian Renaissance* presents a very useful description of the early supporters of the project of a citizen militia in Florence in the fourteenth and fifteenth centuries. For further discussions of the key historical figures of this period see also Pocock, *The Machiavellian Moment*, 200–04, and Skinner, *The Foundations of Modern Political Thought*, Chapter 4.

12 Bruni analyzes the Florentine decision to allow exemptions from military service in exchange for payments to the state for hiring foreign and outside soldiers (*pecunia reipublicae soluta qua peregrini externique conducerentur milites*): "The only sure effect of this was the to render the city's own population unwarlike, so that the citizens would look to others to defend their own fortunes, and would not know how to defend themselves or fight for their country. These and many similar mistakes are committed by governors who lack experience, and though small in the beginning, such errors later give birth to massive harms." Leonardo Bruni, *The*

History of the Florentine People, (Cambridge, MA: Harvard University Press, 2007), Book 7, 101, and Book 8, 1–4 and 22–35.

13 Quoted from Hans Baron, *The Crisis of the Early Italian Renaissance*, 432. Notably, Machiavelli composes his militia of both citizens but also *sudditi* (subjects) who do not enjoy the same advantages and the same rights and are often exposed to a very different set of economic, biomedical, legal and political circumstances than citizens as a legal category. As Yves Winter argues in "The Prince and His Art of War: Machiavelli's Military Populism," *Social Research* 81, no. 1 (Spring 2014): "Incorporating subject populations poses the non-negligible risk that subject-soldiers may turn their weapons against their masters" (180).

14 On the development of this new caste of warriors, see for instance Guido Ruggiero, *The Renaissance in Italy: a Social and Cultural History of the Rinascimento* (Cambridge: Cambridge University Press, 2015), 163–5.

15 Baron, *The Crisis of the Early Italian Renaissance*, 430–31, and Bruni, *The History of the Florentine People*, Book 9, 1–11.

16 In "Civic Humanism and Florentine Politics" (223–46), Najemy convincingly describes this power shift as the consequence of a conflict, not between despotism and republicanism, but between, "two very different kinds of republicanism," which "confronted each other in this period of transformation, and civic humanism was the intellectual expression and ideological product of the ascendancy and triumph of the newer form of Florentine republicanism…civic humanism's real antagonist—the enemy it sought to defeat—was less the duke of Milan than the popular, guild republicanism that had periodically surfaced to challenge the hegemony of the elite in the thirteenth and fourteenth centuries" (81). See also Becker, *Florence in Transition* (Baltimore: Johns Hopkins Press, 1968), Chapter 3. For the meaning of terms like *optimati, nobili, popolani,* and *plebei* in the context of Florentine political life, see H. C. Butters, *Governors and Government in Early Sixteenth Century Florence* (Oxford: Clarendon Press, 1985), Chapter 1.

17 See Becker, "Economic Change and the Emerging Florentine State," *Studies in the Renaissance* 13 (1966): 14, and *Florence in Transition*, 151–200.

18 In *War and Society in Renaissance Florence,* Bayley attributes the increasing Florentine reliance on the *forestieri* as the inevitable adaptation of Florentine military and diplomatic strategy to a host of factors whose coincidence made the citizen militia an increasingly less attractive, and decidedly less effective, option. Bayley contests Bruni's argument that psychological factors were really to blame in the republic's increasing reliance on the *forestieri*. The increasing domestic constraints on the traditional war-making class—the nobility—in Florence made them just as unreliable protectors of the Florentine regime as the farmers and peasants who, as the backbone of the rural militia, found themselves increasingly bound to more and more burdensome contracts to the great landowning urban

families whose own rivalries made effective cooperation in the field questionable. The territorial expansion of Florentine territory made extended campaigns necessary, but fighting these campaigns with Florentine citizens proved supremely disruptive to industrial and agricultural necessities. See Bayley, *War and Society in Renaissance Florence*, Chapters 1 and 4.

19 See Bayley, *War and Society in Renaissance Florence*, 219–315, and John Najemy, *A History of Florence, 1200–1575* (Malden, MA: Blackwell Publishing, 2006), Chapter 7.

20 Bayley, *War and Society in Renaissance Florence*, 178–89. Bayley's analysis of the classical sources for this tradition indicates how the issue of the value and effectiveness of the citizen militia is linked by later writers like Petrarch and Boccaccio to the theme of the survival of Roman virtues in the face of Italy's inundation by the barbaric, "Germanic" *condottiere* whose "attributes of *levitas, feritas, perfidia* were constantly threatening to inundate the ancient Roman qualities of *gravitas, humanitas, fides*" (188).

21 As Bayley observes: "Amid these converging problems, it was fatally easy for Florence to turn to the large bodies of foreign professional troops, who, appearing at the critical juncture of the mid-fourteenth century, pressed their services upon her with such persistence. In the hard logic of military affairs, it was arguable that, if these formidable experts were not employed by Florence, they would be engaged by her foes, by Milan or Pisa" (Bayley, *War and Society in Renaissance Florence*, 50–2). See also William Caferro, *John Hawkwood: An English Mercenary in 14th Century Italy* (Baltimore: Johns Hopkins University Press, 2006), Chapter 3; Guido Ruggiero, *The Renaissance in Italy: A Social and Cultural History of the Rinascimento*, 163–5; Mikael Hörnquist, "Machiavelli's Military Project and the *Art of War*," 112–27, and Anthony Molho, *Florentine Public Finances in the Early Renaissance, 1400–1433* (Cambridge, MA: Harvard University Press, 1971), Chapter 2.

22 During this rebellion the citizen militia failed to muster, and the military suppression of the revolt was achieved only through the energies of Michele di Lando and the arrival of a large force of condottieri. See Bayley, *War and Society in Renaissance Florence*.

23 Bayley, 194, and Najemy, *A History of Florence, 1200–1575,* Chapters 6 & 7.

24 For instance, Bayley outlines the arguments of an anonymous fourteenth-century text, *Pulcher tractatus de materia belli*, which, while affirming the value of the citizen militia, nevertheless doubted the militia's competence and capacity to engage in the exacting standards of the "new art of war" without endangering the entire life of the state each time it engaged the enemy. See Bayley, *War and Society in Renaissance Florence*, 183–4, and Alfred Pichler, *Der pulcher tractatus de materia belli* (Graz-Wien-Leipzig: Leuschner & Lubensky, 1927).

25 *Prince,* Chapter 12.

26 For three very different discussions of the relationship between *virtù* and *fortuna*, see Strauss, "Three Waves of Modernity," in *An Introduction to Political Philosophy: Ten Essays* (Detroit: Wayne State University Press, 1989), 86–7; Sasso, *Niccolò Machiavelli* (Bologna: Il Mulino, 1993), 436; Vatter, *Between Form and Event,* Part II, Chapters 3 and 4.
27 Including Moses.
28 In "Machiavelli's Militia and Machiavelli's Mercenaries," Maury Feld adopts this view when he distinguishes mercenaries from citizen militiamen. For Feld, Machiavelli equates popular religion with popular government: "Military service is the popular cult of the state. The people assembled under arms represent the active presence of divinity in a civic context…The purchase of military service is a simonical practice, a traffic in what is holy. In hiring its defenders, the state both profanes itself and corrupts its citizens and its servants" (86).
29 *Prince,* Chapter 6, 130.
30 *"Costui spense la milizia vecchi, ordinò della nuova; lasciò le amicizie antiche, prese delle nuove; e come ebbe amicizie e soldati che fussino sua, possé in su tale fondamento edificare ogni edificio, tanto che lui durò assai fatica in acquistare e poca in mantenere"* (My emphasis, *Prince,* Chapter 6, 133).
31 Polybius, *The Histories,* 1.9.
32 I do not believe that Machiavelli means the example of this chapter to be Cesare Borgia for two reasons: 1) On the basis of the ambiguous relationship between Alexander VI and Duke Valentino/Cesare Borgia, discussed in detail below; 2) The statement by Machiavelli that appears to recommend the actions of the Duke in this chapter could refer with equal grammatical right to either one of two dukes mentioned in that same paragraph—the Duke of Milan, i.e., Francesco Sforza, *or* Duke Valentino, i.e., Cesare Borgia. Both are discussed in the same paragraph and, before Machiavelli makes the statement customarily taken to imply the career of Borgia as being worthy of imitation, he makes reference to "what was said above" concerning the laying of foundations. Sforza's career is the one discussed in the passage above. Given the way Machiavelli mentions the career of Sforza throughout the *Prince*, and elsewhere, it would seem just as plausible a reading that the Duke being referred to as worthy of imitation is, in fact, Francesco Sforza and that it is Pope Alexander VI who is being held up as worthy of imitation to then Pope Leo X, Giovanni de' Medici. See John Najemy, "Machiavelli and Cesare Borgia: A Reconsideration of Chapter 7 of 'The Prince,'" 543–9.
33 *"E questi tali sono quando è concesso ad alcuno uno stato o per danari o per grazia di chi lo concede." Prince,* Chapter 7, 133.
34 See Goodwin's vivid description of the relationship between the Sultan and his administrators in *Lords of the Horizons* (New York: Henry Holt and Company, 1998), Chapters 6 and 7.

35 *"Questi stanno semplicemente in su la volontá e fortuna di chi lo ha concesso loro, che sono dua cose volubilissime e instabili..."* (*Prince*, Chapter 7, 134)
36 *Prince*, Chapter 7, 44.
37 *"... ed è di tanta virtù, che non solamente mantiene quelli che sono nati principi, ma molte volte fa gli uomini di privata fortuna salire a quel grado"* (*Prince*, Chapter 14, 157).
38 See Alfredo Bonadeo, "The Role of the People in the Works and Times of Machiavelli," *Bibliothèque d'humanisme et renaissance* 32, no. 2 (1970), especially 363–4, for the project to implement a *renovatio militiae*.
39 Commenting on the importance of the art of command, Winter argues in "The Prince and His Art of War": "The concluding claim of *Art of War*, then, is that the crucial knowledge for the prince is not the art of commanding but of creating an army" (176). Examining the passage from *Art of War*, Book 7, shows that Colonna considers both skill sets crucial: "Non basta adunque in Italia il sapere governare uno esercito fatto, ma prima è necessario saperlo fare e poi saperlo comandare" (Machiavelli, *Opere* 1, 686). See Mansfield, *Machiavelli's Virtue*, 192.
40 The argument could be made that Sforza owed his rise to the assistance of Filippo Maria Visconti (1392–1447), then Duke of Milan, marriage to whose daughter, Bianca Maria, legitimized Sforza's accession to the title of duke. At the same time, Machiavelli's account of their relationship in the *Florentine Histories* clearly shows that he believed Sforza ascended to the duchy *despite* all the machinations of Filippo Maria.
41 However, as noted above, the *Prince* is also, of course, addressed to the "acquisitive," or "mixed," prince. "Acquisitive princes" are established princes who are "new" in the sense of having acquired a new people through the territory they have seized. Gennaro Sasso in *Studi su Machiavelli* (Naples: A. Morano, 1958), 87–8, indicates that the possibilities open to the wholly new prince were markedly different than those of acquisitive princes: "*Nel primer caso [the mixed state] il principe è ereditario in tutto, salvo che per la parte aggiunta al suo stato antiquo: se perdesse la parte nuova gli rimarebbe quella antiqua e non per questo, quindi, cesserebbe di essere principe. Nel secondo caso [Francesco Sforza], il principe è al tutto nuovo, perché il suo esser principe dipende unicamente dal principato nuovo da lui conquistato: se lo perdesse, tornerebbe ad essere, di principe, privato.*" See also the discussion of mixed forces in Chapter 5 of the present work.
42 *Prince*, Chapter 12..
43 Or because their father made the error of building a fortress there; as Machiavelli states at *Prince*, Chapter 20: "*Alla casa Sforzesca ha fatto e farà più guerra el castello di Milano, che vi edificò Francesco Sforza, che veruno altro disordine di quell stato.*"
44 This phrase, *the know-how of command*, does not describe a general, *scientific* body of knowledge abstracted from time and respect. It is a knowledge *of* tactics whose

meaning and effectiveness depend on the contexts in which they are deployed (see Chapter 3 of the present work). As Fontana in *Hegemony and Power* notes concerning the knowledge Fabrizio Colonna professes to possess in the *Art of War*: "Such a knowledge, therefore, as it uproots the preexisting and accepted conceptions of the world, presupposes simultaneously rooting itself within a historically specific subject, whose very emergence will represent the negation of the established knowledge. If the latter understands itself as the product of thought and contemplation, and since the new knowledge, which attempts to oppose and overcome it, understands itself as the continual product of an active interaction with social reality—then this new knowledge is necessarily compelled to address a subject existing within the social reality." On the other hand, Fontana's reading gives the impression that for Machiavelli there exists a single, intended unitary subject for his texts, i.e., that there is some appointed "one," or even "ones," to whom Machiavelli's texts are addressed. This ignores how the analyses in the *Prince* could benefit various figures named in its pages including several Italian *condottieri*, Pope Leo X, Lorenzo de Medici, the French, the Swiss, the Spanish—even the Ottoman Sultan! For a formulation sensitive to the multi-intentionality of Machiavelli's texts, see Strauss in *Thoughts on Machiavelli*, 115–16, 141–2, 143–4. See also note 39 above.

45 Or the Carthaginian general, Hannibal or even Hiero II. See *Prince*, Chapter 17, and Chapter 5 of the present work.
46 *Prince,* Chapter 7, 44.
47 Oliverotto da Fermo, a mercenary captain whom Machiavelli describes in *Prince*, Chapter 8, as owing his rise to crime, clearly saw the relationship between the two; Machiavelli has him describing the "greatness of Pope Alexander and of Cesare Borgia, his son, and of their undertakings" prior to the very crime that will seal his momentary accession to power. Oliverotto was shortly afterward strangled at Sinigaglia on the orders of the duke (or the pope?) in 1502.
48 *Prince,* Chapter 11.
49 Machiavelli gives a narration of this episode in "A Description of the Method Used by Duke Valentino in Killing Vitellozzo Vitelli, Oliverotto da Fermo, and Others," in *Opere* 1, 16–22. On Borgia's use of cruelty in the Romagna, see Yves Winter, *Machiavelli and the Orders of Violence* (Cambridge University Press: Cambridge, 2018), 103–07.
50 *Prince*, Chapter 17: "Era tenuto Cesare Borgia crudele; nondimanco quella sua crudeltà aveva racconccia la Romagna, unitola, ridottola in pace e in fede." (162) At this point one, of course, has to wonder whether Duke Valentino might not also, after unifying central Italy, have found himself one morning similarly divided. Notice also how later in the chapter Hiero II managed his army—organized according to Machiavelli like the Italian *condottieri*—by having it cut to pieces.

51 Ultimately, there is a question of how far Cesare ever came to act outside of the influence of his father. C. H. Clough in "Niccolo Machiavelli, Cesare Borgia, and the Francesco Troche Affair," *Medievalia et humanistica* fasc. 17, old series (1966), 129–49, argues convincingly that Borgia acted increasingly (if covertly) independently of Alexander VI, and that the goals of the two became ever more divergent.

52 See Najemy, "Machiavelli and Cesare Borgia," 552–4.

53 Much emphasis has been placed on Machiavelli's apparent admiration for the figure of Cesare, but it is important to remember here that a considerable gap existed between the historical Cesare and the version that Machiavelli portrays, and Machiavelli himself signals awareness of that gap. As C. H. Clough notes (ibid., 142): "Machiavelli as a Florentine official had taken part consistently in blocking Cesare's moves at the expense of Florentine territory; territory which had little love for Florence itself, it should be remembered. Cesare Borgia was not a hero for Machiavelli at this time but an antagonist that Machiavelli with some justifiable pride could believe he had outwitted. It is against this experience that Machiavelli's comments on Cesare in the *Prince* should be judged." Consider Machiavelli's own observations concerning Borgia in his *Legazioni*, especially those of October 10 and November 10, 1502: "*Et questo signore da calen' di octobre in qua ha speso meglio che 60 mila ducati; il che mi ha, manco di dua di fa, testificato et affermato messer Alexandro, tesaurieri. Il che io ho scripto volentieri alle Signorie vostre, acciò che elle veghino che, quando un altro è messo in disordine, elli non spende manco di quelle, né è anche meglio servito da e' soldati che si sieno loro, et per adverso che è armato bene et di arme sue fa e' medesimi effecti dovunque e' si volta.*" (*Opere* 2, 729) See also John Najemy, "Machiavelli and Cesare Borgia: A Reconsideration of Chapter 7 of 'The Prince'."

54 At the same time, the relationship between Alexander VI and Duke Valentino would serve as an excellent model for any other pope who might find himself in such an instrumental relationship with a strategically situated relative, such as Leo X did.

55 Certainly Machiavelli describes many specific people as "princes." However, many passages in Machiavelli also support the notion of a "prince" that exceeds being identified with an individual, autonomous actor. For instance, the *Discourses* shows us that there are bodies, like the Roman Senate, that are in fact composed of *many individuals* and which are noteworthy because their history is a show of the *virtù*—not of individual, autonomous actors—but of a composite body's antagonisms discharging its effects. Thus, this phrase, *effectual authority*, implies a determinate set of signs that operates "authoritatively" for a certain group or groups of people to the extent that their appetites, or desires, are determined through—i.e. coerced by—the circuit of *simulacra* shed by the "aggregate prince." See M. Vatter (*Between Form and Event*, II, Chapters 3 and 4, and Chapter 5 of the

present work) for the influence of Lucretius on Machiavelli's discussion of mixed forces.

56 Thus in *Discourses* 1.14 Machiavelli relates that, before the consul Papirius wished to engage the Samnites in the pivotal conflict of the struggle between the Romans and the Samnites, Papirius consulted the *prince of the chicken men* for the sake of knowing the auguries. This "prince" is later killed in the battle by a spear in the back after having been placed in the front ranks of the army by Papirius for having apparently lied about the pecking of the chickens.

57 See *Discourses* 2.15. See also Livy, *History of Rome*, 20.37; 23.30; 24.28. Machiavelli shows in the *Discourses* that the Romans used their allies so successfully to augment Rome that they subsequently became servants (clients?) in all but name. This alliance was so important to Hiero II that when his son, Gelo, advocated an alliance with the Carthaginians, he died so quickly afterward that suspicion for his death fell even upon Hiero himself.

58 Mansfield in *Machiavelli's Virtue*, 235–8, points to this ambiguity around princely power when he invokes the framework of *indirect government* as an alternative to the framework of direct government articulated by classical thinkers. For Mansfield: "Classical political science takes the fact about any society that is most obvious to any member or observer of the society, who rules, and designates it the most important fact. It considers most important what seems most important to the citizen or statesman. Machiavelli proposed to replace this notion of direct government with indirect government carried on by a hidden power. Instead of ruling in open light, government would be *management*. Machiavelli speaks frequently of managing (*manneggiare*) men in the up-to-date, business-school sense of the term: ruling without seeming too."

59 And in doing so he followed the examples of other mercenary armies and commanders like the Great Company, which held Athens for sixty-three years after capturing it from Water of Brienne, and the Provençal adventurer, Montréal d'Albarno, whose own "Great Company" seized forty-four castles along the east coast of Italy; see William Caferro, *John Hawkwood*, 64–7.

60 *Prince*, Chapter 12, 150.

61 As Mockler in *The Mercenaries*, 48 notes: "if mercenaries were faithless, it is at least arguable that they were mere amateurs in treachery when compared with their employers." See also Gilbert's account of the Florentine reasoning on Vitelli's fate in *Machiavelli and Guicciardini*, 43; Bayley, *War and Society in Renaissance Florence*, 9–15; and Skinner, *The Foundations of Modern Political Thought*, especially 75–84.

62 As Machiavelli indicates in the *Prince*, Chapter 12, Hannibal's reputation for inhuman cruelty "*sua inumana crudeltà*" united an army composed of *infinite kinds of men* so effectively that for a long time it overcame the citizen army of the Romans. Hannibal's employment of cruelty parallels that of the cruelty deployed by Cesare

Borgia/Remirro da Orco in unifying the Romagna. See *Prince,* Chapter 7, and Winter's discussion of cruelty and reputation in *Machiavelli and the Orders of Violence,* 103–10.

63 See the extended discussion of Hannibal in Chapter 5, section 4 of the present work.
64 The discussion of auxiliaries starts in Chapter 12.
65 *Prince,* Chapter 7, 150.
66 See Fabrizio Colonna's discussion of the market dynamics facing the professional soldier in the *Art of War,* Book 1; Caferro, *John Hawkwood,* Chapter 6, and Ruggiero, *The Renaissance in Italy,* 162–5.
67 I agree with Claude Lefort's assessment, *Le travail de l'oeuvre Machiavel,* 562–3, that Machavelli's criticism of the *condottieri* concentrates on how money substitutes for the people's political role where use of money and mercenary forces frame the space of imaginary power: "...*il pointe la division qui s'est instituée entre le militaire et la politique et l'associe à la fonction que joue l'argent dans la guerre; avec la remarque que des princes sans armes payent des hommes armés et sans sujets il nous contraint à reconnaître que le discrédit actuel de l'infanterie se déduit de cette fonction; il nous laisse le soin de recoller l'argument en cours avec celui du dixième chapitre, c'est-à-dire de conclure que* l'argent est venu occuper dans les sociétés modernes la place laissée vide par le peuple. *Mais à la même lumière on voit se dessiner une autre chaîne d'éléments substituables dans l'analyse: les condottieri qu'on est tenté de tenir pour responsables de la corruption des institutions militaires n'existent eux-mêmes qu'en raison de l'absence de l'agent réel de la puissance; ils occupent ainsi la position de la force imaginaire qui avait été déjà identifiée à l'argent. Nous ne devons pas seulement admettre que leur stratégie est déterminée par la nécessité où ils se trouvent de se faire payer; la valeur de cette stratégie s'impose comme la valeur de l'argent à l'imagination des* principi..." See also Becker, *Florence in Transition,* Chapter 3.
68 Thus *condotta* were signed with the condottieri by different states both to fight and also *not* to fight, since it was very much in the interests of the condottieri to stir up business for themselves if there were no enterprise ready at hand. Mockler, *The Mercenaries,* 42–5, and Caferro, *John Hawkwood,* 80 and 90–4; Sánchez-Parga, *Poder y política en Maquiavelo* (Rosario: Homo Sapiens Ediciones, 2005), 164. Caferro, *John Hawkwood,* 90–4, explains how when official hostilities ended mercenaries pivoted to peacetime deployment by forming bands that turned to extortion of individuals and cities. With such a vibrant market in contract force, violence did not end with declarations of peace. See Ruggiero, *The Renaissance in Italy,* 162–5, and Lee, *The Ugly Renaissance: Sex, Greed, Violence and Depravity in an Age of Beauty* (New York: Anchor Books, 2015), 210.
69 And it was a common occurrence that with the end of hostilities the balance yet owed to their paid professionals would simply be canceled. Bayley describes four

types of *condottas* that the Florentines negotiated with their captains—the *condotta a soldo intero, a mezzo soldo, in aspetto,* and *la condotta di garanzia*. For reasons of economy, employers of *condottieri* attempted to frame short-term contracts, and the *condottieri* used a variety of techniques to extend the length and amount of their pay, the most effective of which involved a mixture of slowing down the tempo of operations and opening up negotiations with the opposing power, thereby lengthening the term of service and provoking a bidding war to retain them. Bayley shows how the conditions placed upon the *condottieri* slackened considerably between the end of the fourteenth century and the beginning of the sixteenth century. By the time of the great *condottieri* captains, like Francesco Sforza, even the minimal requirement of mustering the mercenary troops for review by the civilian authority before the disbursement of funds would take place had been waived as a matter of practice. See Bayley, *War and Society in Renaissance Florence*, 9–15; Caferro, *John Hawkwood*, 76–81, and Lee, *The Ugly Renaissance*, 207–08.

70 *Prince*, Chapter 12, 150–1. This time of the *condottieri* had its origins from the 1350s onward but was at its height from 1454–94, stretching from the Peace of Lodi—in which the five great Italian powers accepted a balance of power arrangement amongst themselves—to the first invasion by the French in 1494. See Baron, *The Crisis of the Early Italian Renaissance*, 412–39; Bayley, *War and Society in Renaissance Florence*, Chapters 1 and 4; Mockler, *The Mercenaries*, 42–73; Lee, *The Ugly Renaissance*, 205–33; Najemy, *A History of Florence, 1200–1575*, Chapters 5 and 7 and Waley, "The Army of the Florentine Republic from the 12th to the 14th Century," 70–108.

71 And were feared by the French, Spanish, and Germans, especially in the period from 1350–1430. See Bayley, *War and Society in Renaissance Italy*, Chapter 1; Mockler, *The Mercenaries*, Chapter 3; Ruggiero, *The Renaissance in Italy*, 177–8; and Waley, "The Army of the Florentine Republic from the 12th to the 14th Century."

72 This logic operated according to axioms such as reducing risk of death during conflict and the importance of maintaining perceived threats among the greater and lesser powers throughout the peninsula. Far from being ignorant of these conditions, Machiavelli spells them out, even tracing the genealogy of its development at the end of Chapter 12 of the *Prince*, thereby enhancing the usefulness of the system to a potential prince in the form of a critique of this industry, its strengths and weaknesses. See also Caferro, *John Hawkwood*, Chapter 3.

73 For the distinction between "Italian" and "Continental" (*a gorgia*) styles of fighting, see the rules Italian mercenary commanders routinely observed in their conflicts, outlined by Cecil Clough, "The Romagna Campaign of 1494: a significant military encounter," 214–15. As Clough points out, the French success in the Romagna campaign was not simply due to the Italian use of mercenaries and the French use of

native troops, since, "quite apart from the Milanese contingent in the Romagna, the French army there included Bernard Stuart d'Aubigny with Scots who were foreign mercenaries as well as a sizeable company of Swiss, all from beyond the Alps. Hence it was not so much that Italian military ineptitude lay in the employment of mercenaries, as Machiavelli claimed. Leaving aside the obvious lack of political unity on the peninsula and the self-interest that took its place, the issue was that the French army was not trammeled by the imitation of supposed classical models and the associated chivalry; the French fought to win at all costs with utter ruthlessness." On the "mixed" and multinational nature of the armies, see also Caferro, *John Hawkwood*, 79–81.

74 As Burckhardt states in his, *The Civilization of the Renaissance in Italy*, 13: "They must have been heroes of abnegation, natures like Belisarius himself, not to be cankered by hatred and bitterness…At the same time, and through the force of the same conditions the genius and capacity of many among them achieved the highest conceivable development." See also Lee, *The Ugly Renaissance*, 212–33.

75 Machiavelli consistently argues that when a difference exists between the roles of prince and captain a functional problem emerges in principalities. See, for instance, *Prince*, Chapters 3 and 14, and *Discourses* 3.6. For a discussion of contemporary defense procurements and the growing market in contract force that reflects on Machiavelli's fifteenth-century critique of mercenaries, see Deborah Avant, *The Market for Force*, 60 and 113–38.

76 They may not possess, though, the requisite intention from a host of causes. Some of these causes stem occasionally from lack of opportunity. Some are due to conflicted intentionalities. See the story of Giovampagolo Baglioni at *Discourses* 1.27 and sections III–V of Sean Erwin, "Mixed Bodies, Agency and Narrative in Lucretius and Machiavelli," *Époché: A Journal of the History of Philosophy* 24, no. 2 (Spring, 2020): 337–56.

77 See Lee, *The Ugly Renaissance*, 208–09 and 232–3 on the "conflicted" honors Florence bestowed on the English mercenary, John Hawkwood, and that Cosimo de Medici paid to Sigismondo Pandolfo Malatesta.

78 See John Najemy, *A History of Florence, 1200–1575*, 402–03.

79 *Prince*, Chapter 12. Alberigo da Conio is also Alberigo da Barbiano, whom Machiavelli describes in book 1 of the *Florentine Histories*, sections 34–5 in the following terms: "In these times there were many soldiers in Italy—English, German, and Breton—some led by those princes who at various times had come to Italy, and some sent by the pontiffs who were then in Avignon. All the Italian princes made their wars with them for a long time, and how there emerged Ludovico da Conio, from the Romagna, who formed a company of Italian soldiers named for St. George. The virtue and discipline of which in little time took away the reputation of foreign arms and returned it to Italian arms (*la virtù e disciplina del quale in poco*

tiempo tolse la reputazione alle armi forestiere e ridussela negli Italiani), which the princes of Italy used afterwards in the wars they fought together." Here Machiavelli recognizes the strength Italian mercenary forces originally had, that they were successful at a particular time and that later, from various determinate causes, they no longer demonstrated that original effectiveness.

80 Machiavelli tells the story of the Sforza and the Braccio in his *Florentine Histories*, especially Books 4 through 6. There Machiavelli relates the conflict between Francesco Sforza and Niccolò Piccinino which ended in the defeat of Niccolò and in the legitimation of Francesco, who became heir to the throne of Milan when he married the daughter of Filippo Maria Visconte.

81 It is interesting to note that Machiavelli's description of Braccio's ambition against the Church shows how the papacy—like all other Italian regimes—was equally subject to the dynamics structuring Italy's mercenary market.

82 That the Florentines knew and calculated correctly Sforza's intentions and knew how critically dependent the regimes of Sforza and Bracchio were on external financing, see *Florentine Histories*, Books 5 and 6.

83 Bayley in *War and Society in Renaissance Florence*, Chapters 1–4, lays out these dynamics. Becker in *Florence in Transition*, 151–5, attributes the main cause for the formation of the *Monte* and its meteoric increases to the need to finance mercenary forces in the fourteenth and fifteenth centuries. See also John Najemy, *A History of Florence, 1200–1575*, Chapter 7.

84 Ruggiero, *The Renaissance in Italy*, 172–5, details the tactics employed by Gian Galeazzo Visconti in his conquest of Northern Italy. Ruggiero shows how Visconti's overall strategy centered on reducing his exposure to the economic demands imposed by the the new condottieri economy in the second half of the fourteenth century.

85 Jorge Delgado, *Bajo el signo de Circe* (Buenos Aires: Ediciones del signo, 2006), 93, emphasizes the role that *gloria* played in the careers of many *condottieri*. For a similar assessment see Burckhardt, *The Civilization of the Renaissance in Italy*, part I.

86 But it was also the factor that revealed mercenary commanders as semi-autonomous, political players in their own right. Lee in *The Ugly Renaissance*, 212–24, describes two periods of mercenaries, the first in the thirteenth century and the second in the fourteenth. The second generation of mercenaries differed from the first in their dependence on Italian captains drawn from the younger sons of noble houses with land at their disposal. The troops they led were better trained and equipped and the captains themselves were often paid extravagantly due to their semi-autonomy. As Lee concludes: "In a sense, it was an attempt to turn mercenaries into citizen armies," *The Ugly Renaissance*, 213.

87 The founder of the first "Great Company," Roger de Flor, was killed by his employer, the Byzantine Emperor Adronicus, who feared the "Company" would grow too

powerful in the wake of its spectacular success during the Byzantine civil war; see William Caferro, *John Hawkwood*, 64–5.

88 Machiavelli assisted in the management of this war and was intimately aware of the circumstances surrounding Vitelli's death. As Caferro, *John Hawkwood*, 76, describes the relationship between patrons and *condottieri*: "One cannot overemphasize the degree of distrust that existed between the two sides." See also Bayley, *War and Society in Renaissance Florence*. 243–4, for the truly Byzantine negotiations and conspiracies between Vitelli, the Florentines, the French, and the Venetians.

89 See Mockler, *The Mercenaries*, 48–9.

90 See *Prince,* Chapters 7 and 18. In Chapter 18, Machiavelli names "deception" a mode of force for combating men. Machiavelli gives the meaning of deception a specific sense: to successfully combat men in this way, a prince must learn to use the *promise*. This includes both understanding how to keep and when to break a promise; it also includes knowing how to color the decision to break a promise with the appearance of necessity. The knack of negotiating and failing to fulfill the terms of fifteenth-century *condotte* for contract force would certainly fit with the promissory structure of this form of combat. See Caferro, *John Hawkwood*, Chapter 3.

91 See Burckhardt, *The Civilization of the Renaissance in Italy*, part I. With the technically unskillful mercenary captains, this proportion is reversed for the simple reason that they practice their art so poorly. Through their incompetence they rob their patrons of what they don't deserve. They receive money and supplies, yet they frequently lose the lands and empire of their patrons as, indeed, befell the Venetians at the battle of Vailà in 1509.

92 "*L'ordine che egli hanno tenuto è stato, prima, per dare reputazione a loro proprii, avere tolto reputazione alle fanterie: feciono questo perché, sendo sanza stato e in sulla industria, e' pochi fanti non davono loro reputazione e gli assai non potevano nutrire...*" (*Prince*, Chapter 12)

93 As Caferro, *John Hawkwood*, 67, explains: "Mercenary bands were corporate in structure. The bands emphasized their corporate nature by referring to themselves not as 'armies,' strictly speaking, but as 'societies,' the same term used by contemporary Italian businesses. When marauding as free companies, the bands took the name 'society of societies,' a label stressing that they were a collection of businesses—corresponding to individual military brigades—linked together for the enrichment of its members." As Hawkwood explains, the aim of military campaigns was economic attrition: "Offensives were designed first and foremost to inflict financial pain," with the goal of financial pressure destabilizing the enemy socially and politically; ibid., 82.

94 This story is much more developed in the second section of the *Discourses* and especially in Books 4–6 of the *Florentine Histories*.

95 Despite the praise Machiavelli assigns to the "Socratically-minded" head of the Achaean league, this is the only mention Machiavelli makes of Philopoemon in his published writings, including *The Art of War*. This can hardly be said of Francesco Sforza whose name and example appears throughout the *Prince*, the *Discourses*, the *Art of War*, and, of course, the *Florentine Histories*, which can easily be read as the story/comedy of his transition from being an illegitimate mercenary captain to the "by marriage" made-legitimate prince of Milan.

96 To be supplemented, or even displaced, by the art of the *condotta*?

97 On this, see Jérémie Barthas, *L'argent n'est pas le nerf de la guerre: essai sur un prétendue erreur de Machiavel* (Rome: École Française de Rome, 2011), 329–90; Becker, *Florence in Transition*, Chapter 3; Molho, *Florentine Public Finances in the Early Renaissance, 1400–1433*.

98 Becker, *Florence in Transition*, 153, notes that as early as 1427 the Florentine *Monte* had reached the sum of 8,000,000 florins, "an amount of money approximately equal to the total wealth of the Florentine populace. In other words the state debt had grown until it was equal to the entire capital of the Florentine citizenry; thus the entire state budget would not suffice to pay the carrying charges."

99 Such a critique is implicitly guided by the following question: "what are the *grounds* through which decision-making processes acquire the validity, i.e., the persuasive force, sufficient to sustain the value of the conclusions reached such that some group attempts to secure themselves practically through force structured in this way?"

100 Machiavelli himself indicates the distinct fatal weaknesses of Spanish and French arms in his evaluation of them at Prince, Chapter 26. He evaluates the Swiss limitations at both *Discourses* 2.12 and *Prince,* Chapter 26, where they are described as being "ruined by Spanish infantry."

Chapter 4

1 An earlier version of this chapter appeared as the article, "The Metabolism of the State: Instrumental and Aleatory Aspects of Auxiliaries in Machiavelli," published with *Epoché: A Journal for the History of Philosophy* 20, Issue 1 (Fall 2015): 81–104. https://doi.org/10.5840/epoche201572750

2 Few commentators recognize, much less develop, the function of the category of auxiliary arms in Machiavelli. Patrick Coby's treatment of the theme in Chapter 5 of *Machiavelli's Romans* (Oxford: Lexington Books, 1999) stands out for his acknowledgment of the different employments Machiavelli makes of his definitions of mercenary and auxiliary force. He even refers to the Campanian episode, though passes over the strangeness of Machiavelli's use of Capua as an example of the use of

auxiliary arms. Timothy Lukes' article, "Martialing Machiavelli: Reassessing the Military Reflections" (*The Journal of Politics* 66, no. 4 (2004): 1089-1108), analyzes the themes of mercenaries and auxiliaries and concludes that Machiavelli's treatment of the distinction between them serves as a criticism of the aristocracy and to communicate his support for popular influence in civil affairs. Harvey Mansfield, *Machiavelli's New Modes and Orders* (Chicago: University of Chicago Press, 1979) especially 247–59, lays out Machiavelli's distinction between mercenaries, auxiliaries, and mixed forces and analyzes how Machiavelli deploys these different qualities of force in *Discourses*, Book 2. Similarly, Nathan Tarcov, "Arms and Politics in Machiavelli's Prince," in *Entre Kant and Kosovo*, ed. Anne-Maire de Gloannec and Aleksander Smolar (Paris: Presses de Sciences Po, 2003), 109–21, distinguishes between mercenary and auxiliary arms and emphasizes how established republican political leadership and the ambitious captains of republican forces may possess very different expectations for the troops they lead. Finally, Louis Althusser in *Machiavelli et nous* (Paris: Editions Tallandier, 2009) distinguishes between mercenaries, auxiliaries, and mixed armies, delineates Machiavelli's distinct ways of reasoning about each, and carefully defines *and problematizes* Machiavelli's notion of an army of one's own.

3 "*Le arme ausiliiare , che sono l'altre inutili, sono quando si chiama uno potente che con le sua arme ti venga a difendere. . .Queste arme possono essere buone e utile per loro medesime, ma sono, per chi le chiama, quasi sempre dannose: perché, perdendo, rimani disfatto; vicendo, resti loro prigione*" (*Prince* 13, 154). All page references to Machiavelli refer to Machiavelli's *Opere*, Volumes 1–3, ed. Corrado Vivanti (Torino: Einaudi-Gallimard, 1997).

4 "*Colui adunque che vuole non potere vincere, si vaglia di queste arme, perché sono molto piú pericolose che le mercennarie. Perché in queste è la coniura fatta, sono tutte unite, tutte volte alla obbedienza d'altri*" (*Prince* 13, 154).

5 In which case they are no longer auxiliaries in the sense Machiavelli employs this term here but allies.

6 "*De militibus auxiliariis, mixtis et propriis.*"

7 "*Quale pericolo porti quel principe o quella republica che si vale della milizia ausiliare o mercenaria*" (*Discourses* 2.20, 381).

8 "*Se io non avessi lungamente trattato in altra mia opera quanto sia inutile la milizia mercenaria ed ausiliare e quanto utile la propria, io mi stenderei in questo discorso assai piú che non faro*" (*Discourses*, 2.20, 381).

9 Commentators take this as a reference to the *Prince*, Chapters 12 and 13. See, for instance, Mansfield's note in Machiavelli (2009, 175n1) and Mansfield, *Machiavelli's New Modes and Orders* (247–53), and also Atkinson and Sices' note in *The Sweetness of Power: Machiavelli's Discourses & Guicciardini's Considerations* (Dekalb: Northern Illinois University Press, 2002), 220, n1. Atkinson and Sices recognize Machiavelli's

critique of these arms in the *Art of War*. For a similar analysis that includes discussion of the *Art of War* in sixteenth-century Italy, France, and England, see Sydney Anglo's *Machiavelli: The First Century* (Oxford: Oxford University Press, 2005).

10 The reference to the *Prince* is doubly important here because Chapter 2.20 is placed at the end of a series of chapters in Section 2 of the *Discourses* that treat themes very familiar to readers of the *Prince*. See especially, *Discourses* 2.16–19.

11 Given that auxiliary arms are organized independently and fall under the authority of some prince or republic (although very possibly financed by those receiving the aid), while the soldiers and possibly the captains of mercenary arms are hired by the prince or republic in need, the distinction between the two types of arms is clearly a tenuous one at best, with the labeling of forces as mercenary or auxiliary depending on whether they are described from the standpoint of the one employing or the one lending such arms. This seems to have been the case even during the early Republic's employment of external forces as a way to address the Roman army's classic deficiencies of skilled light troops (velites) and calvary. See Cheesman, *The Auxilia of the Roman Imperial Army* (Oxford: Clarendon, 1904) for the early Roman republic custom of calling *externi* allies despite being functionally mercenaries. See also Mansfield's reading of Machiavelli's *Art of War*, in *Machiavelli's New Modes and Orders,* 201–02.

12 For Machiavelli, the principality and the republic are not as distinct as has been argued by some commentators. As Vickie Sullivan and John Scott argue in, "Patricide and the Plot of the Prince: Cesare Borgia and Machiavelli's Italy" (*American Political Science Review* 88, no. 4: 887–900): "Not only does he insist on calling the leading men of the republic 'Princes', but he shows how the devious maneuverings of these leading men kept the mass of citizens from exercising control in the regime (*Discourses,* 1.47–48, 3.11). Moreover he shows how a republic can overcome the problem, endemic and dangerous to republics, that of slowness to act (*Discourses,* 1.59, 3.6) by infusing itself with the resoluteness, even the despotic character, of princely regimes (*Discourses,* 3.1). Machiavelli does not consider princes and republics to be completely separate or to be contradictory in nature" (897).

13 However, one could easily infer from these distinctions that having arms of one's own implies having men who are willing to lay down their lives for their country. However, as Lynch rightly argues in his commentary on the *Art of War*, trans. and ed. Christopher Lynch (Chicago: University of Chicago Press, 2003), 179–226: "But to state an obvious point, it is killing, being able to kill, and seeming to be able to kill rather than dying that brings victory to the army and glory to the captain. The question ... is not how to get men to want to die for their prince, city or country but how to 'keep them in the field' so that they can and will 'fight well' for their captain" (201).

14 Machiavelli's treatment exaggerates their uselessness so greatly as to render suspect both the policies of the prince or republic that would depend on such arms and the ideologies as well as the theoretical underpinnings whose values structure the logics guiding such flawed decision making.
15 See Coby, *Machiavelli's Romans*, 139, for his explanation of the role auxiliaries play in the relationships between weak and strong states.
16 In addition, it is important to remember that Machiavelli prescribes certain "remedies" to the faithlessness of mercenaries, such as Hannibal's inhuman cruelty (*Prince*, 17). Similarly, the Romans' reliance on auxiliaries from their allies after those allies had been transformed into Roman "client-states" would presumably not pose the same risks such reliance might have had for less powerful princes or republics.
17 "*Queste arme possono essere utile e buone per loro medesime, ma sono, per chi le chiami, quasi sempre dannose; perché, perdendo, rimani disfatto: vincendo, resti loro prigione*" (*Prince*, 13).
18 *Prince*, 13.
19 As Machiavelli indicates in the story of Giovampagolo Baglioni in *Discourses* I.27, Julius II had the great virtue of being the darling of fortune. See also *Prince* 25.
20 The troops employed by Julius II at Ravenna did not, strictly speaking, constitute auxiliary forces as defined here by Machiavelli. Ferdinand of Spain gave clear instructions to his ambassador Vich in Rome that the troops he had loaned to Julius II for the defense of church lands needed to remain under Spanish control. In the battle of Bologna in January 1512 and the battle of Ravenna on April 11, 1512, it was the Spanish viceroy, Cardonna—leader of the combined Spanish and papal troops—who was defeated by the French under Gaston de Foix. The Swiss were actually papal mercenaries headed by Cardinal Schiner. Technically, given Machiavelli's definitions of the compositions of forces, this did not constitute an auxiliary army, but rather a "mixed" force. The Swiss did not spontaneously *rise up* but had been carefully courted by Julius II for years and had been maneuvered, under threat of excommunication, into acting on his behalf; see Christine Shaw, *Julius II: The Warrior Pope* (Oxford: Blackwell, 1993) 292–96.
21 Francesco Guicciardini, *Storie fiorentine dal 1378 al 1509* (Milan: RCS Libri SpA, 1998).
22 See Donald Nicol, *The Last Centuries of Byzantium, 1261–1453*, 2nd ed. (Cambridge: Cambridge University Press, 1993), 235–43.
23 For instance, on the management of the defects of mercenary force, see the treatment of mercenary force in this work and Christopher Lynch, "War and Foreign Affairs in Machiavelli's *Florentine Histories*," *The Review of Politics* 74: 1–26 (2012): especially 15, note 32.
24 The difference between the discussions of mercenaries in the *Prince* and in the *Discourses* is striking. The term "mercenario" itself occurs only four times in the

entire *Discourses*, and three of those occurrences happen in 2.19 and 2.20. The only *discussion* of this theme in the *Discourses* occurs in Chapter 1.43, where Machiavelli attributes the *uselessness* of mercenary soldiers to the differences between armies that fight for their own glory and those that fight for the glory of someone else. He likens mercenary arms to Roman arms under the Decemvirate, who *had the same virtue* as Roman armies always had, but "because in them was not the same disposition, they did not make their customary effects" (*Discourses* 99–110). This treatment contrasts greatly with the *Prince*'s treatment of the theme where "mercenary" occurs twenty times in Italian (*mercenario*) and once in Latin (*mercenariis*), and Machiavelli's deployment of the term reflects his definition of it.

25 Machiavelli treats these two types of soldiers—mercenaries and auxiliaries—as if they constitute a single topic for the purposes of his discussion. The closing statements of 2.19 imply that the topic of mercenary and auxiliary forces falls under the greater genus of incorrect or errant "modes of acquisition" employed by princes and republics. Thus, he sets his reader up to expect *Discourses* 2.20 to discuss mercenary and auxiliary soldiers as modes of *errant* acquisition.

26 "*Perché i soldati ausiliari sono quegli che un principe o una republica manda capitanati e pagati da lei in tuo aiuto*" (*Discourses*, 2.20, 381).

27 342 BC.

28 "*Le quali legioni, marcendo nell'ozio, cominciarono a dilettarsi in quello, tanto che, dimenticata la patria e la reverenza del senato, pensarono di prendere l'armi ed insignorisi di quel paese che loro con la loro virtù avevano difeso, parendo loro che gli abitatori non fussono degni di possedere quegli beni che non sapevano difendere*" (*Discourses*, 2.20).

29 "*La quale cosa presentita, fu da' romani oppressa e corretta.*" (*Discourses*, 2.20)

30 "*Colui, adunque, che vuole non potere vincere, si vaglia di queste armi; perché sono molto più pericolose che le mercenarie. Perché in queste è la ruina fatta: sono tutte unite, tutte volte alla obedienzia di altri*" (*Prince*, 13).

31 Mansfield in *Machiavelli's New Modes and Orders* also notes the strangeness of Machiavelli's use of the term "auxiliaries" in this chapter: "It is very strange, moreover, for Machiavelli to call the Roman legions auxiliaries of the Capuans who had surrendered themselves to Rome for protection (II, 9); they were more of a protecting garrison, if not an army of occupation. And the legions were preparing to plunder the 'prince' under whose insignia they had come and with whose pay they were kept, for Capua, according to the previous chapter, was an acquisition harmful to the Romans" (252).

32 "I say therefore anew that of all the other quality soldiers, the auxiliaries are the most dangerous, because with those [soldiers], the prince or the republic that employs them in its aid does not have any authority; only the one that sends them has authority over them. Because auxiliary soldiers are, as I have said, those that are sent

by a prince, under his captains, under his insignias, and paid for by him as was this army that the Romans sent to Capua [*Perché gli soldati ausiliari sono quegli che ti sono mandati da uno principe, como ho detto, sotto i suoi capitani, sotto sue insegne e pagati da lui.*]" (*Discourses* 2.20).

33 The chief peculiarity of this particular example is that these troops revolt without an ambitious captain to lead them. On this point, see Tarcov, "Arms and Politics in Machiavelli's *Prince*" (118) who discusses the possibilities open to '"ambitious generals" commanding auxiliary forces relative to that prince or republic that has sent them into the field; see also, *Discourses* 1.29–31.

34 Livy, *History of Rome*, 7.32–41.

35 345–343 BC.

36 Livy, *History of Rome* , 7.29–30.

37 However, it is clear from the wording of the ambassador's speech that he clearly understood even the role of Roman "ally" to be close to the role of subject. As he states: "Vobis arabitur ager Campanus, vobis Capua urbs frequentabitur; *conditorum, parentium, deorum immortalium numero nobis eritis*; nulla colonia vestra erit, quae nos obsequio erga vos fideque superet" (Book 7.30, 19–20; emphasis mine). Nevertheless, the Senate refuses this entreaty, publicly stating that their commitment to their old treaty of friendship with the Samnites has first importance: "*tamen tanta utilitate fides antiquior fuit*."

38 For a discussion of how this change of status continues to figure in the relations between the Romans and Campanians, see also Livy, *History of Rome*, 8.2.

39 Livy describes the reasoning of the Romans following the complete capitulation of the Campanians as similarly due to reasons of honor: "Then now it seemed honor not to betray those who had surrendered [*Tum iam fides agi visa deditos non prodi*]." (*History of Rome*, 7.31, 7–8)

40 At the Battle of Ravenna, April 1512.

41 This is also true of Machiavelli's other two examples in Chapter 13 of the *Prince*. For the first, Machiavelli relates how the Florentines agreed to pay the French 10,000 ducats for delivering Pisa to them. In the other, he discusses how John Cantacuzene made use of Ottoman troops in the Greek civil wars of 1350–53. In both examples, the auxiliaries employed satisfy Machiavelli's definition of this type of army. But when considered more closely, these two examples expand Machiavelli's basic definition of auxiliaries. The authority that binds troops in unity to a prince does not necessarily depend on holding a territory. In the first example, the French, Spanish, and Swiss troops in the conflict were bound by being *Christian* troops and, as such, would be united and obedient to the prince of that sect. As Christian troops, they were at least forces of mixed loyalty—they expressed allegiance to their king and at the same time to an extraterritorial source of authority, the pope. It is important to remember the Swiss pike were encouraged to fight for Julius II at Ravenna because

he threatened them with excommunication. As Strauss in *Thoughts on Machiavelli*, argues concerning these themes: "There is a certain similarity between a militia proper and a spiritual militia. The problem concerning the militia proper can be reduced to the alternatives of a citizen army and an auxiliary army; these alternatives have a certain similarity with the alternatives of a citizen priesthood and a priesthood subject to a foreign head. According to Machiavelli, there is a certain similarity between the rule exercised by ancient Rome over other cities and countries and that exercised by papal Rome: the rule of both is to some extent indirect" (102). See also Lynch, "War and Foreign Affairs in Machiavelli's *Florentine Histories*," especially 15.

42 "*Ma sendo i campani oppressati, e ricorrendo a Roma fuora della opinione de'romani e de'sanniti, furono forzati, dandosi i campani ai romani, come cosa loro defendergli, e pigliare quella guerra che a loro parve non potere con loro onore fuggire*" (*Discourses* 2.19).

43 At the end of Machiavelli, *Discourses*, 2.19.

44 As Livy describes the soldiers' reasoning at *History of Rome* 7.39: "Was it fair that their surrendered subjects should enjoy that fertile and agreeable tract, while they, exhausted with campaigning, wrestled with the arid and noxious soil around the city [Rome], or endured the ruinous usury that had fastened on the city and was increasing from one day to the next?" It is interesting to note that the issues of plebeian debt play a contributing role in many of Livy's stories. See for instance the part it plays in Livy, *History of Rome* 6.11–20, in the circumstances surrounding the death of Manlius Capitolinus.

45 See Livy, *History of Rome*, 7.27, 3–4, 7.41, 4–6, and 7.42, 1–4.

46 However, Livy does have the conspirators suggest that there was suffering beyond the crippling levels of indebtedness they had experienced at the hands of the Senate and the nobility.

47 Gaius Marcius Rutulus.

48 Marcus Valerius Corvus.

49 There were, of course, two earlier secessions of the plebeians. The first secession, during which the army withdrew to the Sacred Mount, ended with the creation of the plebeian tribunes and was also clearly attributed to the fact that the plebs were generally drowning in debt and the Senate was initially unwilling to negotiate measures for relief (see ibid., especially 2.24–32). The second secession took place during the reign of the decemvirs. It occurred when the decemvir Appius Claudius was driven by lust to enslave a daughter of the pleb Lucius Verginius. Verginius killed his daughter rather than allow her to submit to enslavement and rape. This episode caused the army to secede once again, this time withdrawing to the Aventine and then to the Sacred Mount, holding out until the decemvirs resigned and the tribuneship was restored (see ibid., 3.44–54).

50 Ibid., 7.40. In the aftermath of the insurrection, the Senate agrees with Corvus that none of the seditious soldiers should be punished, and they pass a "sacred law" to that effect. More importantly, however, a "military law" is passed that prevents any centurion's name from being struck from the lists for service. Service in the army protected soldiers against having their goods seized as a consequence of their indebtedness and being on the lists assured the soldiers that they would receive a share of the spoils of a campaign. (ibid.,7.41). See also the end of 7.42, where Livy acknowledges that the annalists do not agree about the consequences of this sedition and that the tribune, Lucius Genucius, proposed that it be entirely unlawful to lend with interest. From this consideration, Livy concludes that the sedition had great strength: "*Quae si omnia concessa sunt plebi, apparet haud parvas vires defectionem habuisse.*" On the importance of the *lex sacrata*, see Ogilvie, *A Commentary on Livy, Books I–V* (Oxford: Oxford University Press, 1965), 313–14. However, it is notable that the conspiracy that motivated the legions to attempt to seize Capua for their own was, indeed, foiled, and the plebeian debts were not canceled.

51 Livy suggests that more than the two legions were involved. Designs spread from the troops stationed in Capua to the whole army. The consuls began quietly to disperse the troublemakers. One cohort of troops became aware of this stratagem and began to intercept any soldier sent back to Rome. They continued doing so until they became quite numerous. As Livy states, "*Iam valida admodum numero manus erat nec quicquam ad iusti exercitus formam praeter ducem deera*" (*History of Rome*, 7.39).

52 In Livy's version, the conspiracy is sustained due to the level of the soldiers' indebtedness and much of that debt was held by the patricians of the Senate. In fact, the soldiers' conspiracy to secede from Rome is motivated for this very reason: "*Nondum erant tam fortes ad sanguinem civilem nec praeter externa noverant bella, ultimaque rabies secessio ab suis habebatur*" (ibid., 7.39). Machiavelli himself also emphasizes this point. Livy's description of the beginnings of the insurrection only refers to the soldiers' "having forgotten their fatherland." Machiavelli, in his retelling of Livy's story, repeats Livy's phrase, "having forgotten the fatherland," in Italian and then adds, "and their reverence for the Senate" (*Discourses* 2.19). Machiavelli's addition emphasizes that the core issue in this story is the disobedience of the soldiers to the authority of Rome and to the Roman senators *in particular*.

53 Machiavelli *Art of War*, 625.

54 It is important to note that Livy himself says that in the account of the events surrounding the revolt of the garrison, "in no single instance do the ancient authorities agree, except that there was a sedition and it was composed" (Livy, *History of Rome*, 7.42; "*Adeo nihil, praeterquam seditionem fuisse eamque compositam inter antiques rerum auctores constat*"). So this is Livy's story. But Livy

also conveys his understanding that the Roman soldiers who seceded were motivated to conspire to seize Capua and subsequently to take arms against Rome because of the economic burden of their personal debt brought on by the practice of usury in Rome. The lack of agreement among authorities about how the conspiracy came about and how it was subsequently resolved highlights the fact that Livy made many choices as he composed the details of the story and its conclusion. In another context, Strauss in, *Thoughts on Machiavelli*, also draws attention to Livy's authorial strategy: "It would appear then that Machiavelli stands in the same relation to Livy in which Livy stands to some of his characters: he states what he regards as the truth through sentences of Livy often unquoted but always alluded to; Machiavelli's Livy is a character of Machiavelli" (141).

55 Lefort, *Le travail de l'oeuvre Machiavel* (Paris: Gallimard, 1972), 562–63, argues convincingly that Machavelli's criticism of the *condottieri* focuses on how money comes to occupy the political role once occupied by the people; replacing "real" power, money, and mercenary force function to delimit and occupy the space of imaginary power. Miguel Vatter, *Between Form and Event: Machiavelli's Theory of Political Freedom* (Dordrecht: Kluwer, 2000) describes this imaginary power as "negative liberty," which is "the effect of a political process initiated by the state against the people in order to subsume their desire for freedom as no-rule into its strategy of foundation" (128). Instead of genuine or authentic political freedom, the people are reconciled to the demands of the political form through the right to private property, subjugating their desire for freedom ("no-rule") to a civil function within the state. Machiavelli's own emphasis on private property follows this same vein, as the transformation of the desire of the people for no-rule into the freedom to own, i.e., the right to enjoy property unmolested by the prince. See especially Vatter, *Between Form and Event,* Chapter 6, and also Lynch, "War and Foreign Affairs in Machiavelli's *Florentine Histories*," 20–5.

56 On this see, for instance, Machiavelli, *Florentine Histories,* Book 5, section 1.

57 Lefort, *Le travail de l'oeuvre Machiavel,* 552.

58 Barthas, *L'argent n'est pas le nerf de la guerre: essai sur un prétendue erreur de Machiavel* (Rome: École Française de Rome, 2011), 345.

59 Ibid., 345. See also Becker "Economic Change and the Emerging Florentine State" (*Studies in the Renaissance* 13 (1966): 7–39) on the correlation between Florence's mounting public debt (the *Monte*) and its transition in the fourteenth and fifteenth centuries from drawing its army from the *popolo* to increasing, debt-driven expenditures on mercenaries.

60 Ibid., 14. See also *Discourses,* 2.10, 2.18, and 2.30 where Machiavelli makes the case that disarming the people is done to loot them. As he states at *Discourses* 2.30, addressing the common policy of disarming the people shared by the Florentines, the Venetians and the King of France: "*Il che tutto nasce dallo avere disarmati i popoli*

suoi, ed avere piú tosto voluto quell re e gli altri prenominati, godersi un presente utile, di potere sacheggiare il popoli, e fuggire uno immaginato piú tosto che vero pericolo, che fare cose che gli assicurino e faccino i loro stato felici in perpetuo" (408).

61 Barthas, *L'argent n'est pas le nerf de la guerre*, 347.
62 See Fabrizio's response to Cosimo's question in the *Art of War*, Book 1 (Machiavelli, 554–5), about whether it is better for states to possess small paid standing forces or large forces that receive stipends only during times of war.
63 As Barthas argues in "Machiavelli, the Republic and the Financial Crisis," in *Machiavelli on Liberty and Conflict*, ed. David Johnston, Nadia Urbinati, and Camila Vergara (Chicago: The University of Chicago Press, 2017): "From 1406, the eligible citizen had to own shares in the public debt, that is, he had to be a creditor to the government" (267). Payments over a certain threshold entitled citizens to shares of several funded debts, which had the effect of making Florence's Great Council into a company of shareholders. Still, as Barthas notes, "the republic was not a debtor in the same way toward all creditors who did not attain the same material and symbolic benefits" (267).
64 Anthony Molho, *Florentine Public Finances in the Early Renaissance* (Cambridge, MA: Harvard University Press, 1971), especially Chapters 2 and 4.
65 For contemporary treatments of this issue, see P. W. Singer, *Corporate Warriors* (Ithaca: Cornell University Press, 2003); and Deborah Avant *The Market for Force* (Cambridge: Cambridge University Press, 2005).
66 Malanima, *La formazione di una regione economica: la Toscana nei secoli XIII-XV* (*Società e storia* XX, Milan: Italy, 1983), 229–69, 260, quoted from Barthas, *L'argent n'est pas le nerf de la guerre*, 358.
67 Machiavelli, *Art of War*, Book 1, 537–8.
68 Ibid., 541–2.
69 *Prince*, 9.
70 See Philip Pettit, *Republicanism: A Theory of Freedom and Government* (Oxford: Oxford UP, 1997) for the notion of *non-domination* as a third option to both the republican notions of freedom as non-interference and freedom as self-mastery, especially Chapter 1, sections 3 and 4. See also Funes, *La desunión república y no-dominación en Maquiavelo* (Buenos Aires: Editorial Gorla, 2004), 33.
71 For similar formulations to *Discourses* 1.5, see also *Discourses* 1.16 and 1.55; *Prince* 9 and *Florentine Histories* 1.12 and 3.1.
72 Jean-Claude Zancarini, "Les humeurs du corps politique" (*Laboratoire Italien* I: 25–33), 26. John Najemy argues in "Machiavelli, the Militia, and Guicciardini's Accusation of Tyranny," in *Della tirannia: Machiavelli con Bartolo*, ed. Jérémie Barthas (Florence: Leo S. Olschki Editore, 2007), that to counter the charges of tyrannical ambitions raised by the prospect of the militia project, Machiavelli redefines the notion of tyranny "away from the simple realization of illicit ambitions

and desires by one man, and toward a more complex analysis that emphasizes the crucial role of class antagonisms, the resulting growth of factions, and the transformation of political authority and military power in conditions in which public law and institutions break down in the increasing privatization of conflicts...Machiavelli saw tyranny as an aspect, or result, of the *corruzione* that, in his theoretical lexicon occurs when political and military institutions alike fall into the hands of overmighty private citizens" (99).

73 Parel, *The Machiavellian Cosmos* (New Haven, CT: Yale University Press, 1992), 106.
74 Ibid., 144–5.
75 Vickie Sullivan, *Machiavelli's Three Romes* (Dekalb: Northern Illinois University Press, 1996), 68. See especially 70–80 and Sullivan's analysis of how the passion for acquisition manifests differently between the people and a sub-group of the nobles. Markus Fischer in *Well Ordered License* (Boston: Lexington Books, 2000) analyzes the psychology of human action in a way that strongly supports Sullivan's assessment. See especially 62–7. See also Parel, *The Machiavellian Cosmos*, for an identification of the drives motivating the *popolo* and *plebs* in *Florentine Histories*, Book 3.
76 Sullivan, *Machiavelli's Three Romes*, 71.
77 In referring to the plebs desire for unseen goods, Sullivan importantly suggests that the "desire to acquire" does not operate as a sufficient and exhaustive explanatory principle for humoral conflict. Stefano Visentin in *La virtù dei molti. Machiavelli e il repubblicanesimo olandese della seconda metà del seicento*, ed. Luca Sartorello and Stefano Visentin (Pisa: Edizioni ETS, 2006) outlines the complexity of Machiavelli's passion to acquire. In discussing the malice of the people, Visentin draws attention to the irreducible differential between the desire to acquire and the power to make something one's own. As he explains, this malice of spirit ("*malignità dello animo*") originates, "*nella presenza in ogni individuo di una discrasia tra il desiderio e la potenza, dalla quale nasce l'inimicizia tra gli uomini: la cupidità di ottenere—e che tuttavia si immagina essere raggiungibile—, e non il semplice desiderio di acquistare, è dunque la principale fonte del dissidio*" (241). Visentin's formulation here problematizes the status of imagination in Machiavelli. Is imagination a distinct capacity for the Florentine, or is imagination an effect of the differential experienced between desire and the sensation of power?
78 For instance, in *Florentine Public Finances in the Early Renaissance,* Molho outlines how prominent Florentines in the fourteenth and fifteenth centuries used personal connections with officials charged with tax assessment and the collection of forced loans, then adds: "...one's power in the city could be measured to a large extent by the success one met in avoiding payment of one's proper taxes" (75).
79 See Parel, *The Machiavellian Cosmos*, 107.
80 Gerald Sfez in *Machiavel, la politique du moindre mal* (Paris: Presses Universitaires de France, 1999) locates the nature of *umore* in a compulsion to disequilibrium and

a kind of excess: "This rationality stems from the tension between the character of excess of the humor considered in itself [*le caractère de démesure de l'humeur considérée en elle-même*] and the search for a balance among the humors themselves. Irrepressible, the humor is a tendency toward disequilibrium and is put to the ceaseless test of the loss of all equilibrium [*l'humeur déséquilibre et expose à l'épreuve incessante de la perte de tout équilibre*], although to speak of the political relation in terms of humors is to speak of them in terms of the search for an equilibrium in disequilibrium [*la recherche d'un équilibre dans le déséquilibre*]" (209–10). See also Lynch, "War and Foreign Affairs in Machiavelli's *Florentine Histories*," 22–3.

81 As Lefort, *Le travail de l'oeuvre Machiavelli*, describes this relationship: "The reversal of perspectives does not authorize us to judge that the latter is the only legitimate one. We need only admit that every society is divided between the dominators and the dominated, and that the external signs of freedom conceal a factual inequality, the consequences of which lend themselves to several arrangements" (488).

82 Gabriele Pedullà, *Machiavelli in Tumulto* (Roma: Bulzoni Editore, 2011), underlines the importance of the class drives receiving a check by contrasting two types of fear that condition collective behavior: the negative kind he terms "*paura-sospetto*" and the beneficial kind, "*paura-freno.*" This second type "*induce alla temperanza e alla continenza, dissuadendo gli animi inquieti dall'intraprendere azioni nocive alla collettività*" (243–44). In describing this second type, Pedullà marshals Lucretius' *De rerum natura*, Book 5, for support. Though Pedullà links *paura-freno* to the fear of the laws and the *metus poenarum*, the threat posed by the militia to the designs of the *grandi* and the apparently salutary effects that secession can have for preserving liberty may form an additional instance of *paura-freno* that, strictly speaking, suspends the normal functioning of the *metus poenarum* and acts as an extra-legal event.

83 During her analysis of Salvestro Medici's speech before the popular council at *Florentine Histories* 1.10, Michelle T. Clarke in *Machiavelli's Florentine Republic* (Cambridge: Cambridge University Press, 2018) emphasizes the unpredictability of the humors and the difficulty, if not impossibility, of managing them. On her reading, Salvestro resigned because his attempt to foment outrage against the Twelve failed. Machiavelli uses the episode to emphasize that, "it is foolish to believe that one can effectively manage such 'humors' to one's advantage once they have been 'set in motion'" (108, n. 17).

84 John McCormick, *Machiavellian Democracy* (Cambridge: Cambridge University Press, 2011), 33. See also ibid., 44, and Parel, *The Machiavellian Cosmos*, 145.

85 Louis Althusser in *Machiavelli et nous* (Paris: Editions Tallandier, 2009) clearly articulates the degree to which the army as a national institution is central to this project of securing the people to the state; see especially 156.

86 "*Se vuoi avete letto gli ordini che quelli primi re fecero in Roma, e massimamente Servio Tullo, troverrete che l'ordine delle classi non è altro che una ordinanza per potere*

di subito mettere insieme uno esercito per difesa di quella città" (Machiavelli, *Art of War*, 550).

87 This question will be investigated in more detail in the last chapter.
88 See McCormick, *Machiavellian Democracy*, 45.
89 The discussion of the *umori* in Machiavelli may certainly have its origins in Galenic medicine. Commmentators from Bausi (Machiavelli, Niccolò. *Discorsi sopra la prima deca di Tito Livio*, 2001, v. 2, 524–5, note 15) to Yves Winter in *Machiavelli and the Orders of Violence* (Cambridge: Cambridge University Press, 2018, 129–30) assume a Galenic framework at work here. However, where Galen argues on the basis of four humors so, as well, does Lucretius. The Galenic approach to the humors seeks balance and harmony where the four humors act as flows within a mixed body. Unlike Galen, Lucretius notably does not argue that the humors in the body can be balanced but they can be—at least in part—"put off" (*depellere*, *De rerum natura*, 3.321).
90 Where Galen postulates equilibrium between the humors as the principal condition of health, Machiavelli consistently speaks of the humors in disequilibrium (see note 80 above) with marked tendencies toward excess if not blocked. Further, Machiavelli's political humors are not equal. He frequently identifies one of the humors—that of the *grandi*—as more harmful than that of the *ignobili*. Finally, these humors show in places an odd plasticity that argues against absolute distinctions. For instance, the *humor* of the people under certain circumstances can shift and begin to exhibit characteristics of the *nobili*. This is not possible in a Galenic framework but *is* thinkable within a Lucretian one. Despite the Galenic echoes, the restlessness of Machiavelli's body politic with its roots in the incessant *kinēsis* of the humors overlaps more with Lucretian physiology than with the Galenic framework.
91 As Pierre-François Moreau argues in *Lucrèce. L'âme* (Paris: Presses Universitaires de France, 2002), 34–5:
"*D'où résulte l'impossibilité de le nommer? Mais alors, en quoi rend-il possible la sensation si sa seule force est d'être aptitude extrême au mouvement? On peut désormais se douter de la réponse: précisément la sensation n'est que mouvement. Son 'secret' n'est donc pas un mystère: il est logique qu'elle prenne sa source dans un élément de pure mobilité; si l'on ne dit rien d'autre de lui, ce n'est pas qu'il soit inconnaissable—c'est qu'il n'y a rien d'autre à en dire parce qu'il n'est rien d'autre.*"
92 Yves Winter emphasizes the performative feature of plebeian violence in *Machiavelli and the Orders of Violence* (Cambridge: Cambridge University Press, 2018; see especially 179–86). As he aptly notes: "popular vengeance needs to be relished with the senses" (182).
93 "*quorum ego nunc nequeo caecas exponere causas, nec reperire figurarum tot nomina quot sunt principiis, unde haec oritur varianta rerum.*" (Lucretius, *De rerum natura*, 3.316–318)

94 Ibid., 3.320–322. Here Lucretius ascribes to reason so much power over the influence of the characters that, "*nil inpediat dignam dis degree vitam.*"
95 However, even in the *Prince* the account is more complex than Machiavelli's first presentation of it suggests. In *Prince* 19, he emphasizes the humoral dilemma the emperors confronted: "*Ed è prima da notare che, dove nelli altri principati si ha solo a contendere con la ambizione de' grandi e insolenzia de' populi, gl'imperadori romani avevano una terza difficoltà, di avere sopportare la crudeltà e avarizia de soldati...Ed e' piu di loro, massime di quegli che come uomini nuovi venivono al principato, conosciuta la difficultà di quesi dua diversi umori, si volgevano a satisfare a' soldati stimando poco lo iniuriare el populo.*" Later in the passage, Machiavelli repeats the identification of the soldiers as an additional humor when he reasons about doing good or bad deeds. Instead it is necessary to do those things that satisfy the most powerful humor, "*o populi o soldati o grandi.*"
96 Machiavelli, *Florentine Histories* 2.33, 405–06.
97 Machiavelli, *Florentine Histories* 2.36, 412.
98 See *Florentine Histories* 3.1: "*vincendo il popolo, i nobili privi de' magistrati rimanevano, e volendo racquistargli era loro necessario con i governi, con lo animo e con il modo di vivere, simili ai popolani non solamente essere ma pare*" Machiavelli, *Florentine Histories* 2.33, 424.
99 Jean-Claude Zancarini, "Les humeurs du corps politique," 27–9, including notes 12 and 13.
100 Machiavelli, 738.
101 Livy has the legionnaires complaining about the particularly poor soil they are forced to work around Rome.
102 As J. G .A. Pocock states in *The Machiavellian Moment* (Princeton: Princeton University Press, 1975): "[Unlike Venice,] Rome resolved upon empire, upon a daring attempt to dominate the environment, and consequently upon innovation and upon a *virtù* which would enable her to control the disorder which her own actions had helped her to cause. She had therefore to arm the people, to suffer the strife caused by their demands for more power and to make concessions to those demands. The arming of the plebeians contributed to Rome's military greatness; the struggle between the orders to the consolidation of a mixed government; but some continuing disequilibrium, yet to be analyzed, to shortening the life of Roman liberty."
103 Machiavelli makes this connection explicit at *Discourses* 1.6 by situating a link between political freedom and conquest: "If someone wished, therefore, to order a republic anew, he would have to examine whether he wished it to expand like Rome in dominion and in power or truly to remain within narrow limits. In the first case it is necessary to order it like Rome and make a place for tumults and universal dissensions, as best one can; for without a great number of men, and well armed, a republic can never grow, or, if it grows, maintain itself." (215) In

discussing how money both does and does not functions as the sinew of war, Barthas, in *L'argent n'est pas la nerf de la guerre*, argues: "*l'argent est et, sans contredit, n'est pas la nerf de la guerre; il n'est pas la nerf de la guerre au sens où l'opinion commune entend qu'il l'est, c'est-à-dire comme force structurelle essentielle; et il est la nerf de la guerre dans un sens différent du sens commun, mais facilment acceptable, comme moteur de l'excitation et appât, motif des conflits et donc lieu d'un point de vue fécond pour les analyser. Le duxième indique ce qui est la force structurelle essentielle reellement en verité. No non pas l'argent mais l'homme, les armes propres, la population en armes. . .*" (389).

104 And as Vatter, in *Between Form and Event*, explains, this is the key to understanding the relationship between political freedom and the historically imposed requirement to expand that Machiavelli imputes to all states: "The republican modality of political life, in a first moment, opens the state to the outside so that un-formed matter may enter into it. In the second moment, the introjected matter re-opens the state from the inside, from a position in which the people have gained *potestas*, that is, have managed to arm their desire for freedom. The whole second book of the *Discourses on Livy* can be read as the analysis of this second understanding of politics as war. It illustrates the way in which the external war for empire is from the start, turned inwards and employed for the war between the people and the nobles" (110).

105 Ibid: "[W]hether the [revolutionary] changes have internal or external causes, in no case does the political and legal order control their advent: the return to beginnings is something that 'happens' to the state and the state has no control over these events" (255). Vatter takes Machiavelli's state to be a function of its historicity, with no transcendent vantage point independent of the conflict of the *umori*; and this includes the phenomenon of *virtù*. As Filippo Del Lucchese reads Vatter on this point in "*La città divisa: Esperienza del conflitto e novità politica in Machiavelli*" in *Machiavelli: Immaginazione e contingenza*, ed. Luca Sartorello and Stefano Visentin (Pisa: Edizioni ETS, 2006): "Machiavelli situates human existence and activities in the relational and conflictual field of the relation between virtù and fortune. As Vatter correctly contends, this dynamic is inexhaustible not because of the ontological 'constency' of *virtù* and its prevalence on and against *fortuna*, but because of their common contingent character [*è inesauribile non tanto per la 'consistenza' onotologica della virtù e la sua prevalenza 'su' e 'contro' la fortuna, quanto per il loro comune carattere contingente*]. *Virtù* and *fortuna* do not pre-exist their encounter [*riscontro*], but they exist only in and through the conflicts that determine the field of these human actions" (25). See also Del Lucchese's treatment of this theme in Chapter 5 of *Conflict, Power and Multitude in Machiavelli and Spinoza* (New York: Continuum, 2009).

106 This conclusion becomes more thinkable the more one moves away from the notion of the state as a substantial form and toward the state as the product of differentials

between mixed bodies organized into recurrent circuits, i.e., *practices*. As Michel Foucault describes the difference in *Sécurité, territoire, population* (Paris: Gallimard/Seuil, 2004): "*On ne peut parler de l'État-chose comme si c'était un être se développant à partir de lui-même et s'imposant par une mécanique spontanée, comme automatique, aux individus. L'État c'est une pratique. L'État ne peut pas être dissocié de l'ensemble des pratiques qui ont fait effectivement que l'État est devenu une manière de gouverner, une manière de faire, une manière d'avoir rapport au gouvernment*" (282).

107 As Winter argues this point in "The Prince and His Art of War: Machiavelli's Military Populism," *Social Research* 81, no. 1 (Spring 2014): "The relation between war and politics is hence mediated not through the synecdochal relation of prince and general but through the juxtaposition of two distinct perspectives: that of the prince who is summoned to create an army to liberate Italy and that of his armed subjects whose shared practices may initiate a political education that exceeds the prince's control" (186).

Chapter 5

1   Machiavelli's analyses of the cases of French and Carthaginian mixed forces occur in sections 3 and 4 below.
2   "nec, si materiem nostram collegerit aetas/post obitum rursumque redegerit ut sita nunc est/atque iterum nobis fuerint data lumina vitae/pertineat quicquam tamen ad nos id quoque factum/interrupta semel cum sit peretentia nostri" (Lucretius, *De rerum natura*. (Cambridge, MA: Harvard University Press, 1992, 3.847–851)).
3   See *De rerum natura*, 3.879–892.
4   Moreau, *L'âme*, 124.
5   "sed quia semper aves quod abest, praesentia temnis/inperfecta tibi elapsast ingrataque vita/et nec opinanti mors ad caput adstitit..." (*De rerum natura* 3.957–959).
6   "cedit enim rerum novitiate extrusa vetustas/semper, et ex aliis aliud reparare necesset;/nec quisquam in barathrum nec Tartara deditur atra: materies opus es tut crescent postera saecla,/quae tamen omnia te vita perfuncta sequentur;/nec minus ergo ante haec quam tu cecidere, cadentque./Sic alid ex alio numquam desistet oriri/vitaque mancipio nulli datur, omnibus usu" (*De rerum natura* 3.962–972).
7   See also his interpretation of the myth of Sisyphus in the following passage.
8   "*essendo le cose umane sempre in moto, o le salgano o le scendano*" (Machiavelli, *Opere* 1. (Turin: Einaudi-Gallimard, 325)).
9   Machiavelli, *Opere* 1, 326.
10 "*ma variando quegli ancora che i tempi non variino, non possono parere agli uomini quelli medesimi, avendo altri appetiti, alti diletti, altre considerazioni nella vecchiezza che nella gioventù*" (Machiavelli, *Opere* 1, 326).

11 Machiavelli, *Opere* 1, 326.
12 "*se non è tutto nuovo, ma come membro: che si può chiamare tutto insieme quasi misto...*" (Machiavelli, *Opere* 1, 120).
13 "*...li uomini mutano volentieri signore, credendo migliorare, e questa credenza li fa pigliare l'arme contro a quello: di chi e' s'ingannano, perché veggono poi per esperienza avere piggiorato*" (Machiavelli, *Opere* 1, 120).
14 He then lost Milan again to Louis XII in 1500 at the Battle of Novara, when the Duke's Swiss mercenaries capitulated to the French to avoid being pitted against the Swiss troops employed by the French.
15 As he states: "Because, having given reputation to the Swiss, he has debased [*invilito*] all of this arms because he has extinguished entirely the infantry and had made his men of arms obligated to the virtue of others. Because, being accustomed to fight with the Swiss, it does not seem to them able to win without them. From here springs why the French against the Swiss are not enough and without the Swiss, against others, they do not try. Therefore the armies of France have become mixed, part mercenary and part their own. Arms such as these are altogether better than simple auxiliaries or simple mercenaries, and much inferior to one's own" (Machiavelli, *Opere* 1, 56).
16 Machiavelli also refers to this change in Chapter 13 when he mentions the support the French gave to Borgia during his campaign to take the cities of Imola and Forlì. To support Borgia on this campaign, the French lent him not French troops but a contingent of 4,000 *Swiss* soldiers. See also John Najemy in "Machiavelli and Cesare Borgia: A Reconsideration of Chapter 7 of 'The Prince'", *The Review of Politics* 75, no. 4 (2013): 543–9. See, too, Cecil Clough, "The Romagna Campaign of 1494: A Significant Military Encounter," in *The French Descent into Renaissance Italy, 1494–5: Antecedents and Effects*, ed. David Abulafia (Variorum: Farnham, 1995), 191–216.
17 "*Perché da quello principio cominciorno a enervare le forze dello imperio, e tutta quella virtù, che si levava da lui, si dava a loro*" (Machiavelli, *Opere* 1, 120). The prolonging of military commands was another main cause contributing to its downfall; see *Discourses* 3.24.
18 See, for instance, *Prince* 12 where he describes the emergence of an industry of mercenary forces in Italy during the fourteenth and fifteenth centuries that displaced the former modes of military organization.
19 As Caferro (*John Hawkwood*, 80) emphasizes, fifteenth-century armies were as a rule mixed forces: "States rarely relied on a single band during wars but usually hired several mercenary contingents as well as native troops and auxiliaries from other cities. Although officials did their best to try to coordinate them, these multinational armies often did not get along among themselves." Not only were frictions among soldiers of different nationalities an issue, but the dynamics of the mercenary market

often prompted employers to hire any soldier they could in order to corner the market and reduce the number of soldiers available to their rivals.

20 "... *misto di infinite generazioni di uomini, condotto a militare in terra aliena*" (Machiavelli, *Opere* 1, 164).
21 Livy, *History of Rome*, v. 5, Books XXI–XXII (Cambridge, MA: Harvard University Press, [1929] 1996), XXI, ch. 21–3.
22 Many of the examples of agents of cruelty Machiavelli presents in his works span the divide between successful captains and princely contenders, and whether or not they actually commit cruel acts, a "*nome del crudele*," makes them effective in both spheres. As Winter acknowledges, "Cruelty's political effects materialize in the field of phenomena. An analysis of cruelty must therefore pay special attention to these circuits of mediation, that is, to the ways in which cruelty is performed, represented, interpreted and narrated." See Yves Winter, *Machiavelli and the Orders of Violence*, 107.
23 "*più licenza che alla disciplina militare non si conveniva*" (Machiavelli, *Opere* 1, 164).
24 "Ante omnes Q. Fabius natum eum ad conrumpendam disciplinam militarem arguere; sic et in Hispania plus prope per seditionem militum quam bello amissum" (Livy, *History of Rome*, 29.19).
25 "*questa sua qualità dannosa non solum si nascose, ma gli fu a memoria*" (Machiavelli, *Opere* 1, 164).
26 Machiavelli, *Opere* 1, 475.
27 See Plutarch, *The Lives of the Noble Grecians and Romans*, "Life of Pyrrhus."
28 "*tanto che Scipione, per rimediare a questo inconveniente, fu costretto usare parte di quella crudeltà che elli aveva fuggita*" (Machiavelli, *Opere* 1, 475).
29 Machiavelli, *Opere* 1, 477.
30 "*E però diceva un uomo prudente, che a tenere una republica con violenza, conveniva fusse proporzione da chi sforzava a quel che era forzato. E qualunque volta questa proporzione vi era, si poteva credere che quella violenza fusse durabile; ma quando il violentato fusse più forte che il violentante, si poteva dubitare che ogni giorno quella violenza cessasse*" (Machiavelli, *Opere* 1, 477).
31 Machiavelli, *Opere* 1, 312.
32 Machiavelli, *Opere* 1, 311.
33 Machiavelli, *Opere* 1, 312.
34 Livy, *History of Rome*, 8.6. Livy at one point terms this a civil war—"Fuit autem civili maxime bello pugna similis"—so close and equally matched were the two peoples and armies in every respect; see also Livy, 8.7.
35 Livy, ibid., 8.8, states: "Exanimati omnes tam atroci imperio nec aliter quam in se quisque destrictam cernentes securem, metu magis quam modestia quievere."
36 In the chapters (8.8–8.10) that follow Torquatus' execution of his son, Livy describes at length the *new* military orders employed in the battle that gave the victory to Manlius Torquatus over the Latins.

37 Machiavelli, *Opere* 1, 477.
38 Machiavelli, *Opere* 1, 478.
39 Machiavelli, *Opere* 1, 479.
40 Compare this to John Najemy's discussion of *Discourses* 1.37 and how Caesar became Rome's first tyrant in "Machiavelli, the Militia, and Guicciardini's Accusation of Tyranny," in *Della tirannia: Machiavelli con Bartolo*, ed. Jérémie Barthas (Florence: Leo S. Olschki Editore, 2007): "Caesar became Rome's first tyrant, not because he acquired the title and powers of a Dictator, but because he was the *capo* of one of these private factions no longer under the control of public law and the magistrates. This gave him followers—*partigiani and soldiers*—who were more his than the republic's" (102).
41 This should of course be contrasted with *Prince* 17.
42 See Livy, *History of Rome*, 28.24–29.
43 The case of Manlius Torquatus shows that terror *can* frighten and paralyze, stifling agency, but may also heighten auto-regulation. Torquatus leads the Romans to victory against an evenly matched opponent despite the fact—which Livy notes— that the Roman army was transitioning between two disciplinary orders: the phalanx formation to the manipular. Machiavelli has Fabrizio Colonna emphasize in Book II of the *Art of War* how the only troops who qualify as veterans were those for whom the disciplinary practices he recommended had already become second nature. As explained in Chapter 2 above, the shift from phalanx formations to manipular formations was not simply a matter of soldiers lining up differently: it required habituation to new classes of weapon and new ways of performing physically on the field. Manlian *asprezza* governed troops who were, from a disciplinary perspective, *new*. Despite these obstacles, the Romans defeat the Latins and Livy emphasizes that they do so because they have Torquatus for their captain.
44 According to this logic, a pope like Julius II functioned much like a Hannibal did, leading mixed troops composed of "infinite generations of men." See Leo Strauss, *Thoughts on Machiavelli* (Chicago: University of Chicago Press, 1958) 102. See also Christopher Lynch, "War and Foreign Affairs in Machiavelli's *Florentine Histories*," *The Review of Politics* 74 (2012): 1–26.
45 "*Venendo dunque un uomo così fatto a grado che comandi, desidera di trovare tutti gli uomini simili a sé, e l'animo suo forte gli fa comandare cose forti e quel medesimo, comandate che le sono, vuole si osservino*" (Machiavelli, *Opere* 1, 477).
46 "*subito a quelli marinai apparve innanzi uno gentiluomo che era l'anno davanti stato loro capitano loro, per amore di quello si partirono e lasciarono la zuffa*" Machiavelli, *Opere* 1, 480.
47 This is hardly surprising, since within a Lucretian context the subjective and objective domains are not two distinct spheres but extensive and subjective arrays of bodies that differ according to degrees of mobility, size, and shape only.
48 Machiavelli, *Opere* 1, 289.

49 Machiavelli describes Claudius, quoting Livy 3.36 inaccurately, as, "Appio finem fecit ferendae alienae personae." Livy has, "*Ille finis Appio alienae personae ferendae fuit.*"
50 Machiavelli *Opere* 1, 287: "*...à volere con violenza tenere una cosa, bisogna che sia più potente chi sforza, che chi è sforzato. Donde nasce che, quelli Tiranni, che hanno amico lo universale, et inimici i grandi, sono più sicuri, per essere la loro violenza sostenuta da maggiore forze, che quella di coloro, che hanno per inimico il Popolo, et amica la nobilità.*"
51 "*Per che con quello favore bastano à conservarsi le forze intrinsiche...*"
52 Otherwise, Machiavelli explains, intrinsic forces are not enough ("*non bastano le forze intrinsiche*") and a would be tyrant has to find support by appealing to the outside ("*di fuora*"). Those who choose this second route must do so in three ways: by acquiring foreign satellites ("*satelliti forestieri*") that would act as the tyrant's guard, arming the countryside (*il contado*) to perform the role the plebe should perform, and joining up with neighboring powers that defend him. See also Najemy's analysis of the career of Appius Claudius and the reasons behind his downfall in "Machiavelli, the Militia, and Guicciardini's Accusation of Tyranny," 102–05.
53 Machiavelli emphasizes here, as he does elsewhere, the effects that differences of political and military leadership can have on the spheres of the military and the political. Here he does so by contrasting Rome's political and military leadership under the leadership of Appius Claudius–who does not lead the troops against the Sabines and Volsci–with the example of Nabis in the same chapter who united the roles of captain and prince. The implication is that the question of *arma propriis* ultimately depends as much on the performance of the magistrates who make up the political leadership as it does on the military leadership.
54 At 1.43 Machiavelli first explains the reason for the poor performance of Rome's armies under the decemvirate and then again rehearses the arguments for the importance of, "arming oneself with one's own subjects" and eschewing the use of mercenaries. In the final sentences of the chapter, he returns to the issue of Rome's armies and how they once again behaved as "arms of one's own" with the downfall of the decemvirs. The implication of the chapter's organization is that: (1) for a time Rome did not possess arms of its own; and (2) the city regained arms of that status only by re-capturing the *animo* of the troops, not in some vague general sense, but once again as subjectively organized into *arma propriis*.

Conclusion

1 As Yves Winter argues in "The Prince and His Art of War: Machiavelli's Military Populism," *Social Research* 81, no. 1 (Spring 2014): "More important, what makes the

army a functioning and effective whole is not its hierarchy, nor the skill of its captain but the coherence and cohesion that are produced through shared bodily and spatial practices. An army is a collective subject that is produced through a series of shared practices" (174).

2 Stefano Visentin, "La virtù dei molti. Machiavelli e il reppublicanesimo olandese," in *Machiavelli: Immaginazaione e contingenza*, eds Filippo Del Lucchese, Luca Sartorello, and Stefano Visentin (Pisa: Edizioni ETS 2006), 217–52): "L'aspetto paradossale del rapport tra il principe e la moltitudine consiste dunque nella necessità di una separazione, di una rottura che il primo compie nei confronti della passioni e dei desideria della second, che deve saper allontanare ed anzi contrapporre a sé" (251).

3 Ibid., 251.

4 On this, see Machiavelli, *Opere* 1, especially 637–40.

5 In the same book, he also lays out the tactics a captain should use to extinguish or generate in his troops the desire to act by startling them (*sbigottirgli*) or igniting them with scorn (*sdegnare*) (ibid., 624–5).

6 Machiavelli, *Opere* 1, 503: "Giudicando adunque il popolo, nella elezione a' magistrati, secondo quelli *contrassegni* che degli uomini si possono avere piú veri, e quando ei possono essere consigliati come i principi, errano meno de' principi."

7 Livy, *History of Rome*, 24.8: "...eadem vos cura qua in aciem armati descenditis" (197).

8 Ibid., 204. Livy notes that the grave dangers facing Rome spared Quintus Fabius from being suspected of making a power grab. On the contrary, people praised his, "magnitudinem animi," because he knew the republic had need of a, "summo imperatore," and that he was without doubt that one and that he counted, "minoris invidiam suam, si qua ex ea re oreretur, quam utilitatem rei publicae fecisset."

9 Or when he affirms that an army should not be led into battle that lacks confidence, since that itself proves the most certain sign (*segno*) of failure: "E sopra tutto ti debbi guardare di non condurre l'esercito ad azzuffarsi che tema o che in alcuno modo diffidi della vittoria; perche il maggiore segno di perdere è quando non si crede potere vincere" (Machiavelli, *Opere* 1, 623). Also, as Colonna affirms in Book 6: "E perché a frenare gli uomini armati non bastono né il timore delle leggi, né quegli degli uomini, vi aggiugnevano gli antichi l'autorità di Iddio; è pero con cerimonie grandissime facevano a' loro soldati giurare l'osservanza della disciplina militare, acciò che contrafaccendo, non solamente avessero a temere le leggi e gli uomini, ma Iddio; e usavano ogni industria per empiergli di religione" (Ibid., 655).

10 Ibid., 624–6.

11 For Machiavelli's reading of Moses, see Alison Brown, "Savonarola, Machiavelli and Moses," in *The Medici in Florence*, Florence: Leo S. Olschki Editore and Perth: University of Western Australia Press, 1992; Warren Montag, "'Uno Mero Esecutore': Moses, *Fortuna*, and *Occasione* in the *The Prince*" and Miguel Vatter,

"Machiavelli and the Republican Conception of Providence" in *The Radical Machiavelli: Politics, Philosophy and Language*, eds. F. Del Lucchese, F. Frosini, and V. Morfino (Leiden: Brill, 2015); also Thierry Ménissier, *Machiavel ou la politique du centaure* (Paris: Hermann Éditeurs, 2010), Chapter 7.
12 Ibid., 132.
13 Ibid., 231.
14 Ibid., 231.
15 On the relationship between Machiavelli and Savonarola's 1498 sermons on Moses, see Fabio Frosini, "Prophecy, Education and Necessity: Girolamo Savonarola between Politics and Religion" in *The Radical Machiavelli*, eds. F. De Lucchese, F. Frosini, and V. Morfino (Leiden: Brill, 2015), 230–3.
16 Machiavelli, *Opere* 1, 492.
17 Earlier in the passage, Machiavelli describes the source of this envy that Moses opposed successfully and Savonarola unsuccessfully. Here Machiavelli also clearly indicates that Savonarola in the end failed to be persuasive since his sermons continued to be full of accusations and invectives against the wise of the world, which, according to Machiavelli's interpretation of the friar, was how in fact he spoke and wrote about the wise.
18 John Najemy, "Papirius and the Chickens, or Machiavelli on the Necessity of Interpreting Religion," *Journal of the History of Ideas*, 60, no. 4 (October, 1999): 678.
19 Ibid., 678. The religious spirit of the Romans extended throughout the ranks from rank-and-file soldiers to the formation's captain-interpreter, though its demands for observance manifested in the militia's distinct strata differently. As Najemy concludes concerning the Roman use of religion: "This is the crux of Machiavelli's view of Roman religion: complete respect for the ceremonies, prayers, and rituals, not out of cynical concern for appearances, but because that respect was the foundation of obedience to the laws, of *educazione,* of loyal and disciplined armies in short, of *civiltà*; and, at the same time, skillful interpretation, as necessity requires of the strictures and demands of religion" (675).
20 See sections 1 and 2 of Chapter 5 above and Chapter 1, section 8.
21 For instance, see Miguel Vatter, "Machiavelli and the Republican Conception of Providence," 262–7.

Bibliography

Aelianus, *De instruendis aciebus*. Translated by Theodorus Gaza. Rome: Eucharius Silber, 1487.
Althusser, Louis. *Écrits philosophiques et politiques*. Paris: Éditions Stock/IMEC, 1995.
Althusser, Louis. *Machiavelli and Us*. New York: Verso, 1999.
Althusser, Louis. *Machiavelli et nous*. Paris: Editions Tallandier, 2009.
Anglo, Sydney. *Machiavelli—The First Century*. Oxford: Oxford University Press, 2005.
Avant, Deborah. *The Market for Force*. Cambridge: Cambridge University Press, 2005.
Baron, Hans. *The Crisis of the Early Italian Renaissance*. Princeton: Princeton University Press, 1966.
Barthas, Jérémie. "Machiavelli in Political Thought from the Age of Revolutions to the Present." In *The Cambridge Companion to Machiavelli*, edited by John Najemy, 256–73. Cambridge: Cambridge University Press, 2010.
Barthas, Jérémie. *L'argent n'est pas le nerf de la guerre: essai sur un prétendue erreur de Machiavel*. Rome: École Française de Rome, 2011.
Barthas, Jérémie. "Machiavelli, the Republic and the Financial Crisis." In *Machiavelli on Liberty and Conflict*, edited by David Johnston, Nadia Urbinati and Camila Vergara, 257–79. Chicago: The University of Chicago Press, 2017.
Bayley, C.C. *War and Society in Renaissance Florence*. Toronto: University of Toronto Press, 1961.
Becker, Marvin. "Economic Change and the Emerging Florentine State." *Studies in the Renaissance* 13 (1966): 7–39.
Becker, Marvin. *Florence in Transition, v. 2*. Baltimore: Johns Hopkins Press, 1968.
Bertelli, Sergio; Gaeta, Franco. "Noterelle machiavelliane: Un codice di Lucrezio e di Terenzio." *Rivista storica italiana* 73 (1961): 544–55.
Black, Robert. *Machiavelli*. London: Routledge, 2013.
Black, Robert. "Machiavelli and the Militia." *Italian Studies* 69, no. (2014): 41–50.
Bonadeo, Alfredo. "The Role of the People in the Works and Times of Machiavelli." *Bibliothèque d'humanisme et renaissance* 32, no. 2 (1970): 351–78.
Brown, Alison. *The Medici in Florence*. Florence: Leo S. Olschki Editore and Perth: University of Western Australia Press, 1992.
Brown, Alison. *The Return of Lucretius to Renaissance Florence*. Cambridge, MA: Harvard University Press, 2010.
Brown, Alison. "Prefazione alla edizione italiana." In *Machiavello e Lucrezio*. Translated by Andrea Asioli, 8–11. Rome: Carocci editore S.p.A., 2013.

Brown, Alison. "Lucretian Naturalism and the Evolution of Machiavelli's Ethics." In *The Radical Machiavelli,* edited by F. Del Lucchese, F. Frosini, and V. Vittorio, 105–127. Leiden: Brill, 2015.

Bruni, Leonardo. *History of the Florentine People, volumes II & III.* Cambridge, MA: Harvard University Press, 2007.

Burckhardt, Jacob. *The Civilization of the Renaissance in Italy.* Translated by S. G. C. Middlemore. Vienna: Phaidon Press, 1932.

Butters, H.C. *Governors and Government in Early Sixteenth Century Florence, 1502- 1519.* Oxford: Clarendon Press, 1985.

Caferro, William. *John Hawkwood: an English Mercenary in 14th Century Italy.* Baltimore: Johns Hopkins University Press, 2006.

Chabod, Federico. *Machiavelli and the Renaissance.* London: Bowes and Bowes, 1958.

Cheesman, G. L. *The Auxilia of the Roman Imperial Army.* Oxford: Clarendon, 1904.

Cicero, Marcus Tullius. *De finibus.* Translated by H. Rackham. Cambridge, MA: Harvard University Press, 1914.

Cicero, Marcus Tullius. *De natura deorum. Academica.* Translated by H. Rackham. Cambridge, MA: Harvard University Press, 1951.

Clarke, Michelle T. *Machiavelli's Florentine Republic.* Cambridge: Cambridge University Press, 2018.

Clough, Cecil. "Niccolo Machiavelli, Cesare Borgia, and the Francesco Troche Affair," *Medievalia et humanistica* fasc. 17, old series (1966), 129–49.

Clough, Cecil. "The Romagna Campaign of 1494: A Significant Military Encounter." In *The French Descent into Renaissance Italy, 1494–5: Antecedents and Effects,* edited by David Abulafia, 191–216. Variorum: Farnham, 1995.

Coby, Patrick. *Machiavelli's Romans.* Oxford: Lexington Books, 1999.

Cohen, Eliot. "A Revolution in Warfare," *Foreign Affairs* 75, no.2 (March/April, 1996): 37–54.

Colish, Marcia. "Machiavelli's Art of War: A Reconsideration," *Renaissance Quarterly* v. 51, (1998): 1151–68.

Dain, Alphonse. *Histoire du texte d'Élien le Tacticien des origines à la fin du Moyen Âge.* Paris: Société d'édition "Les Belles lettres," 1946.

De Grazia, Sebastiana. *Machiavelli in Hell.* New York: Vintage Books, 1989.

Delgado, Jorge Velázquez. *Bajo el signo de Circe.* Buenos Aires: Ediciones del signo, 2006.

Della Valle, Giovanni Battista. *Vallo.* Venetia: Nicolò d'Aristotile, 1529.

Del Lucchese, Filippo. "La città divisa: Esperienza del conflitto e novità politica in Machiavelli." In *Machiavelli: Immaginazione e contingenza,* edited by Filippo Del Lucchese, Luca Sartorello, and Stefano Visentin, 17–29. Pisa: Edizioni ETS, 2006.

Del Lucchese, Filippo. *Conflict, Power and Multitude in Machiavelli and Spinoza.* New York: Continuum, 2009.

Dotti, Ugo. *Niccolò Machiavelli; La fenomenologia del potere.* Milan: Feltrinelli Editore, 1980.

Eliano. *Eliano— La "Tactica Theoria": Testo critic, traduzione e comment dei Capitoli I–XXVII*, edited by Filippo Di Cataldo, dissertation, Università degli studi di Catania, 2009–10.

Eltis, David. *The Military Revolution in Sixteenth Century Europe*. New York: Barnes & Noble, 1998.

Erwin, Sean. "A War of One's Own. Mercenaries and the theme of *arma aliena* in Machiavelli's, *Il Principe*." *British Journal of the History of Philosophy* 18, no. 4 (2010): 541–74.

Erwin, Sean, "Mixed Bodies, Agency and Narrative in Lucretius and Machiavelli," *Époché* 24, no. 2 (Spring 2020): 337–56.

Euclid. *The Thirteen Books of the Elements, v. 2*. Translated by Thomas L. Heath. New York: Dover, 1956.

Evrigenis, Ioannis. *Fear of Enemies and Collective Action*. Cambridge: Cambridge University Press, 2008.

Feld, Maury. "Machiavelli's Militia and Machiavelli's Mercenaries." In *The Military, Militarism, and the Polity*, edited by Michel Martin and Ellen McCrate, 79–92. New York: The Free Press, 1984.

Finch, Chauncey. "Machiavelli's Copy of Lucretius," *Classical Journal* 56 (1960): 29–32.

Fischer, Markus. *Well Ordered License*. Boston: Lexington Books, 2000.

Fontana, Benedetto. *Hegemony & Power*. Minneapolis: University of Minnesota Press, 1993.

Foucault, Michel. *Il faut défendre la société*. Paris: Gallimard/Seuil, 1997.

Foucault, Michel. *Sécurité, territoire, population*. Paris: Gallimard/Seuil, 2004.

Foucault, Michel. *Surveiller et punir: Naissance de la prison*. Paris: Gallimard, 1975.

Fournel, Jean-Louis. "Il genere e il tempo delle parole: dire la guerra nei testi machiavelliani." In *The Radical Machiavelli*, edited by Filippo Del Lucchese, Fabio Frosini, and Vittorio Morfino, 23–38. Leiden: Brill, 2015.

Frosini, Fabio. "Prophecy, Education and Necessity: Girolamo Savonarola between Politics and Religion." In *The Radical Machiavelli*, edited by Filippo Del Lucchese, Fabio Frosini, and Vittorio Morfino, 219–36. Leiden: Brill, 2015.

Funes, Ernesto. *La desunión república y non-dominación en Maquiavelo*. Buenos Aires: Editorial Gorla, 2004.

Gigandet, Alain. *Lucrèce. Atomes, mouvement*. Paris: Presses Universitaires de France, 2001.

Gilbert, Felix. *Machiavelli and Guicciardini*. Princeton: Princeton University Press, 1965.

Gilbert, Felix. "Machiavelli: The Renaissance of the Art of War." In *Makers of Modern Strategy*, edited by Peter Paret, 2–25. Princeton: Princeton University Press, 1944.

Goodwin, Jason. *Lords of the Horizons*. New York: Henry Holt and Company, 1998.

Gramsci, Antonio. *Quaderni del carcere, v. 2,* edited by Valentino Gerratana. Turin: Guilio Einaudi, 1977.

Grimal, P. "*Elementa, primordia, principia dans le poème de Lucrèce.*" In *Mélanges de philosophie, de littérature et d'histoire ancienne offerts à Pierre Boyancé*, 357–66. Rome: École française de Rome, 1974.

Guicciardini, Francesco. *Storie fiorentine dal 1378 al 1509*. Milan: RCS Libri SpA, 1998.

Hale, J. R. "A Humanistic Visual Aid. The Military Diagram in the Renaissance." *Renaissance Studies* 2, no. 2 (Oct. 1988): 280–98.

Hall, Bert. *Weapons and Warfare in Renaissance Europe*. Baltimore: Johns Hopkins University Press, 1997.

Hörnquist, Mikael. "Perché non si usa allegare I Romani: Machiavelli and the Florentine Militia of 1506." *Renaissance Quarterly* v. 55 (2002): 148–91.

Hörnqvist, Mikael. *Machiavelli and Empire*. Cambridge: Cambridge University Press, 2004.

Hörnquist, Mikael. "Machiavelli's Military Project and the *Art of War*." In *The Cambridge Companion to Machiavelli*, edited by John M. Najemy, 112–27. Cambridge: Cambridge University Press, 2010.

Hulliung, Mark. *Citizen Machiavelli*. Princeton: Princeton University Press, 1983.

Jurdjevic, Mark. *A Great & Wretched City*. Cambridge: Cambridge University Press, 2014.

Landon, William. "Bridging the Supposed Chasm: Tyranny, Republicanism and Lucretius' Influence on *The Prince* and *The Discourses*." In *Machiavelli's Prince: Traditions, Texts and* Translations, edited by N. Gardini and M. McLaughlin, 63–79. Rome: Viella, 2017.

Lefort, Claude. *Le travail de l'oeuvre Machiavel*. Paris: Gallimard, 1972.

Livy, Titus. *History of Rome*. Translated by B. O. Foster. Cambridge, MA: Harvard University Press, 1967.

Lucretius. *De rerum natura*. Translated by W. H. D. Rouse. Cambridge, MA: Harvard University Press, 1975.

Lukes, Timothy. "Martialing Machiavelli: Reassessing the Military Reflections." *The Journal of Politics* 66, no. 4 (2004): 1089–1108.

Lynch, Christopher. "Interpretive Essay." Commentary in *Art of War*, by Niccolò Machiavelli, 179–226. Translated and edited by Christopher Lynch. Chicago: University of Chicago Press, 2003.

Lynch, Christopher. "War and Foreign Affairs in Machiavelli's *Florentine Histories*." *The Review of Politics* 74 (2012): 1–26.

Machiavelli, Niccolò. *Arte della guerra*. Florence: li Heredi di Philippo di Giunta, 1521.

Machiavelli, Niccolò. *Arte della guerra*. Florence: li Heredi di Philippo di Giunta, 1528.

Machiavelli, Niccolò. *I sette libri dell'arte della guerra di Nicolo Machiavelli, cittadino e segretario fiorentino*. Venice: 1550.

Machiavelli, Niccolò. *Art of War*. Translated by David Lynch. Chicago: University of Chicago Press, 2005.

Machiavelli, Niccolò. *Opere, volume 1*. Edited by Corrado Vivanti. Turin: Einaudi-Gallimard, 1997.

Machiavelli, Niccolò. *Opere, volume II*. Edited by Corrado Vivanti. Turin: Einaudi, 1999.
Machiavelli, Niccolò. *Opere, volume III*. Edited by Corrado Vivanti. Turin: Einaudi, 2005.
Machiavelli, Niccolò. *Discorsi sopra la prima deca di Tito Livio*. Edited by Giorgio Inglese. Rizzoli Editore: Milan, 1984.
Machiavelli, Niccolò. *Discorsi sopra la prima deca di Tito Livio*. Edited by Corrado Vivanti. Turin: Einaudi, 2000.
Machiavelli, Niccolò. *Discorsi sopra la prima deca di Tito Livio*. Edited by F. Bausi. Rome: Salerno Editrice, 2001.
Machiavelli, Niccolò. 2009. *Discourses on Livy*. Translated by Harvey C. Mansfield and Nathan Tarcov. Chicago: University of Chicago Press.
Machiavelli, Niccolò, James B. Atkinson, David Sices, and Francesco Guicciardini. *The Sweetness of Power: Machiavelli's Discourses & Guicciardini's Considerations*. Dekalb: Northern Illinois University Press, 2002.
Malanima, Paolo. 1983. *La formazione di una regione economica: la Toscana nei secoli XIII-XV*. In *Società e storia*, XX, 229–69. Milan: Italy, 1983.
Mallett, Michael. *Mercenaries and their Masters: Warfare in Renaissance Italy*. Havertown: Pen and Sword, 2019.
Mallett, Michael. "The Theory and Practice of Warfare in Machiavelli's Republic." In *Machiavelli and Republicanism*, edited by Gisela Bock, Quentin Skinner, and Maurizio Viroli, 173–80. Cambridge: Cambridge University Press, 1990.
Mansfield, Harvey. "Bruni and Machiavelli on Civic Humanism." In *Renaissance Civic Humanism*, edited by James Hankins, 223–4. Cambridge: Cambridge University Press, 2000.
Mansfield, Harvey. *Machiavelli's Virtue*. Chicago: University of Chicago Press, 1996.
Mansfield, Harvey. *Machiavelli's New Modes and Orders*. Chicago: University of Chicago Press, 1979.
McCormick, John. *Machiavellian Democracy*. Cambridge: Cambridge University Press, 2011.
Ménissier, Thierry. *Machiavel ou la politique du centaure*. Hermann Éditeurs: Paris, 2010.
Mockler, Anthony. *The Mercenaries*. New York: Macmillan Company, 1969.
Molho Anthony. *Florentine Public Finances in the Early Renaissance*. Cambridge, MA: Harvard University Press, 1971.
Montag, Warren. "'Uno Mero Esecutore': Moses, *Fortuna*, and *Occasione* in the *The Prince*." In *The Radical Machiavelli*, edited by Filippo Del Lucchese, Fabio Frosini, and Vittorio Morfino, 237–49. Leiden: Brill, 2015.
Moreau, Pierre-François. *Lucrèce. L'âme*. Paris: Presses Universitaires de France, 2002.
Morfino, Vittorio. "Tra Lucrezio e Spinoza: la 'filosofia' di Machiavelli." In *Machiavelli immaginazaione e contingenza*, edited by Filippo Del Lucchese, Luca Sartorello, and Stefano Visentin, 67–110. Pisa: Edizioni ETS, 2006.

Morfino, Vittorio. "*Lucrezio e la corrente sotterranea del materialismo.*" In *Lucrezio e la modernità, I secoli XV–XVII,* edited by Filippo Del Lucchese, Vittorio Morfino, and Gianfranco Mormino, 33–59. Naples: Bibliopolis, 2011.

Najemy, John. "Civic Humanism and Florentine Politics." In *Renaissance Civic Humanism,* edited by James Hankins, 75–104. Cambridge, MA: Cambridge University Press, 2000.

Najemy, John. *A History of Florence, 1200–1575.* Malden, MA: Blackwell Publishing, 2006.

Najemy, John. "Machiavelli, the Militia, and Guicciardini's Accusation of Tyranny." In *Della tirannia: Machiavelli con Bartolo,* edited by Jérémie Barthas, 75–108. Florence: Leo S. Olschki, 2007.

Najemy, John. "Machiavelli and Cesare Borgia: A Reconsideration of Chapter 7 of "The Prince"," *The Review of Politics* 75, no. 4 (2013): 543–9.

Najemy, John. "Papirius and the Chickens, or Machiavelli on the Necessity of Interpreting Religion." *Journal of the History of Ideas* 60, no. 4 (October, 1999): 659–81.

Nicol, Donald. *The Last Centuries of Byzantium, 1261–1453,* 2nd ed. Cambridge: Cambridge University Press, 1993.

Ogilvie, R. M. *A Commentary on Livy, Books I–V.* Oxford: Oxford University Press, 1965.

Palmer, Ada. *Reading Lucretius in the Renaissance.* Cambridge, MA: Harvard University Press, 2014.

Parel, Anthony. *The Machiavellian Cosmos.* New Haven, CT: Yale University Press, 1992.

Pedullà, Gabriele. *Machiavelli in Tumulto.* Rome: Bulzoni Editore, 2011.

Pedullà, Gabriele. "Machiavelli the Tactician: Math, Graphs, and Knots in *The Art of War.*" In *The Radical Machiavelli,* edited by Filippo Del Lucchese, Fabio Frosini, and Vittorio Morfino, 81–101. Leiden: Brill, 2015.

Pettit, Philip. *Republicanism: A Theory of Freedom and Government.* Oxford: Oxford University Press, 1997.

Pichler, Alfred. *Der pulcher tractatus de materia belli—ein Beitrag zur Kriegs- und Geistesgeschichte des Mittelalters.* Graz-Wien-Leipzig: Leuschner & Lubensky, 1927.

Pieri, Piero. *La crisi militare italiana nel rinascimento.* Riccardo Ricciardi Editore: Naples: 1934.

Pigeaud, J.-M. *La physiologie de Lucrèce.* In *Revue des études latines* 58 (1980): 176–200.

Plato. *Laws, Books I–VI.* Translated by R.G. Bury. Cambridge, MA: Harvard University Press, 1926.

Plato. *Republic.* Edited and Translated by Chris Emlyn-Jones and William Preddy. Cambridge, MA: Harvard University Press: 2013.

Plutarch. *The Lives of the Noble Grecians and Romans.* Translated by John Dryden. Modern Library: New York, 1992.

Pocock, J. G. A. *The Machiavellian Moment.* Princeton: Princeton University Press, 1975.

Polybius, *The Histories*. Translated by W. R. Paton. Cambridge, MA: Harvard University Press, 1922.
Prezzolini, Giuseppe. *Machiavelli*. Translated by Gioconda Savini. Rome: Gherardo Casini Editore, 1967.
Rahe, Paul. *Against Throne and Altar*. Cambridge: Cambridge University Press, 2008.
Rahe, Paul. "In the Shadow of Lucretius." *History of Political Thought* 28, no. 1 (2007): 30–55.
Roecklin, Robert. *Machiavelli and Epicureanism*. Lanham, MD: Lexington Books, 2012.
Rogers, Clifford. "Tactics and the Face of Battle." In *European Warfare: 1350–1750*, edited by Frank Tallett and D. J. B. Trim, 203–35. Cambridge, UK: Cambridge University Press, 2010.
Ruggiero, Guido. *The Renaissance in Italy: a Social and Cultural History of the Rinascimento*. Cambridge: Cambridge University Press, 2015.
Sánchez-Parga, José. *Poder y política en Maquiavelo*. Rosario: Homo Sapiens Ediciones, 2005.
Sasso, Gennaro. *Niccolò Machiavelli*. Bologna: Il Mulino, 1993.
Sasso, Gennaro. *Studi su Machiavelli*. Naples: A. Morano, 1958.
Sfez, Gérald. *Machiavel, la politique du moindre mal*. Paris: Presses Universitaires de France, 1999.
Shaw, Christine. *Julius II: The Warrior Pope*. Oxford: Blackwell, 1993.
Singer, Peter Warren. *Corporate Warriors*. Ithaca, NY: Cornell University Press, 2003.
Skinner, Quentin. *Machiavelli*. New York: Hill & Wang, 1981.
Skinner, Quentin. "The Idea of Negative Liberty; philosophical and historical perspectives." In *Philosophy in History*, edited by Richard Rorty, Jerome B. Schneewind, and Quentin Skinner, 209–10. Cambridge: Cambridge University Press, 1980.
Skinner, Quentin. *The Foundations of Modern Political Thought, volume I*. Cambridge: Cambridge University Press, 1978.
Snyder, R. Claire. *Citizen Soldiers and Manly Warriors*. Lanham, MD: Rowan & Littlefield, 1999.
Spackman, Barbara. "Politics on the Warpath: Machiavelli's Art of War." In *Machiavelli and the Discourse of Literature*, edited by Albert Russell Ascoli and Victoria Kahn, 179–95. New York: Cornell University Press, 1993.
Strauss, Leo. *An Introduction to Political Philosophy: Ten Essays*. Detroit: Wayne State University Press, 1989.
Strauss, Leo. *Thoughts on Machiavelli*. Chicago: University of Chicago Press, 1958.
Sullivan, Vickie. *Machiavelli's Three Romes*. Dekalb: Northern Illinois University Press, 1996.
Sullivan, Vickie, and John Scott. "Patricide and the Plot of the Prince: Cesare Borgia and Machiavelli's Italy." *American Political Science Review* 88, no. 4 (1994): 887–900.

Tarcov, Nathan. "Arms and Politics in Machiavelli's Prince." In *Entre Kant and Kosovo*, edited by Anne-Maire de Gloannec and Aleksander Smolar, 109–21. Paris: Presses de Sciences Po, 2003.

Taylor, Frederick Louis, *The Art of War in Italy, 1494–1529*. Cambridge: Cambridge University Press, 1921.

Tutrone, Fabio. *Blood, Sweat and Tears. The Changing Concepts of Physiology from Antiquity into Early Modern Europe.* Leiden: Brill, 2012.

Valturio, Roberto. *De re militari.* Verona: Nicolai, 1472.

Vatter, Miguel. *Between Form and Event: Machiavelli's Theory of Political Freedom.* Dordrecht: Kluwer, 2000.

Vatter, Miguel. "Machiavelli and the Republican Conception of Providence." In *The Radical Machiavelli: Politics, Philosophy and Language*, edited by Filippo Del Lucchese, Fabio Frosini, and Vittorio Morfino, 250–70. Leiden: Brill, 2015.

Vegetius Renatus, Flavius. *Epitoma rei militaris,* edited by M. D. Reeve. Oxford: Clarendon Press, 2004.

Verrier, Frédérique. "Machiavelli and Fabrizio Colonna nell''Arte della guerra,': il polemologo sdoppiato." In *Niccolò Machiavelli—politico storico letterato*, edited by Jean-Jacques Marchand, 175–87. Rome: Salerno Editrice, 1996.

Visentin, Stefano. "*La virtù dei molti. Machiavelli e il repubblicanesimo olandese della seconda metà del seicento.*" In *Machiavelli: immaginazione e contingenza*, edited by Luca Sartorello and Stefano Visentin, 217–52. Pisa: Edizioni ETS, 2006.

Waley, Daniel. "The Army of the Florentine Republic from the Twelfth to the Fourteenth Century." In *Florentine Studies: Politics and Society in Renaissance Florence*, edited by Nicolai Rubinstein, 70–108. Evanston: Northwestern University Press, 1968.

Wicht, Bernard. "Les suisses comme révélateur du project Machiavélien de milice." In *Niccolò Machiavelli—politico storico letterato*, edited by Jean-Jacques Marchand, 235–45. Rome: Salerno Editrice, 1996.

Winter, Yves. *Machiavelli and the Orders of Violence*. Cambridge: Cambridge University Press, 2018.

Winter, Yves. "The Prince and His Art of War: Machiavelli's Military Populism," *Social Research* 81, no. 1 (Spring, 2014): 165–91.

Xenophon, *Scripta minora*. Translated by G.W. Bowersock. Cambridge, MA: Harvard University Press, 1968.

Zancarini, Jean-Claude. "Les humeurs du corps politique." *Laboratoire Italien* I (2001): 25–33.

Index

Aelianus Tacticus, 9–10, 37–51, 107, 121, 139n8, 140n23, 142n35
agency, 14–15
Agincourt, battle of, 138n4
aging, 103, 104, 144n55
Albizzi, Rinaldo degli, 17–18
Alexander the Great, 31, 58
Alexander VI, Pope, 59–60, 61, 155n54
allies, 2
Altoviti, Guglielmo, 93
anima, 22–9, 35, 100, 121, 134–5n44
animo, 28–32, 35
    of horses, 32–5
animus, 26–7, 28–9, 35, 100, 121
anti-teleological physics, 19
Aristotle, 55
armed force
    qualitative dimension, 8–9
    qualities of, 1, 2, 8–9
arms of others, 2, 3, 8–9, 53, 62–4, 80, 122, 127
    critique of, 82–3
    dangers of, 96–7
    see also mercenaries
arquebusiers, 38, 138n4
Art of War, 4–5, 81, 89
    Aelianus Tacticus' influence, 9–10, 37–51
    aim, 7–8
    audience, 41–2
    Book 3, 6–7
    Colonna's discussion, 3, 20–5, 25–6, 29–32, 32–3, 34, 37, 42–3, 43–6, 46–9, 49–51, 123
    diagrams, 10, 40–2, 48, 140–1n24
    legion–phalanx hybrid, 28
    Lucretian influence, 9, 13–36, 50
    opening, 85
    project, 40
    publication, 19
    on state indebtedness, 83–4
    strategy types, 34
    technical character, 7
    usage of *animo*, 28–32
artillery, 6–7
ataraxía, 14
atomic bodies, internalized conditioning, 50
atomic elements, 45
atomic mechanics, 101
atomic physics, 108
atomic swerve, the, 14
atomism, 15, 18, 20–5, 35
atomist physics, 15, 16, 33, 25–6, 36, 132n14
authority, 4–5, 81, 156n55
autonomy, 95, 145n63
    princely, 61–2
auxiliaries, 2, 16, 53, 63, 73–97, 121, 163n2, 164n11
    as a commodity, 84–5
    danger of, 73–4, 77–8, 81, 94–7, 106, 167n32
    definition, 77, 168n41
    in *Discourses*, 74, 76–81, 86, 95–6, 97
    economies of force, 82–6
    effectiveness, 73
    examples, 75–6
    humoral theory, 86–95, 96
    instrumentality, 82–6
    M's account of, 122
    obedience, 74–5
    in *Prince*, 73–4, 74–6, 77, 78, 82, 86, 96, 97
    Roman army, 77–81, 164n11
    uselessness, 74

banking innovations, 84
Barthas, Jérémie, 82–3
Battalion/brigade organization, 15–16, 20–1, 22–6, 44–5, 143–4n51
battlefield, unpredictability of, 49
Becker, Becker, 82–6
bioengineering, 16

Black, Robert, 6
bodies of war, 16–17
Borgia, Cesare, 1, 1–2, 6, 14–15, 57, 59–61, 149n7, 152–3n32, 155n53
Brown, Alison, 13, 131n4
Bruni, Leonardo, 54–5
Buondelmonte, Zanobi, 2

capidieci, 22–3, 42, 49, 123, 143–4n51
capital accumulation, 82–3, 85
capo, 118–9
captains
   authority, 4–5
   oratory, 125
   as prophet, 125–7
   reputation, 115–6, 157n62
   role, 123
   see also leadership
Capua, Roman occupation of, 77–81, 86, 88, 94–5, 95–6, 122, 168n44, 168n46, 169–70n52, 169n49, 169n50, 170n54
Cardona, Ramón de, 78
cavalry, 136n78
   defects of, 32–5
   tactics, 39
Chabod, Federico, 7
Charles VII, King of France, 106–7
Church, the, 69
civic humanism, 54, 149n16
civic virtue, 54
civil war, 81
civilizations, collapse of, 17
Claudius, Appius, 117–9, 120, 182n53
clinamen, 14, 33–4
clinamen, the, 14
colonies, 106
Colonna, Fabrizio, 3, 8, 14, 15, 20–5, 25–6, 29–32, 32–3, 34, 37, 42–3, 43–6, 46–9, 49–51, 84, 123, 136n64, 145–6n67, 149n9
command
   art of, 59, 153n39, 154n44
   and submission, 89
compatibilization, 92
composite bodies, 16, 17, 19–20, 24–5, 35, 50
compound bodies, cavalry, 33
condottieri, 62, 64, 68, 84, 158n70
   contracts, 157–8n69, 158n69
   critique of, 70–1, 170n55
   dependence on, 54–5
   effective and ineffective, 64–5, 71
   intentions, 66–7
conflict, industry of, 68–9
conquest, 176n103
corporeality, 14–15
Corvinus, Valerius, 110–4, 116, 117, 120, 122
courage, 38
cruelty, 60, 109, 110, 115–6, 157n62, 179n22
Cyrus, 56, 114

Darius I, 57–8, 61
Darius III, 58
David, 1–2
De instruendis aciebus (Aelianus Tacticus), 10, 37, 38–43, 45
De rerum natura (Lucretius), 9, 13, 15, 32, 105, 140–1n24
   atomism, 132n14
   atomist physics, 25–6, 36
   bodies of war, 16–17
   explanation of *clinamen*, 33–4
   humoral theory, 90–2
   M's marginal notations, 18, 133n26
   on mixed bodies, 99–102, 103–4
   and motion, 26–7
death, fear of, 101–2, 127
debt, function of, 82–6
deception, 161n90
decision-making, 123–5
desires, 103
diagrams, 40–2, 48, 140–1n24
Diogenes Laertius, 14
disciplinary practices, 180–1n43
disciplinary regimes, 35, 83–4, 92, 107, 122–3
discipline, 45–6, 46, 49–51, 111, 113, 120, 121–2, 145–6n67, 180–1n43
discontent, 103–4
Discourses, 1, 2, 16, 20, 61, 125, 126, 141n28
   audience, 3
   auxiliaries in, 74, 76–81, 86, 95–6, 97
   discussions of mercenaries, 53
   humoral theory, 86, 87, 90, 92
   importance of renewal, 18–19

Lucretian influence, 13, 17, 102–4
   mixed bodies in, 103
   mixed forces in, 108–19, 119
   on state indebtedness, 83
distancing, 122, 127
doubling by flank, 44–5, 142n35
doubling by line, 44, 45–6

ecclesiastical principalities, 60
economies of force, 82–6
effectual authority, 61
Eltis, David, 38
emotions, 27, 30–1
Epicureanism, 13, 14
Epicurus, 14
equine swerve, critique of the, 32–5
estrangement, 122, 127
ethical themes, 13
Euclid, 146n68

Fabius, Quintus, 123–5
Ferdinand I, King of Spain, 78
Fermo, Oliverotto da, 154n47
fighting styles, 159n73
firearms, 6–7, 38, 138n4
Fischer, Markus, 88
flags, 22, 25, 45
Florence, 5, 6, 126–7, 150n18
   banking innovations, 84
   bans teaching of Lucretius, 19
   civic humanism, 149n16
   dependence on condottieri, 54
   humoral theory, 92–3
   riots, 1382, 55
   state indebtedness, 82–6, 171n59
   tumults, 87
   use of auxiliaries, 76
   use of mercenaries, 66–7, 68
Florentine Histories, 16, 20, 160n79, 160n80
   bodies in, 17–18
   discussions of mercenaries, 53
   humoral theory, 86–7, 87, 92–3
   Lucretian influence, 17
Foix, Gaston de, 78
force, economies of, 82–6
force categories, 5
formations, 39
   reordering, 46, 51

fortuna, 55–6, 58, 61
Foucault, Michel, 132n19
Fournel, Jean-Louis, 6–7
free will, 13, 14, 33
freedom, 176n103, 176n104

gentlemen, 112
Gilbert, Felix, 4
glory, 88
Goliath, 1–2
good arms, 62
Gramsci, A., 7
grandi, 74
Greeks, Ancient, 141–2n32, *see also* phalanx tactics
guides, 22–3, 25, 39
Gustavus Adolphus, 138n1

Hale, J. R., 40
Hannibal, 63, 99, 108–10, 115–6, 120, 122, 145n64, 157n62, 181n44
Hiero II, , 1–3 56–7, 61, 149n7
Hieronymous, 2, 61
historical concerns, 15
honor, 88
Hörnquist, Mikael, 6
horses, *animo* of, 32–5
human body, the, 17–8, 19, 20, 25–8, 100, 145n63
   composite, 35
   in flux, 102–4
humoral theory, 173n80, 174n83
   examples, 92–4
   Galenic tradition, 90–1, 174–5n90, 174n89
   gradations, 93–4
   Livy and, 94–5
   Lucretian account, 90–2
   M's account of, 86–90, 90–1, 92, 92–4, 94–5, 96

identity, 100–1, 103, 119
illustrations, 40–2
inconsistencies, 5
indirect government, 156n58
individual soldiers
   placement of, 38–40, 45–8, 49, 121
instrumentality, auxiliaries, 82–6
internalized conditioning, 50

intrinsic forces, 118
Italian campaign, Louis XII, King of France, 105–7, 178–9n16

John VI Cantacuzene, Emperor, 76, 167–8n41
judgment, 104
Julius II, Pope, 75–6, 78, 165n20, 181n44

Latin War, 113–14
leadership, 109, 109–19, 120, 182n53
legion–phalanx hybrid, 28–32
liberty, 7
Livy, 77–81, 86, 88, 89, 95–6, 104, 110, 113, 123–5, 167n39, 168n44, 169–70n52, 170n54
Louis XI, King of France, 99, 106, 119
Louis XII, King of France, 178n15
    Italian campaign, 105–7, 178–9n16
Lucretius, 9, 127, 135–6n60
    atomist physics, 15, 25–6, 36, 132n14
    bodies of war, 16–17
    explanation of *clinamen*, 33–4
    on the human body, 25–6
    influence, 9, 13–36, 50, 102–4, 121, 131n4, 133n26
    on mixed bodies, 99–102, 108, 119
    and motion, 26–7
    primordia, 16, 17–20, 90, 91, 92, 119, 121, 140–1n24, 140n24
    in *Prince*, 104–8
    teaching ban, 19
    umori, 90–2
Lukes, Timothy, 3

McCormick, John, 4–5, 89–90
Malanima, Paolo, 85
Manlian commands, 113–14
manoeuvres, 39–40, 43–6, 48–9, 142n35
Mansfield, Harvey, 4–5
Marc Antony, 34
marching order, 43–4, 48–9
martial bodies, 16–7
martial choreographies, 37
martial practices, internalized, 37
Maurice of Nassau, 138n1
Medici, Giovanni de', 93
memory, continuity of, 100–1

mercenaries, 1–2, 2, 16, 53–71, 74, 99, 121, 151n21, 160–1n86, 166n24
    astutely employed, 67–8
    comparison with one's own arms, 57–62
    consequences of employing, 67–70
    cost of, 82–6
    critique of, 53, 54–5, 62–4, 69, 70–1, 122, 147n4
    danger of, 157–8n69, 161–2n93
    dependence on, 54–5
    difficulties with, 63–4
    effective and ineffective, 64–5
    examples of use, 65–7
    importance, 3
    industry of war, 68–9
    intentions, 66–7
    patrons, 65
    qualities, 63
    role, 53
    usefulness, 63
    uselessness, 74
    utility, 71
mercenary captains, ambitions, 66–7, 67–8
Michele, Don, 6
Milan, 62, 66, 69, 105
military and military forces, M's discussions of, 3–9
military discipline, emphasis on, 4
military force, 4
military formations, Lucretian, 16
military policy, 4–5
military practice, non-professional character of, 46
military values, 38
militia, 8, 54, 121
    as alternative to dependence on mercenaries, 70
    composite bodies, 149n13
    composition, 129–30n16
    disciplinary regime, 83–4, 92, 107
    draftees roles, 136n64
    Florentine, 5, 6
    legion–phalanx hybrid, 28
    as mixed bodies, 17
    organizational structure, 89–90
    physical force, 4
    quality, 84
    shared subjective framework, 81

mixed bodies, 14, 16, 17, 18–19, 50, 53, 94, 108, 121
   in flux, 102–4
   Lucretian, 99–102, 108, 119
mixed forces, 2, 99–120, 122, 178n15, 179n19
   definition, 99
   in *Discourses*, 108–19, 119
   effectiveness, 110
   lack of fixed character, 119–20
   leadership, 109–19, 120
   in *Prince*, 99, 104–8, 119
   quality, 108–9, 117–19
mixed principalities, 104–8
Molho, Anthony, 84
Moreau, Pierre-François, 91
Morfino, Vittorio, 14–5
Moses, 56, 125–7, 184n17
motion, 26–7, 35

Najemy, John, 6, 127, 149n16
Naples, 66
natural determinism, 14
naturalism, 16–7, 132–3n21
non-professional, combatants, 16

obedience, 74–5, 95, 113–14
offers, 84
officers, 22–3, 28, 37, 42, 49
   disciplinary role, 50–1
   numbers, 143–4n51
one's own arms, 2, 3, 8–9, 53, 55–62, 62, 65, 96, 97, 125–6
oppression, modes of, 88
optimates, 54–5
oratory, 125
Orco, Remirro de, 60
ordering elements, 22–3
organization, 4
Ottacilius, Titus, 123–5
Ottoman Turks, 58, 167–8n41

Palmer, Ada, 14, 18, 19, 133n26
papacy, the, political criticism of, 8
Papirius, 156n56
Parel, Anthony, 87
Parthians, 34, 136n78
Pedullà, Gabriele, 7, 15
Persian Empire, 57–8

Petrarch, 55
phalanx tactics, 7, 10, 15–16, 38–43, 141–2n32
   comparison to Roman legion, 20–5
   disposition, 44, 45
Philopoemon, 69
physical force, 4
Pisa, siege of, 106, 167n41
Plato, 42, 42–3, 55
pleasures, 103
Plutarch, 104
policymaking, 70
political equality, 112, 115–16
political leadership, 117–19
political power, and military force, 4
politics, and war, 3, 4
Polybius, 2
popular government, 4–5
potential princes, 3
primordia, 16, 17–20, 90, 91, 92, 119, 121, 140n24
Prince, The, 16, 126
   audience, 3
   auxiliaries in, 73–4, 74–6, 77, 78, 82, 86, 96, 97
   discussion of one's own arms, 55–62
   discussions of mercenaries, 53, 54–5, 62–4, 74–5
   Hiero II in, 1
   humoral theory, 86, 87, 92, 93
   Lucretian influence, 104–8
   mixed bodies in, 99
   mixed forces in, 104–8, 119
princely autonomy, 61–2
princely power, 156n58
princes, potential, 3
principalities, mixed, 104–8
professional soldiers, dangers of, 85
promotion structure, 89
prophet, captains as, 125–7
proportion (*proporzione*), 1, 43, 46, 47, 48, 141n28
   importance of observing, 49–51
   in leadership, 111–12
   temporal dimension, 47–8

quasi-professionalization, 85

Rahe, Paul, 13–14
rally points, 49
Ravenna, battle of, 75–6, 165n20
reciprocity, 89
recruitment, 4–5, 84
religion, 13, 125–7, 184n19
renewal, importance of, 18–19
republican political dimensions, 112–3
reputation, 115–16, 157n62
rewards, 88
Roecklin, Robert, 14, 15
Roman army, 6, 106, 145n64
    auxiliaries, 77–81, 164n11
    quality, 117–19, 182n54
Roman legion
    comparison to phalanx, 20–5
    renewal styles, 46–9
    superiority of, 20
Roman renewal styles, 46–9
Rome and the Romans, 2, 34, 39–40, 46–7, 65, 127, 156n56, 156n57, 176n102, 182n53, 183n8, 184n19
    the decemvirate, 117–19, 182n54
    decision-making, 123–5
    Latin War, 113–14
    militia organization, 89
    occupation of Capua, 77–81, 86, 88, 94–5, 95–6, 122, 168n44, 168n46, 169–70n52, 169n49, 169n50, 170n54
    virtue, 104
    wars of expansion, 47
Romulus, 56
Rucellai, Cosimo, 2, 31–2, 134–5n44
Rucellai, Naddo, 93

Salutati, Coluccio, 55
Savanarola, Girolamo, 8, 56, 125–7, 184n17
scholarly reassessments, 3–9
Scipio Africanus, 109, 120, 122, 145n64
sea warfare, 137n88
security, limits of, 69
self-regulation, 24
sensation, 27
Sertorius, 125
service, terms of, 85
Sforza, Francesco, 3, 53, 59, 62, 64, 66, 69, 122, 160n80
Sforza, Muzio Attendolo, 66

shared subjective framework, 81
siege craft, 31
signs, 44–5, 51, 123
signs or characters, troops, 41
simple bodies, 17
small unit tactics, 38–43, 138n1
soul, 25–6, 35, 102, 135–6n60
sound cues, 22–3, 25, 30–1
Spackman, Barbara, 142n44
Spartans, the, 66
state, economies of force, 82–6
state debt, 70, 82–6, 171n79
state institutions, 4
strategy, types, 34
Strozzi, Nanni degli, 54
submission, and command, 89
Sullivan, Vickie, 87–8
Swiss, the, 7, 66
    comparison to Roman legion, 20–5
    pike squares, 15–6, 20–5, 38, 138–9n7, 138n3

tactical language, 142n44
tactics, 20–5, 37
    cavalry, 39
    small unit, 38–43, 138n1
Terence, 13
terminology, 14
terrain, 34, 45
Theseus, 56
thinking, 27
Thomas Aquinas, 55
time, 47
Torquatus, Manlius, 110–14, 115–16, 117, 120, 122, 180–1n43
Tutrone, Fabio, 91

umori, 96, 121, 173n80, 174n89
    Livy and, 94–5
    Lucretian account, 90–2
    M's account of, 86–90, 92–4
unit cohesion, 38
unpredictability, 35

Valentino, Duke, 59–60, 155n50, 155n54
Valle, Battista Della, 40
valor, 38

Vegetius Renatus, Publius Flavius, 39–40, 55
Venice, 66, 67, 68, 116–17
Verrier, Frédérique, 8
violence, theatricality of, 140n19
virtù, 55–6, 58
Visentin, Stefano, 122, 127
Vitelli, Paolo, 68
vocabulary, 6–7

war and warfare
    instruments of, 82
    M's discussions of, 3–9
    M's experience of, 5–6
weapons, 48
Wicht, Bernard, 7
will-to-power, 69
Winter, Yves, 4, 8

Xenophon, 114

Zama, battle of, 145n64
Zancarini, Jean-Claude, 93

www.ingramcontent.com/pod-product-compliance
Lightning Source LLC
Chambersburg PA
CBHW061830300426
44115CB00013B/2323